Supply Chain Management Accounting

Supply Chain Management Accounting

Managing profitability, working capital and asset utilization

Simon Templar

KoganPage

First published in Great Britain and the United States in 2019 by Kogan Page Limited

2nd Floor, 45 Gee Street
London
EC1V 3RS
United Kingdom

c/o Martin P Hill Consulting
122 W 27th Street
New York, NY 10001
USA

4737/23 Ansari Road
Daryaganj
New Delhi 110002
India

© Simon Templar 2019

ISBNs

Hardback   978 0 7494 9805 4
Paperback   978 0 7494 7299 3
Ebook   978 0 7494 7300 6

British Library Cataloguing-in-Publication Data

A CIP record for this book is available from the British Library.

Library of Congress Cataloging-in-Publication Data

A CIP record for this book is available from the Library of Congress.

Typeset by Integra
Print production managed by Jellyfish
Printed and bound in Great Britain by CPI Group (UK) Ltd, Croydon CR0 4YY

CONTENTS

ACKNOWLEDGEMENTS

I would like to acknowledge the support of Julia Swales and Ro'isin Singh from Kogan Page. I am grateful to Kaplan Publishing for their permission to use the accounting definitions fromv the *CIMA Official Terminology* (2005). I would also like to thank Bureau van Dijk for giving me permission to use the finance ratios from their Fame database. I acknowledge Cranfield School of Management who have granted permission for me to use examples of my work as a lecturer at Cranfield University. I also thank the following organizations who have given their permission for me to use their financial information from their annual report and accounts:

- BASF Group;
- Deutsche Post DHL Group;
- Marks and Spencer Group PLC;
- Nestlé Group;
- The Procter & Gamble Company.

Finally, I would like to thank Carolyn Templar, who has read every single word of the manuscript and for her patience and support during the process of authoring this book.

Introduction 01

The rationale for this book came from the author's passionate belief that supply chain (SC) practitioners can have a direct impact on the financial performance of their organizations, their customers and their suppliers. The decisions taken by supply chain specialists don't just impact on cost of operations, but impact on other financial variables including sales revenue, cash-to-cash cycle times and the productivity of the assets deployed by the business. It is important that practitioners are able to understand the impact of their supply chain decisions on the financial performance of the organizations they work for. Therefore, the aim of the book is to introduce and explore the strategically important relationship between supply chain management and management accounting.

The book draws on the author's working experiences in various industries, ranging from 'bananas to telecommunications' in a wide range of different functions, which have included management accounting, sales and marketing, physical distribution management and human resource management.

The book is also underpinned by the author's research interests: his PhD research explored the impact of transfer pricing on supply chain management decisions. Other research interests relate to activity-based costing and supply chain finance, as the author is a co-founder of the Supply Chain Finance Community, a non-profit association that aims to share good practice and new research in an open, collaborative environment; and supply chain costing, as the author was a member of a multi-disciplinary research team jointly funded by the Engineering and Physical Sciences Research Council (EPSRC) and industry which developed a novel process to assess supply chain costs in the food and drink industry.

The final inspiration for the book came from the many fascinating conversations the author has had over the last 10 years as a lecturer with students, fellow academics, employers and practitioners, who have stressed the need for a user-friendly publication that explores the strategically important interface between supply chain management and management accounting, providing the opportunity to gain a greater insight into this special relationship to enhance value for an organization.

There are many more things that I wanted to include in this book, but I decided to focus on five key themes, which are important to me and I hope are of interest to you:

- the relationship between supply chain decisions and financial performance as measured by financial statements, including the income statement, balance sheet and key financial performance indicators;
- the application of traditional (full costing, marginal costing and standard costing) and contemporary (activity-based costing, target costing and total cost of ownership) costing approaches to support supply chain management decision-making;
- the benefits of taking a holistic perspective and increased degree of functional integration between supply chain management, sales and marketing, IT, and management accounting are essential for the future organizational structure;
- the development of financially sustainable supply chain operations incorporating supply chain finance, working capital management and risk management;
- introducing a capital investment appraisal toolkit to build the business case for investing in supply chain assets.

There are nine chapters, and like the themes, there could have been many more.

Chapter 2: Income statement

This chapter recognizes the strategically important relationship between an organization's supply chain operation and the profitability of their business. This chapter describes the role of the income statement (IS), and identifies the different elements that make up a typical IS and those important elements that SC practitioners can influence. The chapter explores and explains the impact of supply chain decisions on the IS and their effect on the financial ratios that are used to evaluate the IS.

Chapter 3: Balance sheet

This chapter introduces you to the balance sheet (BS) of an organization. The BS is basically an accounting equation that illustrates where an organization has raised its funds from and where these raised funds have been invested in the business. You will be able to recognize and explain the impact of supply chain management decisions on the balance sheet (BS) of an organization: for instance, what will be the impact on the balance sheet and the financial ratios that are used to evaluate the BS of introducing vendor-managed inventory (VMI)?

At the end of this chapter you will be able to:

- explain the role of the BS;
- explore the structure of a typical BS;
- identify the different segments that make up a typical balance sheet;
- explain the impact of supply chain decisions on the balance sheet;
- calculate financial ratios that are relevant to evaluating the balance sheet.

Chapter 4: Cash flow and working capital management

This chapter will introduce you to the importance of managing cash flow and working capital management. You will be able to explain the importance of cash flow for any organization by constructing a cash flow forecast for a business. You will be able to identify the components of the cash-to-cash cycle calculation (inventory days, accounts receivables, and accounts payables) and calculate the cash-to-cash cycle time for organizations that make up a supply chain. You will also recognize the importance and impact that your supply chain decisions can have on the management of working capital and appreciate the important relationship between supply chain management, supply chain finance and liquidity.

Chapter 5: Depreciation

This chapter introduces you to the concept of depreciation and explains why organizations use depreciation and how they calculate the depreciation for their organization. You will be introduced to three different methods of depreciation and you will be able to calculate a fixed asset's depreciation and then explain how depreciation impacts on both the income statement and balance sheet of a business.

Chapter 6: Supply chain management and financial performance

This chapter introduces you to the significant impact that your supply chain decisions will have on the financial performance of the organization. It will enable you to explain the relationship between the decisions you are planning to take on a set of the financial ratios that are used by organizations to measure the different aspects of firm performance.

Return on capital employed, a significant financial ratio, will be used as the lens to analyse the important relationship between supply chain decisions and organizational financial performance.

Finally, you will be able to explain the important linkages between SC decisions and an organization's financial statements and the resulting impact of those decisions on the different financial ratios used to evaluate financial performance.

Chapter 7: Marginal costing

In this chapter you are now aware of the different types of cost that are typically found in a supply chain operation, which are fixed and variable. You have seen how changes in output impact on these different cost types. You now recognize that in accounting, marginal cost is the same as the variable cost. You are also able to calculate a product's contribution per unit. You can now derive the break-even point for a product or service by formula and graphically. You can now also apply marginal costing to solve capacity problems with a single constraint and can identify the strengths and weaknesses of applying marginal costing in practice.

Chapter 8: Absorption costing and variance analysis

For hundreds of years organizations have been applying full or absorption costing to calculate the total cost of a product. This chapter introduces you to the application of absorption costing and the use of variance analysis in the context of supply chains. You will explore how a product is costed from the receipt of raw materials to the final delivery to the customer. On your journey you will be able to identify direct and indirect costs that make up a product or service using absorption costing, and recognize the different cost units and cost centres within an organization's supply chain that impact on the product's journey. You will discover the different processes involved in distributing indirect costs to cost units and be able to explain the difference between mark-up and margin. You will recognize the important role that absorption costing has in valuing inventory in a supply chain. Finally, you will be introduced to variance analysis and will be able to calculate price and quantity variances for direct costs:

- Calculate typical price and usage variances for direct costs.
- Recognize the benefits and limitations of absorption costing.

Chapter 9: Contemporary costing methods

This chapter introduces you to three contemporary costing methods used in practice that can have a significant impact on the decisions taken by SC practitioners and contribute to the financial performance of any organization. Of the three costing methods, activity-based cost is the most versatile, as it can be used across all the activities highlighted in Porter's value chain as well as the supply chain operations reference model (SCOR) activities. You will be introduced to the rationale for the adoption of these costing methods in the SC and will be able to identify their benefits and their impact on the different areas of an organization's SC operation.

Chapter 10: Investment appraisal

The chapter highlights the reasons why organizations use investment appraisal techniques to evaluate an investment opportunity. Organizations aim to maximise returns to their stakeholders, obtain value for money and improve liquidity. They also want to reduce risk by comparing different investment opportunities as part of the management duty of stewardship. You will be introduced to six accounting techniques that are used in the appraisal process. Finally, you will recognize the importance of taking a holistic perspective to investment appraisal by incorporating all of the accounting techniques into your decision-making process, not just relying on a single technique.

The book contains examples from theory, practice and case studies and every chapter contains a set of activities and study questions with worked solutions.

Supply chain issues and financial performance

Table 1.1 illustrates the typical supply chain management issues facing organization.

Table 1.1 Typical supply chain management issues facing organizations

• Make or buy decision	• Reducing inventory holding costs
• Returns management	• Cost of serving different customers
• Supplier relationship management	• Investing in non-current assets
• Inventory management	• Reducing logistics costs
• Asset utilization	• Cost visibility in supply chains
• Customer service levels	• Demanding forecasting
• Managing risk	• Ethical supply chain issues
• Supplier audits	• Environmental supply chain issues
• Working capital management	• Improving cash flow
• Cash to cash cycle times	• Taxation aspects of supply chains
• Removing waste in processes	• Managing supply chain complexity
• Supply chain disruption	• New product introductions

Every one of these supply chain issues will have an impact on the financial performance of an organization. Hence the importance of SC practitioners understanding the relationship between their decision and the impact on the financial statements of their organization.

Finally...

I have always seen this book as a journal/logbook, not a textbook, with each chapter providing the reader with examples from theory, practice and my own experiences, like an old recipe book that has been handed down from generation to generation, which has been amended, annotated, added to, and top tips written in the margin. Therefore, I hand this book on to you, to amend it, annotate it and add your own notes and your top tips in the margin.

Remember, the numbers don't make decisions, people do, but also, people's decisions make the numbers; therefore, the narrative behind the numbers is the most significant factor we need to understand and communicate.

The income statement 02

Before we explore and deconstruct the income statement (IS), aka profit and loss account (P&L), I must first pause and issue a 'health warning' and make you aware of the fact that the language and vocabulary of accountancy can often be perplexing, confusing and difficult to comprehend, as often different words are used which refer to the same term and are frequently used interchangeably in a paragraph of text and the spoken word. Here are a couple of examples. The first term is sales, which is the first line of the IS; however, it is also referred to as income, sales turnover or often abbreviated to just turnover, net sales, revenue and the top line. Profit also has many aliases, including earnings, surplus, margin and return. These aliases are used as a substitute for profit; for example in the terms profit before interest and tax (PBIT) and earnings before interest and tax (EBIT) they mean the same thing. You may have also come across the financial ratios return on sales (ROS) and return on capital employed (ROCE); they refer to profit over sales and profit over capital employed. You will be introduced in this chapter to financial ratios that measure profitability; however, we will explore financial ratios later in Chapter 6 (Supply chain management and firm performance). There are many more examples, which will be flagged as we travel together across the accounting landscape.

2.1 Aim and objectives

The aim of this chapter is to recognize the important relationship between the supply chain (SC) and the organization's income statement (IS).

At the end of this chapter you will be able to:

- explain the role of the IS;
- identify the different elements that make up a typical IS;
- identify the different costs that exist within a typical SC;
- explain the impact of SC decisions on the IS;
- calculate financial ratios that are relevant to evaluating the IS.

2.2 The income statement

The IS in its simplest form is just a subtraction sum, which is income minus expenditure: if income is greater than expenditure, a profit is made; however, if income is less than expenditure, a loss would be incurred. Mr Micawber in *David Copperfield* eloquently describes an income and expenditure scenario: 'if a man had twenty pounds a-year for his income, and spent nineteen pounds nineteen shillings and sixpence, he would be happy, but that if he spent twenty pounds one he would be miserable.'

The IS matches the income generated in an accounting period with the relevant expenditure incurred in the same time frame to calculate the organization's profit or loss.

CIMA (1989:5) defines the matching concept as: 'Revenues and costs are matched one with the other and dealt with in the profit and loss account of the period to which they relate irrespective of the period of receipt or payment (SSAP2).'

Christopher (2011:58) argues that SC practitioners need to be conscious of the impact of their decisions on the financial performance of their organization, but also stresses that the organization's pursuit of increasing profits may have unforeseen and unintentional consequences for the business as a whole: 'The bottom line has become the driving force which, perhaps erroneously, determines the direction of the company.'

In a single sentence the IS describes how the revenue stated in the top line is reduced by various cost elements to derive the retained earnings for the year (bottom line). A typical IS format is illustrated in Figure 2.1 for a fictitious company, Mega plc. The first thing to point out is that in the title it states clearly the accounting period, for example the year ending 31 March 20XX; therefore, referring back to the matching concept, all revenues and expenditures will be accounted for in this time period. If a sale to a customer on credit is made on 31 March 20XX, the invoice will be included in the revenue for that year, even though the payment will be received 90 days into the new financial year. The accounting treatment of the transaction (double entry) is that the invoice is included in the revenue figure (credit) in the IS and in the accounts receivables on the balance sheet (debit).

The statement reveals five different profit calculations (bold font), which can be used to analyse the financial performance of the organization from different perspectives, including sales procurement, operations, treasury, tax and investors.

Figure 2.1   Mega plc income statement

Mega plc income statement for the year ending 31 March 20XX	£m
Revenue	200
Cost of sales	80
Gross profit	**120**
Operating expenses	40
Operating profit	**80**
Interest payable	6
Interest received	1
Earnings before tax	**75**
Taxation	23
Earnings after tax	**52**
Dividend	10
Retained earnings	**42**

The five profitability ratios, including their method of calculation and the results for Mega plc, are illustrated in Table 2.1. It is important to note that the denominator in all of these ratios is revenue. These ratios act as milestones, illustrating how revenue is eroded at significant points from the top line to bottom line. In the case of Mega plc, only 21% of its revenue for the year ending 31 March 20XX has been retained in the organization, or in other words, 79% of revenue earned for the year has been expensed in the financial year ending 31 March 20XX.

Table 2.1   Mega plc profitability ratios

Ratio	Formula	Calculation
Gross margin	(Gross profit/ revenue) *100	(£120m/£200m) *100 = 60%
Operating margin	(Operating profit/ revenue) *100	(£80m/£200m) *100 = 40%
Earnings before tax	(Earnings before tax/ revenue) *100	(£75m/£200m) *100 = 37.5%
Earnings after tax	(Earnings after tax/ revenue) *100	(£52m/£200m) *100 = 26%
Retained earnings	(Retained earnings/ revenue) *100	(£42m/£200m) *100 = 21%

Alternatively, a different perspective can be taken, as mentioned earlier – one that focuses on the individual cost elements as a percentage of revenue, as illustrated in Table 2.2. This approach is extremely useful when comparing organizations within the same industrial sector with reference to benchmarking your organization's costs with its competitors.

Table 2.2 Mega plc cost elements as a percentage of revenue

Ratio	Formula	Calculation
Cost of sales %	(Cost of sales/revenue)*100	(£80m/£200m)*100 = 40%
Operating expenses %	(Operating expenses/ revenue)*100	(£40m/£200m)*100 = 20%
Net interest %	(Net interest/revenue)*100	(£5m/£200m)*100 = 2.5%
Taxation %	(Taxation/revenue)*100	(£23m/£200m)*100 = 11.5%
Dividend %	(Dividend/revenue)*100	(£10m/£200m) *100 = 5%

Now have a go at Activity 2.1.

Activity 2.1

Using the information in Table 2.3 extracted from the annual report and accounts of four Mega plc competitors, calculate the five profitability ratios for each company.

Table 2.3 Competitors' income statements

Company	Alpha	Beta	Gamma	Delta
Revenue £m	250	175	225	200
Cost of sales £m	75	80	110	65
Gross profit £m	175	95	115	135
Operating expenses £m	65	40	45	50
Operating profit £m	110	55	70	85
Interest payable £m	0	10	5	6
Interest received £m	2	0	4	2
Earnings before tax £m	112	45	69	81
Taxation £m	35	15	20	25
Earnings after tax £m	77	30	49	56
Dividend paid £m	12	3	10	12
Retained earnings £m	65	27	39	44

(continued)

Table 2.3 *(Continued)*

Ratio	Alpha	Beta	Gamma	Delta
Gross margin %				
Operating margin %				
Earnings before tax %				
Earnings after tax %				
Retained earnings %				

Table 2.4 has been extracted from the Procter & Gamble Company report and accounts for June 2017 (page 36). It illustrates the IS elements for 2017 and 2016 and the percentage change between the two years.

Table 2.4 Procter & Gamble Company consolidated statements of earnings

	Year ended 30 June 2017	Year ended 30 June 2016	
	Amounts in $ millions	Amounts in $ millions	% change
Net sales	65,058	65,299	–0.369
Cost of products sold	32,535	32,909	–1.136
Selling, general and administrative expense	18,568	18,949	–2.011
Operating income	13,955	13,441	3.824
Interest expense	465	579	–19.689
Interest income	171	182	–6.044
Other non-operating income/(expense), net	(404)	325	–224.308
Earnings from continuing operations before income taxes	13,257	13,369	–0.838
Income taxes on continuing operations	3,063	3,342	–8.348
Net earnings from continuing operations	10,194	10,027	1.666

(continued)

Table 2.4   *(Continued)*

	Year ended 30 June 2017	Year ended 30 June 2016	
	Amounts in $ millions	Amounts in $ millions	% change
Net earnings from discontinued operations	5,217	577	804.159
Net earnings	15,411	10,604	45.332
Less: Net earnings attributed to non-controlling interests	85	96	−11.458
Net earnings attributable to Procter & Gamble	15,326	10,508	45.851

In Table 2.5, selected lines related to the organization's continuing operations have been extracted from the Procter & Gamble Company IS, and each line is presented as a percentage of net sales for both years, allowing comparisons to be made between the two accounting periods.

Table 2.5   Income statement as a percentage of net sales

Procter & Gamble Company	% of net sales 2017	% of net sales 2016
Net sales	100.00	100.00
Cost of products sold	50.01	50.40
Selling, general and administrative expense	28.54	29.02
Operating income	21.45	20.58
Interest expense	0.71	0.89
Interest income	0.26	0.28
Other non-operating income/(expense), net	−0.62	0.50
Earnings from continuing operations before income taxes	20.38	20.47
Income taxes on continuing operations	4.71	5.12
Net earnings from continuing operations	15.67	15.36

Both cost of products sold and selling, general and administrative expenses have decreased between 2016 and 2017, resulting in an increase in operating income even though net sales (revenue) has slightly decreased, as illustrated in Table 2.4.

Let us now explore a typical IS using the format in Figure 2.1 and identify the impact that supply chain management (SCM) decisions can have on the individual elements that make up the financial statement. Examples from practice, including extracts from the annual financial reports of organizations, will be used to explore, explain and inform each element of the IS and provide insights into the relationship between SC decisions and their impact on the financial statements.

2.3 Revenue

Revenue is often referred in business as the 'top line'. Let's explore the term *revenue* in more depth using definitions extracted from different organization's report and accounts. Marks and Spencer Group PLC (2018:82) defines revenue as:

> Revenue comprises sales of goods to customers outside the Group less an appropriate deduction for actual and expected returns, discounts and loyalty scheme vouchers, and is stated net of value added tax and other sales taxes. Revenue is recognized when goods are delivered to our franchise partners or the customer and the significant risks and rewards of ownership have been transferred to the buyer.

While Nestlé Group (2017:711) defines the revenue as:

> Sales represent amounts received and receivable from third parties for goods supplied to customers and for services rendered. Revenue from the sales of goods is recognised in the income statement at the moment when significant risks and rewards of ownership of the goods have been transferred to the buyer, which is mainly upon shipment. It is measured at the list price applicable to a given distribution channel after deductions of returns, sales taxes, pricing allowances, other trade discounts and couponing and price promotions to consumers. Payments made to the customers for commercial services received are expensed.

Both of these definitions are important for supply chain practitioners as they identify a number of factors relating to supply chain activities including:

- sales of good calculation;
- returns management;
- distribution;
- channel management;
- promotions.

Revenue is typically reported in the annual report and accounts by:

- time period (year and quarter);
- geographic region;
- product segment;
- operational division;
- customer segmentation.

Data extracted from Deutsche Post DHL Group 2017 annual report (page 178) and accounts illustrates how the organization discloses their revenue. In Table 2.6 revenue is reported by business segment.

Table 2.6   Deutsche Post DHL Group 2017, revenue by business segment

Segment	%
Post/e-commerce/parcel	30
Express	25
Global forwarding/freight	24
Supply chain	23
Corporate centre/other	2
Consolidation *	−4
	100

* *internal transactions between segments*

Table 2.7   Deutsche Post DHL Group 2017, SC revenue by business segment

Sector	%
Retail	25
Consumer	23
Automotive	14
Technology	12
Life sciences and healthcare	11
Others	8
Engineering and manufacturing	5
Financial services	2
	100

The supply chain segment generates 23% of the organization's total revenue for 2017; the accounts also break down the SC segment's revenue by industrial sector, as illustrated in Table 2.7 (DHL Group, 2017: 69).

The retail sector generates 25% of the revenue for the SC segment, which equates to 5.75% of total revenue; this figure is obtained by multiplying 23% by 25%. The SC sector's revenue is also reported by geographical region, as illustrated in Table 2.8, with 51% of SC revenue derived from the Europe/Middle East/Africa region in 2017 (Table 2.8).

Table 2.8   Deutsche Post DHL Group 2017, SC revenue by region

Region	%
Europe/Middle East/Africa	51
Americas	32
Asia Pacific	17
	100

Revenue growth is extremely important to an organization, their shareholders and the financial markets, and therefore measuring growth is key. Typically, in a set of report accounts you will see the current year compared with the previous one, a five-year summary, and in the notes to the accounts you can also find quarterly revenues. Revenue growth can be measured using index numbers; you will have come across indices when listening to the business news, watching TV news and in newspapers. They are extremely useful for highlighting trends; indices measure stock prices (FTSE 100, Dow Jones and other share price indices), inflation (retail price index), commodities such as oil (Brent crude), copper and currencies. An index measures the change from a specific point in time, typically referred to as the base year, which has a value of 100; future values are then calculated in relation to the base year. Table 2.9 illustrates the construction of an index using revenue data extracted from Nestlé Group Annual Report and Accounts (2017:150–151) for the period 2013 to 2017. Using 2013 as the base year, which is given a value of 100, we can express subsequent years in relation to 2013, by constructing a simple index, using the following approach. The revenue for 2014 (CHFm 91,612) is divided by the revenue (CHFm 92,158) in base year 2013 and then multiplied by 100 to give an index figure for 2014, which is 99.41. The index figure of 99.41 demonstrates that the company revenue has reduced in comparison to 2013 as the index has now decreased below 100. For 2017 the index is 97.43, which illustrates that revenue has decreased by 2.57% over the 5 years since 2013.

Table 2.9 Revenue index

Financial year	2013 CHF millions	2014 CHF millions	2015 CHF millions	2016 CHF millions	2017 CHF millions
Revenue	92,158	91,612	88,785	89,469	89,791
Index	100.00	99.41	96.34	97.08	97.43

Typically, a company's annual report discloses data over a five-year period, as illustrated in Table 2.9. However, the impact of an index is enhanced over a longer time period, and when a chart is used to graphically present the index, it becomes very informative and user-friendly, especially for non-specialists, as illustrated in Figure 2.2. This chart uses revenue from Next plc for the period 2004 to 2018.

Figure 2.2 Next plc revenue index, 2004–2018

SOURCE *Fame* (Bureau van Dijk, 2019)

Activity 2.2

Table 2.10 has been extracted from Deutsche Post DHL Group (2017:178) and illustrates eight years' revenue for the period 2010 to 2017. Using 2010 as the base year (100), calculate a simple index for the period.

Table 2.10 Deutsche Post DHL Group, revenue 2010–2017

Financial year	2010	2011	2012	2013	2014	2015	2016	2017
Revenue €m	51,388	52,829	55,512	54,912	56,630	59,230	57,334	60,444

SC practitioners working with their sales and marketing colleagues can have a positive impact on facilitating revenue creation by designing distribution channels that fulfil customer demand and enhance customer service. This significant point is emphasized by Marks & Spencer Group plc (2018:23): 'Our supply chain must be fit for purpose. It is currently slow, outdated and expensive, and must be improved.'

This statement is followed by (2018:23): 'Commencement of an end-to-end review of our supply chain and logistics network across both businesses to deliver improved efficiency of picking, improved trade utilization and a faster, more reliable service for stores and customers.'

2.4 Cost of sales

CIMA terminology (2005:64) defines cost of sales as:

> The cost of goods sold during an accounting period. For a retail business this will be the cost of goods available for sale (opening stock plus purchases) minus closing stock. For a manufacturing business it will include all direct and indirect production costs.

Therefore, the cost of sales for Mega plc (Figure 2.1) is calculated by taking the opening inventory of £25m, adding the purchases made by the company in the year, which is £85m, then subtracting the closing inventory, valued at £30m, to produce a cost of sales of £80m.

	£m
Opening inventory	25
Plus purchases	85
Minus closing inventory	30
Equals	80

Two inventory management ratios can be derived from the information contained in the cost of sales calculation and are extremely useful and important for SC practitioners: they are inventory days and inventory turnover. The number of days' inventory for Mega plc can be calculated as follows:

$$\text{(average inventory/cost of sales)} * 365 \text{ days}$$

Average inventory is calculated by (opening inventory + closing inventory)/2; therefore the average inventory for Mega plc is (£25m + £30m)/2, which is £27.5m. The number of days' inventory can now be derived for Mega plc: (£27.5m/£80m) *365 = 125 days.

The inventory turnover ratio measures the number of times inventory is turnedover in a financial year and is calculated by dividing the number of days in a year (365 days) by the number of days' inventory held by the organization. So for Mega plc it will be 365/125 = 2.92 per year.

Another key performance indicator used in practice is to measure the cost of sales as a percentage of revenue. Mega plc's cost of sales percentage is £80m/£200m multiplied by 100, which is 40%.

Earlier in this section the CIMA definition of cost of sales highlights two types of cost sales calculations: one for a retailer and one for a manufacturer. This point is illustrated from two examples taken from practice, the first from a retailer (Marks & Spencer Group plc) and the second a manufacturer (Procter & Gamble Company). Marks & Spencer Group plc (2018:84) defines the cost of its finished goods inventories as:

> Inventories are valued on a weighted average cost basis and carried at the lower of cost and net realizable value. Cost includes all direct expenditure and other attributable costs incurred in bringing inventories to their present location and condition. All inventories are finished goods.

There are a number of significant points in the definition – which will be addressed later – in particular the weighted average cost basis and net realizable value. However, the definition provides us with greater insight into the types of SC costs that are included in the inventory valuation. Based on the data contained in Marks & Spencer Group plc's annual report (2018:88), their cost of sales as a percentage of sales was 62.17% (2018), and for the previous financial year it was 61.52%. Their average inventory days were 42.24, with an average inventory turnover of 8.64 times per year.

The Procter & Gamble Company (2017:41) defines their cost of products sold as:

> Cost of products sold is primarily comprised of direct materials and supplies consumed in the manufacturing of product, as well as manufacturing labor, depreciation expense and direct overhead expense necessary to acquire and convert the purchased materials and supplies into finished product.

But this definition also includes other SC costs:

> Cost of products sold also includes the cost to distribute products to customers, inbound freight costs, internal transfer costs, warehousing costs and other shipping and handling activity.

The Procter & Gamble Company sees SC management as an opportunity to reduce the organization's cost of product sold and increase gross profit, as stated in their 2017 (viii) report and accounts:

> The majority of the savings opportunities are in cost of goods sold. We see opportunities ahead in raw and packaging materials, manufacturing expense, transportation and warehousing as we fully synchronize our supply network and replenishment systems from our suppliers to our customers.

Therefore, the decisions taken by procurement and SC practitioners with regard to supplier relationship management, purchasing, inventory management, warehousing and distribution will have a significant impact on the cost of sales calculation.

2.5 Inventory and the income statement

Inventory has a significant impact in the financial statements of an organization. It is included in the cost of goods sold calculation, which determines the gross profit as illustrated in the previous section, but the costs of holding inventory will impact on the operating expenses of the organization as well and hence earnings before interest and tax (EBIT).

There is a strict rule with regard to the valuation of inventory in the financial statements of an organization. The rule is that inventory should be valued at the lower of cost or its net realizable value. Marks and Spencer Group PLC £m (2018:86) defines net realizable value as:

Inventory provisions are recognized where the net realizable value from the sale of inventory is estimated to be lower than it carrying value, requiring estimation of the expected future sale price. The estimation includes judgement on a number of factors including historical sales patterns, expected sales profiles, potential obsolescence and shrinkage.

We can now explore how this would work in practice using a simple example. You are doing an inventory check at your distribution centre at the month end. A stock-keeping unit (SKU), which was purchased for £200 six months ago, is damaged. You would not be able to sell the item for its original value; therefore, you decide to mark it down by 60%. Its net realizable value (NRV) is now £80, so it will be valued at NRV, not its cost, on the IS and balance sheet. The difference between the SKU's cost and NRV of £120 will be written off as damages in the IS. Another NRV example is mark-down due to obsolescence, as a new version of the product supersedes the original and therefore the inventory value is reduced in line with the new value of the item. However, if the NRV was more than cost, the original cost would be used to value the SKU.

Activity 2.3: Net realizable value

You have been supplied with the following information from your distribution centre for the year ending 30 June 20X2. Calculate the value of the inventory and the adjustment that will be required in the IS.

Table 2.11   Closing inventory 30 June 20X2

SKU code	Units	Cost per unit £	Net realizable value £ per unit
QWE123	10	35.00	35.50
QWE456	24	12.00	8.75
BNM123	57	9.00	8.00
ZXC267	80	5.00	6.00
QWE673	20	3.00	3.50
PLM420	36	26.00	23.00

2.6 Inventory valuation methods

In practice, most organizations will typically use one of the following three methods to value inventory in their IS and on their balance sheet:

- first in first out (FIFO);
- last in first out (LIFO);
- average cost (AVCO).

These methods will now be introduced and explained further using a fictitious case study to illustrate how the closing inventory valuation is calculated using each method and then compare the impact of each valuation method on the company's gross profit.

Your company purchases a single SKU and then sells it on to its customers. The company's opening inventory in their regional distribution centre (RDC) was 600 units, valued at £15 per unit, valuing its inventory at £9,000 on 01/01/XX. Table 2.12 illustrates the units received into the RDC from suppliers and the sales dispatched to customers from the RDC during January 20XX.

Table 2.12 RDC receipts and issues for January 20XX

Date	Receipts units	£ per unit	Value £	Issues units	£ per unit	Value £
06/01/XX	800	17	13,600			
07/01/XX				1,000	50	50,000
09/01/XX	1,000	20	20,000			
14/01/XX				1,000	50	50,000
16/01/XX	800	23	18,400			
21/01/XX				1,000	50	50,000
22/01/XX	1,000	25	25,000			
28/01/XX				1,000	50	50,000

Using the data in Table 2.12, this exercise will illustrate and explain how the closing inventory valuation is derived using three inventory valuation methods: FIFO, LIFO and AVCO.

Using the RDC transaction data in Table 2.12, we can now demonstrate the impact that the different inventory valuation methods will have on the calculation of the closing inventory for the month and the company's gross profit.

First in first out (FIFO) method

This method is based on the first unit of inventory that is received from the supplier into the RDC and is the first unit to be issued to the customer. Therefore, the closing inventory in December of 600 units will be included in the first order of 1,000 units dispatched to the customer on 7 January 20XX. The closing inventory valuation for the month of January 20XX is 200 units at £25 per unit, which is £5,000, as illustrated in Table 2.13.

Last in first out (LIFO) method

This method adopts a different approach from FIFO. In LIFO, the last unit received into the RDC is the first unit to be issued to the customer, hence the customer's order of 1000 units dispatched on 7 January 20XX contains 800 units that were received on 6 January plus 200 units from the opening inventory. The closing inventory value at the end of January is 200 units at £15, which equates to £3,000; however, these units were also present in January's opening valuation, as under the LIFO approach they have not been issued as subsequent inventory has been received and has been dispatched to customers, as illustrated in Table 2.14.

Table 2.13 First in first out (FIFO) method

Date	Receipts units	£ per unit	Value £	Issues units	£ per unit	Value £	Inventory units	£ per unit	Value £
01/01/XX							600	15	9,000
06/01/XX	800	17	13,600				800	17	13,600
							1,400		22,600
07/01/XX				1,000	50	50,000	-600	15	-9,000
							-400	17	-6,800
							400	17	6,800
09/01/XX	1,000	20	20,000				1,000	20	20,000
							1,400		26,800
14/01/XX				1,000	50	50,000	-400	17	-6,800
							-600	20	-12,000
							400	20	8,000
16/01/XX	800	23	18,400				800	23	18,400
							1,200		26,400
21/01/XX				1,000	50	50,000	-400	20	-8,000

(continued)

Table 2.13 (*Continued*)

Date	Receipts units	£ per unit	Value £	Issues units	£ per unit	Value £	Inventory units	£ per unit	Value £
							−600	23	−13,800
							200	23	4,600
22/01/XX	1,000	25	25,000				1,000	25	25,000
							1,200		29,600
28/01/XX				1,000	50	50,000	−200	23	−4,600
							−800	25	−20,000
31/01/XX							200	25	5,000

Table 2.14 Last in first out (LIFO)

Date	Receipts units	£ per unit	Value £	Issues units	£ per unit	Value £	Inventory units	£ per unit	Value £
01/01/XX							600	15	9,000
06/01/XX	800	17	13,600				800	17	13,600
							1,400		22,600
07/01/XX				1,000	50	50,000	−800	17	−13,600
							−200	15	−3,000
							400	15	6,000
09/01/XX	1,000	20	20,000				1,000	20	20,000
							1,400		26,000
14/01/XX				1,000	50	50,000	−1,000	20	−20,000
							400	15	6,000
16/01/XX	800	23	18,400				800	23	18,400
							1,200		24,400
21/01/XX				1,000	50	50,000	−800	23	−18,400
							−200	15	−3,000
							200	15	3,000
22/01/XX	1,000	25	25,000				1,000	25	25,000
							1,200		28,000
28/01/XX				1,000	50	50,000	−1,000	25	−25,000
							200	15	3,000

Average cost (AVCO) method

AVCO follows the same receipt and issue approach as FIFO but differs in the method used to value inventory by using a moving weighted average, which will vary every time an order is received into the RDC and dispatched. For instance, at the close of business on 6 January, the inventory in the RDC consists of the opening month's inventory of 600 units at £15, plus a delivery of 800 units received that day, which cost £17 per unit, which equates to £13,600. AVCO uses a weighted average to derive the inventory valuation for 6 January 20XX, which is £16.143, as illustrated in Table 2.15. Using the AVCO method, the closing valuation for January 20XX will be £4,888 = 200 units @ £24,439 (Table 2.16 on page 29).

Table 2.15 Weighted average method

Units	Cost £ per unit	Valuation £
600	15.000	9,000
800	17.000	13,600
1,400	16.143	22,600

Nestlé Group (2017:90) adopts the weighted average method as disclosed in their accounting policies:

> Work in progress, sundry supplies and manufactured finished goods are valued at the lower of their weight average cost and net realizable value.

Here is an interesting dilemma to think about: if three organizations have identical opening inventory valuation, they have the same receipts and sales, but each uses a different inventory valuation method; a different value will be placed on the inventory at the end of the accounting period. This will result in a different cost of sales calculation for each company and hence a different gross profit, as illustrated in Table 2.17, but it also will have implications for the inventory days and inventory turnover ratios.

An organization will state in the notes of its annual report and accounts the method of inventory valuation used in the cost of goods sold calculation. The following table illustrates the policy used from five organizations, which has been extracted from their annual reports from 2017 and provides additional insight into the calculation method.

Table 2.16 Average cost (AVCO) method

Date	Receipts units	£ per unit	Value £	Issues units	£ per unit	Value £	Inventory units	£ per unit	Value £
01/01/XX							600	15.000	9,000
06/01/XX	800	17	13,600				800	17.000	13,600
							1,400	16.143	22,600
07/01/XX				1,000	50	50,000	–1,000	16.143	–16,143
07/01/XX							400	16.143	6,457
09/01/XX	1,000	20	20,000				1,000	20.000	20,000
							1,400	18.898	26,457
14/01/XX				1,000	50	50,000	–1,000	18.898	–18,898
							400	18.898	7,559
16/01/XX	800	23	18,400				800	23.000	18,400
							1,200	21.633	25,959
21/01/XX				1,000	50	50,000	–1,000	21.633	–21,633
							200	21.633	4,327
22/01/XX	1,000	25	25,000				1,000	25.000	25,000
							1,200	24.439	29,327
28/01/XX				1,000	50	50,000	–1,000	24.439	–24,4389
							200	24.439	4,888

Table 2.17 Inventory valuation method and gross profit calculation

Inventory method	FIFO		LIFO		AVCO	
Sales £		200,000		200,000		200,000
Opening inventory £	9,000		9,000		9,000	
Purchases £	77,000		77,000		77,000	
Closing inventory £	5,000	81,000	3,000	83,000	4,888	81,112
Gross profit £		119,000		117,000		118,888
Gross margin %		59.5%		58.5%		59.4%

Activity 2.4

A company purchases a single SKU from a distributor and then resells it on to their customers. The company's opening inventory was 1,000 units valued at £10 per unit, valuing its inventory at £10,000 on 01/01/XX. Table 2.18 illustrates the units received into their RDC and the units sold to their customers during the month of January.

Table 2.18 RDC receipts and issues for January 20XX

Date	Receipts units	£ per unit	Value £	Issues units	£ per unit	Value £
10/01/XX	2,000	12	24,000			
20/01/XX				2,500	20	50,000

Use the data in the table to calculate the closing inventory valuation and gross profit for the business in January using three different inventory valuation methods: FIFO, LIFO and AVCO.

Table 2.19 on page 31 reveals a number of interesting insights with regards to the different inventory valuations method used in practice. For instance, Nestlé Group use different inventory valuation methods in their SC operation with FIFO being adopted for raw materials and purchased finished goods. While a weighted average cost valuation method has been adopted for work in progress (WIP), sundry supplies and manufactured finished goods. P&G use FIFO for product related inventories, but for spare parts they use an average cost method.

Table 2.19 Inventory valuation policy used in practice

Organization	Inventory valuation policy
BASF Group	'Inventories are measured at acquisition cost or cost of conversion based on the weighted average method. If the market price or fair value of the sales product which forms the basis for the net realizable value is lower, then the sales products are written down to this lower value. The net realizable value is the estimated price in the ordinary course of business less the estimated costs of completion and the estimated selling costs.' (2017:179)
Deutsche Post DHL Group	'Inventories are assets that are held for sale in the course of business, are in the process of production, or are consumed in the production process or in the rendering of services. They are measured at the lower of cost or net realizable value. Valuation allowances are charged for obsolete inventories and slow-moving goods.' (2017:117)
Marks and Spencer Group PLC	'Inventories are valued on a weighted average cost basis and carried at the lower of cost and net realizable value. Cost includes all direct expenditure and other attributable costs incurred in bringing inventories to their present location and condition. All inventories are finished goods. Certain purchases of inventories may be subject to cash flow hedges for foreign exchange risk. The Group applies a basis adjustment for those purchases in a way that the cost is initially established by reference to the hedged exchange rate and not the spot rate at the day of purchase.' (2017:98)
Nestlé Group	'Raw materials and purchased finished goods are valued at the lower of purchase cost calculated using the FIFO (first-in, first-out) method and net realizable value. Work in progress, sundry supplies and manufactured finished goods are valued at the lower of their weighted average cost and net realizable value. The cost of inventories includes the gains/losses on cash flow hedges for the purchase of raw materials and finished goods.' (2017:88)

(continued)

Table 2.19 (*Continued*)

Organization	Inventory valuation policy
Procter & Gamble Company	'Inventories are valued at the lower of cost or market value. Product-related inventories are maintained on the first-in, first-out method. The cost of spare part inventories is maintained using the average-cost method.' (2017:42)

2.7 Operating expenses

Operating expenditure is another significant area where SC management practitioners can make a positive impact on the financial performance of their organization. As in the previous sections of this chapter, I will introduce examples to you from practice to highlight the subject area. As you progress through this chapter, I want you to reflect on the organization that you work for now, or organizations that you have previously worked for in the past or an academic institution where you are studying. I would like you to draw on the many examples of operating costs that you are currently experiencing or have experienced in the past, as this will emphasize further the importance of the decisions that you have taken in the past or are about to take.

In this section we will look at operating expenditure from a number of different organization perspectives, including a retailer (Marks & Spencer Group plc), a manufacturer (Procter & Gamble Company), a third-party logistics operator (Deutsche Post DHL Group) and a chemical company (BASF Group), using examples taken from their annual report and accounts to explore this significant cost component of the IS. The objective is to introduce and reveal the types of costs that organizations classify as operating costs, not to make a judgement on their performance.

For a retail perspective of operating costs, I will use examples extracted from the 2018 annual report and accounts of Marks & Spencer Group plc. In 2018, selling and administrative expenses represented just over 32% of the company's revenue for the financial year. Table 2.20 illustrates the breakdown of selling and administrative expenses by type (2018:88).

Table 2.20   Marks & Spencer Group plc, selling and administrative
expenses 2018

Selling and administrative expenses	£m
Employee costs	1,521.0
Occupancy costs	705.6
Repairs, renewal and maintenance of property	94.7
Depreciation, amortization and asset impairments and write-offs before adjusting items	580.6
Other costs	524.3
Selling and administrative expenses	**3,426.2**

Approximately 44.4% of selling and administrative expenses are related
to employee costs, occupancy costs account for 20.6%, with depreciation, amortization, asset impairments and write-offs before adjusting items
responsible for 16.9% of the total.

Taking a fast-moving consumer goods (FMCG) perspective on operating
expenses, Procter & Gamble Company (2017:41) define them as:

> Selling, general and administrative expense (SG&A) is primarily comprised
> of marketing expenses, selling expenses, research and development costs,
> administrative and other indirect overhead costs, depreciation and amortization
> expense on non-manufacturing assets and other miscellaneous operating items.

In 2017, Procter & Gamble Company's selling, general and administrative
expenses were 28.54% of their sales revenue compared with the previous
year's figure of 29.02%, which equates to a reduction of 1.65% (see Table 2.4).

We can now look at operating expenses from a logistics perspective using
Deutsche Post DHL Group as an example. Deutsche Post DHL Group
(2017:113) recognizes operating expenses as: 'Operating expenses are
recognised in income when the service is utilised or when the expenses are
incurred.'

In 2017, Deutsche Post DHL Group's operating expenses increased by
€2,841m, which is just over a 5% increase on the previous year. However,
in 2017, operating expenses were 97.35% of sales revenue compared with
the previous year's figure of 97.67%, hence operating expenses reduced as a
percentage of sales revenue (see Table 2.21).

The previous three examples have come from retail, FMCG and logistics perspectives. The next example is the chemical company BASF Group.

Table 2.21   Deutsche Post DHL Group, operating expenses

Operating expenses	2017 €m	2016 €m
Materials expense	32,775	30,620
Staff costs	20,072	19,592
Depreciation, amortization and impairment losses	1,471	1,377
Other operating expenses	4,526	4,414
Total operating expenses	**58,844**	**56,003**

SOURCE Deutsche Post DHL Group (2017:102)

Table 2.22 illustrates BASF Group (2017:168) operating expenses extracted from their statement of income for the financial years 2017 and 2016.

Table 2.22   BASF Group (2017:168) operating expenses for the financial years 2017 and 2016

	2017 €m	2016 €m	% change
Selling expenses	8,262	7,764	6.41
General administration expenses	1,412	1,337	5.61
Research and development expenses	1,888	1,863	1.34
Other operating expenses	2,949	3,133	–5.87

Depreciation and amortization costs are significant items of operating expenditure for all of the organizations illustrated in this section. The concept of depreciation and amortization is explored further in Chapter 5.

2.8 Net finance costs

Typically, in the IS the net finance costs are reported, but in the notes to the accounts additional information is disclosed, as illustrated in Table 2.23, extracted from the notes of the 2017 accounts of Deutsche Post DHL Group. During 2016–17, the organization's net finance costs were negative and therefore a cost to the business.

Table 2.23   Deutsche Post DHL Group, net finance costs

Financial income	2017 €m	2016 €m
Interest income	55	54
Income from other equity investments and financial assets	1	1
Other financial income	33	35
	89	**90**
Financial costs		
Interest expenses	−282	−302
of which unwinding of discounts for net pension provision and other provisions	*−130*	*−156*
Other financial costs	−200	−82
	−482	**−384**
Foreign currency losses	−18	−65
Net finance costs	**−411**	**−359**

SOURCE Deutsche Post DHL Group (2017:127)

2.9 Earnings before tax

Earnings before tax is derived by deducting from revenue the cost of goods sold, operating expenses and net finance costs. Deutsche Post DHL Group (2017: 36) defines profit before tax for their divisions as:

> EBIT is calculated by deducting materials expense and staff costs, depreciation, amortization and impairment losses, as well as other operating expenses from revenue and other operating income, and adding net income from investments accounted for using the equity method. Interest and other finance costs/other financial income are shown in net financial income/net finance costs.

Table 2.24 illustrates the earnings before tax calculation from the Deutsche Post DHL Group (2017:102) IS. The organization's earnings (profit) before tax for 2017 and 2016 is €3,741m and €3,491m, which equates to a margin of 6.19% and 6.09% respectively.

Earnings before interest and tax margin is a more relevant ratio for accessing the impact of the decisions taken by SC practitioners. EBIT is simply calculated by adding back net finance costs onto earnings before

Table 2.24   Deutsche Post DHL Group, income statement

Income statement €m	2017	2016
Revenue	60,444	57,334
Other operating income	2,139	2,156
Total operating income	62,583	59,490
Materials expense	32,775	30,620
Staff costs	20,072	19,592
Depreciation, amortization and impairment losses	1,471	1,377
Other operating expenses	4,526	4,414
Total operating expenses	58,844	56,003
Net income from investments accounting for using the equity method	2	4
Profit from operating activities (EBIT)	**3,741**	**3,491**
Financial income	89	90
Financial costs	482	384
Foreign currency losses	18	65
Net finance costs	**411**	**359**
Profit before income taxes	**3,330**	**3,132**

tax; for the financial year ending 2017, Deutsche Post DHL Group's EBIT margin is (€3,741m/€60,444m) * 100 = 5.74%.

Taking a retail perspective, let us now explore three profitability ratios using data from Next plc from the period 2004–18:

- gross margin (%);
- EBIT margin (%);
- EBITDA margin (%).

The ratios were extracted from the FAME database (Bureau van Dijk) for the period 2004 to 2018 and are illustrated in Table 2.25 and Figure 2.3.

It can be seen from Table 2.25 and Figure 2.3 that all three profitability ratios have increased over the time period, with the gross margin increasing by 11.65%, EBIT margin increasing 27.92% and the EBITDA margin by 25.72%. Using profitability ratios provides insights into different aspects of the IS and the organizational functions that influence those areas, which will be explored further in section 2.10.

Table 2.25 Next plc, profitability ratios

Ratio	2018	2017	2016	2015	2014	2013	2012	2011	2010	2009	2008	2007	2006	2005	2004
Gross margin (%)	33.44	33.48	34.78	33.59	33.16	31.60	30.38	29.21	29.26	27.77	28.51	27.76	27.85	31.36	29.95
EBIT margin (%)	18.74	20.20	20.76	20.30	19.33	19.51	17.49	16.64	15.55	14.59	16.10	15.41	15.10	15.35	14.65
EBITDA margin (%)	21.75	23.08	23.56	23.17	22.54	22.85	21.01	20.16	19.35	18.16	19.35	18.53	17.71	17.98	17.30

SOURCE Bureau van Dijk (2018)

Figure 2.3   Next plc, profitability ratios

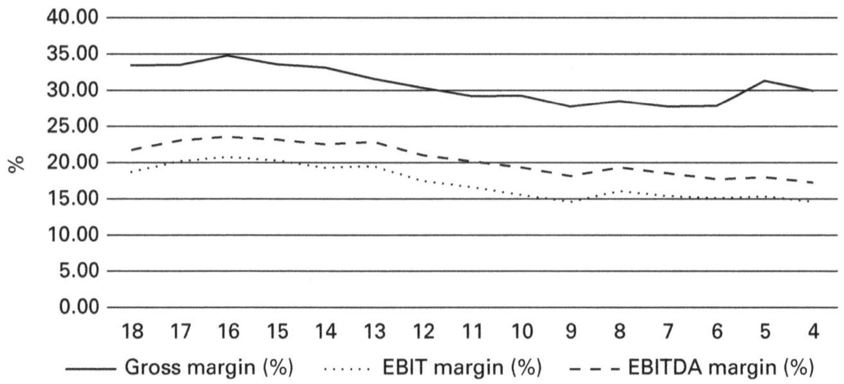

SOURCE Adapted from: Bureau van Dijk (2018)

2.10 Taxation, earnings after tax, dividends and retained earnings

The remaining elements of the IS are grouped together, as typically direct taxation calculations and dividends policy have traditionally been outside the scope of the decisions taken by SC practitioners. However, the relationship between taxation and SC design has attracted a lot of attention in recent years with the emergence of tax-efficient SC management.

Beregheanu *et al* (2010) make the important connection between SC design and tax planning:

> Tax Efficient Supply Chain Management (TESCM) takes as its premise that supply chain design and execution is inherently linked to taxation planning and optimisation, and that tax costs and risks arising from supply chain design should be subject to the same management rigour as the supply chain operating costs.

The significant point here is that when designing a global supply network, it is important to take into consideration the potential tax implications of your design and involve your specialist taxation team at the initial design stages to minimize the risk of incurring an unforeseen tax (indirect or direct) liability.

2.11 SC management and profitability

SC management decisions will have a significant impact on the components of the IS, including revenue, cost of goods sold, operating expenses and taxation.

An organization's profit margin can be increased by enhancing revenue and reducing expenditure, therefore it is important that SC practitioners are able to demonstrate how their decisions impact on these two variables. SC initiatives that can have an impact on revenue and costs will be mapped onto Porter's value chain activities. Porter argues that each of the activities in the value chain need to be considered when focusing on value creation (1985:33–34):

> Competitive advantage cannot be understood by looking at a firm as a whole. It stems from the many discrete activities a firm performs in designing, producing, marketing, delivering and supporting its production. Each of these activities can contribute to a firm's relative cost position and create a basis for differentiation.

Porter (33–34) emphasizes this point further: 'A firm gains competitive advantage by performing these strategically important activities more cheaply or better than its competitors.'

Table 2.26 maps potential initiatives on to supply chain activities. The initiatives identified are not exhaustive, but indicative and can be extended further.

Table 2.26 Maps potential SC initiatives on to supply chain activities

Supply chain activities	Sub activities	Potential SC initiatives
	Supplier relationship management	• Review outsourcing, insourcing and offshoring opportunities; • Review the cost of goods sold calculation; • Assess supplier (supplier audits); • Evaluate supplier relationship management (SRM) opportunities; • Explore the total cost of ownership of procurement decisions.
Up stream	Goods in	• Evaluate factory gate pricing (FGP); • Review Incoterms; • Explore just in time (JIT); • Examine total landed cost (TLC); • Consider Vendor-managed inventory (VMI).

(*continued*)

Table 2.26 *(Continued)*

Supply chain activities	Sub activities	Potential SC initiatives
Conversion	Manufacturing, production and operations	• Identifying non-value activities; • Explore outsourcing, insourcing an offshoring opportunity; • Examine opportunities to reducing waste in business processes.; • Evaluate toll manufacturing.
Down stream	Goods	• Evaluate third-party logistics solutions; • Understanding the cost to serve different customers; • Explore collaboration opportunities with customers, suppliers and competitors.
	Returns management	• Evaluate returns management; • Revise after sales service; • Evaluate customer complaints.
	Customer relationship management	• Review customer relationship management (CRM); • Evaluate functional integration and matrix management opportunities; • Review new product development (NPD) time to market; • Evaluate on-shelf availability performance; • Explore the opportunities to develop value added services; • Examine customer service performance; • Collaboration with customers, suppliers and competitors; • Evaluate on time in full (OTIF) performance.

(continued)

Table 2.26 (*Continued*)

Supply chain activities	Sub activities	Potential SC initiatives
Support	Information technology	• Assess the opportunities associated with artificial intelligence (AI); • Re-evaluate the application of automation; • Review the opportunities relating to big data, cloud technology and analytics; • Assess the application of blockchain and smart contracts; • Evaluate the possibilities of machine learning; • Evaluate the adoption of radio frequency identification (RFID); • Explore the application of robotics with the organization; • Evaluate routing and scheduling technologies; • Explore asset ownership (own, lease or rent); • Identifying and reducing unproductive assets; • Evaluate network design opportunities.
	People management and development	• Evaluate Driver training; • Review alternative remuneration schemes; • Examine future succession planning.
	Overheads	• Review outsourcing opportunities; • Evaluating shared services with competitors.

Here are two examples taken from practice where organizations recognize the significant contribution that the SC can make in enhancing profitability. The first example is from Marks & Spencer plc and was sourced from their 2018 (5) report and accounts under the sub-heading 'Supply chain fit for purpose': 'In order to be a faster and more commercial business we must improve our SC, which is slow, inefficient and expensive.'

The piece then introduces the SC initiatives that are being implemented by Marks & Spencer plc (2018:5), first in clothing and home:

> In Clothing & Home, the announcement of our investment in a new distribution centre at Welham Green is a step towards delivering a single-tier network of national distribution centres. This will enable us to reduce stock holding points which make our store deliveries slow and mean we carry many weeks' more stock than our competitors.

Then in Marks & Spencer plc's (2018:5) food operation:

> In Food we have a high-cost distribution model which limits availability and increases waste. We are rolling out operational improvements across our stores with the aim of improving stock file accuracy, reducing stock held in the back of our stores and ensuring appropriate deliveries.

This chapter has concentrated on the relationship between the IS and the SC; however, I must stress that the role of the SC is not just about taking cost out of business processes. The role of SC goes much further and it is important that we as SC practitioners recognize and understand the pivotal role we play in assisting the creation of shareholder/stakeholder value. I must also state the 'flip side': if the SC fails, it can destroy value. Sadly, we tend to hear about the failures more as they hit the front pages and the news bulletins, rather than the former, which are often taken for granted. This chapter concludes with a quotation which for me sums up the significant role that the SC plays in business.

Ellram and Liu (2002:30) argue that the impact of SC management is not just confined to reducing cost:

> The financial impact of purchasing and supply management goes well beyond cost reduction. It extends to such critical performance areas as business growth, profitability, cash flow, and asset utilization.

They stress the importance of communicating the role of purchase and supply management:

> SC managers need to be able to quantify that broader impact. And then convey that message upward so that top management better understands how purchasing and supply management can contribute to company success.

2.12 Summary

This chapter recognizes the strategically important relationship between an organization's supply chain operation and the profitability of the business. This chapter describes the role of the income statement (IS) from its top line to its bottom line, identifying the different elements that make up a typical IS. The chapter identifies those important elements that SC practitioners can influence, such as the cost of goods sold calculation, choice of inventory valuation method, gross margin calculation and operating expenses. The chapter explores and explains the impact that supply chain decisions can have on the IS by mapping potential SC initiatives onto Porter's value chain activities. The chapter includes examples from practice taken from different industrial sectors, including retailing, manufacturing, logistics, and finance to illustrate the relation between SC and the IS. Finally, a set of important financial ratios that are used to evaluate the IS, which is essential for SC practitioners to know, are introduced and explained.

2.13 References

BASF Group (2017) *Report*, http://report.basf.com/2017/en/ (accessed 15 December 2018)

Bureau van Dijk (2018) www.bvdinfo.com/en-gb/contact-us/office-locations (accessed 18 November 2018)

Beregheanu, M, Dunkerley, G, Sarson, T, and Templar, S (2010) Tax efficient supply chain management: determinants and benefits, in *Logistics Research Network Annual Conference*, Harrogate, UK, 8–10 September

Christopher, M (2011) *Logistics and Supply Chain Management: Creating value-adding networks,* 4th edn, Pearson Education, Harlow

CIMA (2005) *CIMA Official Terminology*, CIMA Publishing, Oxford

Deutsche Post DHL Group (2017) *Annual Report*, https://annualreport2017.dpdhl.com/downloads-ext/en/documents/DPDHL_2017_Annual_Report.pdf (accessed 15 December 2018)

Dickens, C (2016) *David Copperfield*, Bloomsbury Publishing, London

Ellram, LM and Liu, B (2002) The financial impact of supply chain management, *Supply Chain Management Review*, 6 (6), pp 30–37

Marks & Spencer Group Plc (2018) *Annual Report and Financial Statements*, https://corporate.marksandspencer.com/annualreport (accessed 15 December 2018)

Nestlé (2017) *Annual Review*, www.nestle.com/investors/publications#tab-2017 (accessed 15 December 2018)

Porter, M (1985) *Competitive Advantage: Creating and sustaining superior performance*, Free Press, New York

Procter & Gamble Company (2017) *Form 10-K*, www.annualreports.com/Hosted-Data/AnnualReports/PDF/NYSE_PG_2017.pdf (accessed 15 December 2018)

2.14 Solutions to the activities

Activity 2.1

The profitability ratios for Mega plc and their competitors are illustrated in Table 2.27.

Table 2.27   Profitability ratios

Ratio	Mega	Alpha	Beta	Gamma	Delta
Gross margin %	60.0%	70.0%	54.3%	51.1%	67.5%
Operating margin %	40.0%	44.0%	31.4%	31.1%	42.5%
Earnings before tax %	37.5%	44.8%	25.7%	30.7%	40.5%
Earnings after tax %	26.0%	30.8%	17.1%	21.8%	28.0%
Retained earnings %	21.0%	26.0%	15.4%	17.3%	22.0%

Alpha has the highest gross margin of 70%, and the range between the largest and the smallest is 18.9%; therefore, it is worth Mega plc exploring potential procurement scenarios to reduce their cost of sales. Alpha and Delta have operating margins higher than Mega plc's 40%; focusing on Mega's operating expenditure could be an opportunity to improve operating margin. The other three profit ratios are not directly related to SC decisions as they relate to interest, taxation and dividend decisions, which are influenced by decisions taken by other functions. However, there is an argument that in certain circumstances designing SCs can be tax-efficient, which can legally reduce your organization's tax liability.

Activity 2.2

Using 2010 as the base year (100), a simple revenue index has been produced (Table 2.28) using revenue data extracted from Deutsche Post DHL Group's annual report (2017:178) for the financial years 2010 to 2017.

Table 2.28   Deutsche Post DHL Group, revenue 2010–2017

Financial year	2010	2011	2012	2013	2014	2015	2016	2017
Revenue €m	51,388	52,829	55,512	54,912	56,630	59,230	57,334	60,444

Table 2.29 illustrates that the organization's revenue has increased by 17.62% over the eight years

Table 2.29 Deutsche Post DHL Group, revenue 2010–2017 index (Base year = 2010)

Financial year	2010	2011	2012	2013	2014	2015	2016	2017
Index	100.00	102.80	108.03	106.86	110.20	115.26	111.57	117.62

Activity 2.3

The company's closing inventory valuation in their RDC for the six SKUs will be £2,304; this is calculated by taking the lower of cost or net realizable value for each SKU, as illustrated in Table 2.30.

The difference between the total cost and the new valuation of £243, effectively a mark-down, will be written off as a cost in the IS.

Table 2.30 Closing inventory valuation

SKU code	Inventory units	Cost £ per unit	Net realizable value £ per unit	Cost £	NRV £	Lowest £
QWE123	10	35.00	35.50	350	355	350
QWE456	24	12.00	8.75	288	210	210
BNM123	57	9.00	8.00	513	456	456
ZXC267	80	5.00	6.00	400	480	400
QWE673	20	3.00	3.50	60	70	60
PLM420	36	26.00	23.00	936	828	828
				2,547	**2,399**	**2,304**

Activity 2.4

Tables 2.31–2.33 illustrate the three different inventory valuation methods.

Table 2.31   First in first out (FIFO) method

Date	Receipts units	£ per unit	Value £	Issues units	£ per unit	Value £	Inventory units	£ per unit	Value £
01/01/XX							1,000	10	10,000
10/01/XX	2,000	12	24,000				2,000	12	24,000
							3,000		34,000
20/01/XX				2,500*	20	50,000	500	12	6,000
31/01/XX							500	12	6,000

* The value of the inventory issued was £28,000 (£10 x 1000 units plus £12 x 1500 units).

Table 2.32   Last in first out (LIFO)

Date	Receipts units	£ per unit	Value £	Issues units	£ per unit	Value £	Inventory units	£ per unit	Value £
01/01/XX							1,000	10	10,000
10/01/XX	2,000	12	24,000				2,000	12	24,000
							3,000		34,000
20/01/XX				2,500*	20	50,000	500	10	5,000
31/01/XX							500	10	5,000

* The value of the inventory issued was £29,000 (2000 units @ £12 plus 500 units @ £10).

Table 2.33   Average cost (AVCO) method

Date	Receipts units	£ per unit	Value £	Issues units	£ per unit	Value £	Inventory units	£ per unit	Value £
01/01/XX							1,000	10.000	10,000
10/01/XX	2,000	12	24,000				2,000	12.000	24,000
							3,000	11.334	34,000
20/01/XX				2,500*	20	50,000	500	11.334	5,667
31/01/XX							500	11.334	5,667

* The value of the inventory issued was £28,333 (2500 units @ £11.334).

Table 2.34 depicts the three different inventory valuation methods and their impact on the organization's gross profit calculation and margin. It can be seen that if the company uses LIFO, their margin will be less than if they used FIFO, while the margin using AVCO will be between LIFO and FIFO.

Table 2.34   Inventory valuation method and gross profit calculation

Inventory method	FIFO		LIFO		AVCO	
Sales £		50,000		50,000		50,000
Opening inventory £	10,000		10,000		10,000	
Purchases £	24,000		24,000		24,000	
Closing inventory £	6,000	28,000	5,000	29,000	5,667	28,333
Gross profit £		22,000		21,000		21,667
Gross margin %		44%		42%		43.33%

2.15 Study questions

Study question 2.1

Using the information in Table 2.35, which has been extracted from the income statements of four organizations, complete Table 2.36 by calculating the IS ratios for each company.

Table 2.35   Income statement data

Company	Red	Blue	Green	Yellow
Revenue £m	**356**	**784**	**954**	**259**
Cost of sales £m	198	583	769	187
Gross profit £m	**158**	**201**	**185**	**72**
Operating expenses £m	65	121	98	43
Operating profit £m	**93**	**80**	**87**	**29**
Interest payable £m	6	8	12	2
Interest received £m	1	2	2	0
Earnings before tax £m	**88**	**74**	**77**	**27**
Taxation £m	22	20	20	6
Earnings after tax £m	**66**	**54**	**57**	**21**
Dividend paid £m	7	6	8	3
Retained earnings £m	**59**	**48**	**49**	**18**

Table 2.36   Income statement ratios

Ratio	Red	Blue	Green	Yellow
Gross margin %				
Operating margin %				
Earnings before tax %				
Earnings after tax %				
Retained earnings %				
Cost of sales %				
Operating expenses %				
Net interest %				
Taxation %				
Dividend %				

Study question 2.2

The revenue figures in Table 2.37 have been extracted from the Marks & Spencer Group plc annual report (2018:119).

Using 2014 as the base year, complete Table 2.38 by calculating the index numbers for UK, international and total revenue for the period 2014 to 2018.

Table 2.37   Marks & Spencer Group plc, revenue 2014–2018

Financial year	2014 £ millions	2015 £ millions	2016 £ millions	2017 £ millions	2018 £ millions
UK	9,155.7	9,223.1	9,470.8	9,441.7	9,611.0
International	1,154.0	1,088.3	1,084.6	1,180.3	1,087.2
Total	10,309.7	10,311.4	10,555.4	10,622.0	10,698.2

Table 2.38   Marks & Spencer Group plc, revenue index 2014–2018

Financial year	2014	2015	2016	2017	2018
UK	100.0				
International	100.0				
Total	100.0				

Study question 2.3

The company's closing inventory for the end of the financial year is detailed in Table 2.39. Calculate the value of the company's closing inventory.

Table 2.39   Closing inventory check

SKU code	Inventory units	Cost £ per unit	Net realizable value £ per unit
XTX897	20	5.00	5.50
MNU239	80	2.00	3.00
SCT753	55	8.00	7.00
SLT159	60	7.00	7.00
TCT852	30	2.00	2.50
GJT158	50	1.00	1.30
CJT654	40	6.00	6.25

Study question 2.4

Using the financial data for the five companies contained in Table 2.40, calculate the three profitability ratios for each organization.

Table 2.40   Profitability ratios

	Company A	Company B	Company C	Company D	Company E
Sales £m	400	200	600	500	300
Cost of sales £m	100	55	200	150	120
Operating expenses £m	120	70	150	200	100
Depreciation £m	30	20	45	30	25
Gross margin %					
EBIT %					
EBITDA %					

2.16 Study question solutions

Study question 2.1 solution

Company Red has the best set of profitability ratios of the four companies, with Company Green the lowest. Focusing on the key cost lines, Green has the highest cost of sales percentage at 80.61, which means for every £1 of revenue generated by the company, nearly 81 pence equates to the cost of sales, compared with Red, whose figure is just under 56 pence. Although Red has the highest profitability in terms of percentage in sales, the company has the highest operating expenses with 18.26%, compared with Green's 10.27%.

Table 2.41 Income statement data

Company	Red	Blue	Green	Yellow
Revenue £m	356	784	954	259
Cost of sales £m	198	583	769	187
Gross profit £m	158	201	185	72
Operating expenses £m	65	121	98	43
Operating profit £m	93	80	87	29
Interest payable £m	6	8	12	2
Interest received £m	1	2	2	0
Earnings before tax £m	88	74	77	27
Taxation £m	22	20	20	6
Earnings after tax £m	66	54	57	21
Dividend paid £m	7	6	8	3
Retained earnings £m	59	48	49	18

Table 2.42 Income statement ratios

Ratio	Red	Blue	Green	Yellow
Gross margin %	44.38%	25.64%	19.39%	27.80%
Operating margin %	26.12%	10.20%	9.12%	11.20%
Earnings before tax %	24.72%	9.44%	8.07%	10.42%
Earnings after tax %	18.54%	6.89%	5.97%	8.11%
Retained earnings %	16.57%	6.12%	5.14%	6.95%
Cost of sales %	55.62%	74.36%	80.61%	72.20%

(continued)

Table 2.42 (*Continued*)

Ratio	Red	Blue	Green	Yellow
Operating expenses %	18.26%	15.43%	10.27%	16.60%
Net interest %	1.40%	0.77%	1.05%	0.77%
Taxation %	6.18%	2.55%	2.10%	2.32%
Dividend %	1.97%	0.77%	0.84%	1.16%

Study question 2.2 solution

It can be seen from Table 2.43 that the total revenue for the five-year period 2014 to 2018 has increased by 3.77%.

Table 2.43 Marks & Spencer Group plc, revenue index 2014–2018

Financial year	2014	2015	2016	2017	2018
UK	100.00	100.74	103.44	103.12	104.97
International	100.00	94.31	93.99	102.28	94.21
Total	100.00	100.02	102.38	103.03	103.77

UK revenue has increased by nearly 5% over the period; however, international revenue has declined by 5.79%, as illustrated in Figure 2.4.

Figure 2.4 Marks & Spencer Group plc, revenue index 2014–2018

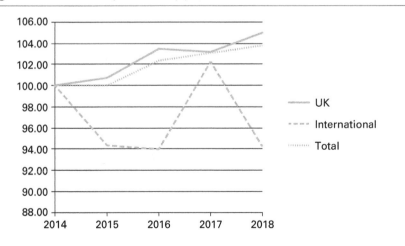

Study question 2.3 solution

The company's closing inventory for the end of the financial year is detailed in Table 2.44. The value of the company's closing inventory is £1,415.00, and the company will have to write off the difference between the cost and lowest value, which is £55.00 in their IS for the financial year.

Table 2.44   Closing inventory valuation

SKU code	Inventory units	Cost £ per unit	Net realizable value £ per unit	Cost £	NRV £	Lowest £
XTX897	20	5.00	5.50	100.00	110.00	100.00
MNU239	80	2.00	3.00	160.00	240.00	160.00
SCT753	55	8.00	7.00	440.00	385.00	385.00
SLT159	60	7.00	7.00	420.00	420.00	420.00
TCT852	30	2.00	2.50	60.00	75.00	60.00
GJT158	50	1.00	1.30	50.00	65.00	50.00
CJT654	40	6.00	6.25	240.00	250.00	240.00
				1,470.00	1,545.00	1,415.00

Study question 2.4 solution

Company A has the highest set of profitability ratios, while Company E has the lowest. Calculating the EBITDA percentage removes the issue of different depreciation policies and allows a comparison to be made on a 'like for like' basis.

Table 2.45   Profitability ratios

	Company A	Company B	Company C	Company D	Company E
Sales £m	400	200	600	500	300
Cost of sales £m	100	55	200	150	120
Operating expenses £m	120	70	150	200	100
Depreciation £m	30	20	45	30	25
Gross margin %	75%	73%	67%	70%	60%
EBIT %	45%	38%	42%	30%	27%
EBITDA %	53%	48%	49%	36%	35%

The balance sheet 03

In the previous chapter, we concentrated on the income statement (IS), focusing on the supply chain relationship with revenue, expenditure and profitability. In this chapter we are going to look at the supply chain infrastructure that needs to be in place to deliver revenue and profitability for an organization as well as look at where the sources of funding came from to pay for it. The information we require to explore and understand these two points is disclosed in the organization's balance sheet (BS) or, as it is also referred to, the 'statement of financial provision'.

Before we explore the statement of financial provision in more depth (I prefer the balance sheet myself), I must also warn you that the BS can take many guises, but fundamentally the different formats all do the same thing, that is, they tell us where the organization has raised its finance 'from' and where the money went 'to'. Typically, the BS is prepared on the last day of the financial year, and the organization can choose any date; typically 31 March and 31 December are preferred, although there are exceptions. An extremely important point to remember is that the BS illustrates the financial position of the organization for just a single day and this is reflected in wording of the BS's title. The title on the statement contains the phrase 'as at', that is, 'on this day'. If you think of a film, for example, as the financial year, a single frame of the film would be the BS. Hence the organization's financial position will be slightly different on the day before (30 December) and the day after (1 January); just as the action in the film changes by a single frame, business transactions in a business change minute by minute. You may also have come across other words to describe the BS, such as photograph, a still, a frozen image, and one point in time.

3.1 Aim and objectives

The aim of this chapter is to introduce you to the BS of an organization and recognize the impact that supply chain management decisions have on this financial statement.

At the end of this chapter you will be able to:

- explain the role of the BS;
- explore the structure of a typical BS;
- identify the different segments that make up a typical balance sheet;
- explain the impact of supply chain decisions on the balance sheet;
- calculate financial ratios that are relevant to evaluating the balance sheet.

3.2 Debits, credits and account types

There are five different account types in business: income, expenditure, asset, liability and equity. Table 3.1 illustrates the five account types that make up the two key financial statements: two form the IS (revenue and expenditure) and the other three make up the BS. From a double-entry perspective, the table also identifies which account types are debits and which are credits; example account items are provided.

Table 3.1 Debits, credits, account types and items

Account type	Statement	Balance	Account item
Income	Income statement	Credit	Revenue
Expenditure	Income statement	Debit	Utility costs
Asset	Balance sheet	Debit	Plant, property and equipment
Liability	Balance sheet	Credit	Accounts payables
Equity	Balance sheet	Credit	Share capital

Every single transaction in business has a double aspect to it: a debit element and a credit one. CIMA (2005:66) defines double-entry bookkeeping as: 'Most commonly used system of bookkeeping based on the principle that every financial transaction involves the simultaneous receiving and giving of value, and is therefore recorded twice.'

The double aspect of a transaction is illustrated with the following example. A company makes a sale to a customer of £1,000, and the buyer is given 90 days to pay for the goods. The double entry is as follows:

- credit revenue (income account) with the value of the sale £1,000;
- debit the accounts receivables account (asset account) of £1,000.

Two days before the sale, the company purchased the item they sold to their customer from their supplier for £600 on payment terms of 120 days. The double entry for this transaction is:

- credit account payables (liability account) with the value of the goods £600;
- debit purchases account (expenditure account) £600.

Ninety days later the customer pays the invoice; the double entry for this transaction is:

- credit the accounts receivables account (asset account) £1,000;
- debit the cash account (asset account) £1,000.

After receiving the cash from the customer, the company now pays £600 to the supplier, who supplied the goods to them on 120 days payment terms. The double-entry for this transaction is as follows:

- debit account payables (liability account) with the value of the sale £600;
- credit the cash account (asset account) £600.

The company sold goods to a customer for £1,000 that cost them £600 and made a profit of £400. This is a simple IS and the two account types used form the IS calculation: income – expenditure = profit (£1,000 – £600 = £400).

The other three accounts (asset, liabilities and equity) relate to the BS. In this simple example there are no liabilities as the accounts payable was cleared. However, there are an asset and a capital account, which form the company's BS:

- cash (asset account) £400 = retained earnings (equity account) £400.

The BS is basically a calculation, where assets = equity + liabilities (debits = credits). This accounting equation will be explored further in the next section.

3.3 Accounting equation

In this section, you will explore further the accounting equation that was introduced to you in the previous section. The accounting equation simply illustrates where an organization obtains its finances 'from' and where it has positioned the money 'into' the business. The equation will always balance, and in its simplest form it is: 'To = From'. The accounting equation illustrates the organization's debits and credits, and it balances because of the double-entry accounting system.

Building on the double-entry transactions in section 3.2, here is a very simplistic illustration to introduce you to the accounting equation using three transactions. You are planning to establish an express courier service between London and Manchester. You have managed to persuade your family and friends to support your venture and they have purchased all of your share issue for £50,000 (equity account); you put the cash into the bank (asset account). Table 3.2 illustrates the accounting equation for this transaction.

Table 3.2 Transaction 1: financing the business

To		= From	
Debits		= Credits	
Current assets: Cash in bank	£50,000	= Equity: Share capital	£50,000
Total assets (TA)	£50,000	Total equity	£50,000

The following day you decide to purchase a delivery van from a garage for £20,000, paying by cash; you now have a non-current asset (delivery van) and the accounting equation will change to reflect this second transaction. Your cash (current asset) will reduce by £20,000 and you now have a non-current asset (delivery van) of £20,000. But your total assets still remain at £50,000 and your equity account is unaffected by this transaction as it only impacts on the asset accounts (see Table 3.3). The business now has two different assets accounts, one that is short term (less than one year) and is referred to as current assets (cash), and a non-current asset account (delivery van), which are long-term assets. It is important that SC practitioners are able to distinguish between these two assets accounts when taking SCM decisions relating to the assets that they manage, for example the make or buy decision.

Table 3.3 Transaction 2: purchasing a non-current asset

To		= From	
Debits		= Credits	
Non-current assets: Motor vehicle	£20,000	Equity: Share capital	£50,000
Current assets: Cash in bank	£30,000 =		
Total assets	£50,000	Total equity	£50,000

You decide that the business needs to raise additional finance. You success-fully present your business case to your bank and they agree to lend you £10,000 over five years. Table 3.4 illustrates the impact of this third transaction on the accounting equation.

Table 3.4   Transaction 3: a long-term loan

To		=	From	
Debits		=	Credits	
Non-current assets:	£20,000	=	Equity: Share capital	£50,000
Motor vehicle			Non-current liability:	£10,000
Current assets:	£40,000		Long-term loan	
Cash in bank			Total equity	£60,000
Total assets	£60,000		and liabilities	

The information in Table 3.4 can now be summarized into the accounting equation in Table 3.5.

Table 3.5   The accounting equation = total assets = equity and liabilities

Total assets £k				=	Total equity and liabilities £k				
NCA	+	CA	=	TA	=	EQ	+	NCL	=	TEL
20	+	40	=	60	=	50	+	10	=	100

The accounting equation simply explains where an organization raises its finances from and where the organization decides to position it in their business. The equation will become more complex as the account types sub-divide, as illustrated in Table 3.6, that is, liabilities divide into current (short term, less than a year) and non-current (long term, more than a year).

Table 3.6   The accounting equation

To	=	From				
Debits	=	Credits				
Assets	=	Capital				
Assets	=	Equity	+	Liabilities		
Non-current+Current assets	=	Equity	+	Non-current	+	Current liabilities
To	**=**	**From**				
Total assets	=	Total equity and liabilities				

The next section explores and expands on the accounting equation as it transforms into the balance sheet.

3.4 The balance sheet

In the introduction to this chapter, I described the BS as a photograph. Now imagine if you could hypothetically press the pause button on a magical business remote control system and for a single moment in time freeze everything that is happening in the business. All activities stop, transactions are on hold, physical flows of goods and services between suppliers and customers stand still, information and financial flows between the nodes in a supply network are paused. Just imagine pressing the pause button on an automotive assembly line and consider the different types of inventory classifications: there will be finished cars, cars partially assembled on the line, parts waiting to be added, sub-assemblies waiting to be installed, steel blanks waiting to be pressed into panels, seats in transit on the motorway from the supplier, and so many more examples. In practice, physical information and financial flows do not stop; they continue on and on. However, from a financial perspective there will be amounts owed to the automotive company from cars sold to dealerships and outstanding payments to suppliers for components at the end of the financial year, and these transactions need to be accounted for in the year they occurred. The matching and accruals concepts, which were introduced in the previous chapter on the IS, also apply to the BS.

Therefore, the BS for a single moment in time illustrates where the organization has raised its finances from and where it has been positioned into the business; it enables the organization to 'take stock' (apologies for the pun) of its financial position, as a value can now be placed on the assets, liabilities and equity accounts. The CIMA terminology (2005:60) defines the balance sheet as:

> Statement of the financial position of an entity at a given date disclosing the assets, liabilities and equity (such as shareholders' contributions and reserves) prepared to give a true and fair view of the entity at that date.

In the introduction to this chapter, I issued a warning concerning the BS ability to take on many appearances. Fundamentally these different formats contain the same information but they report it slightly differently; however, they are all saying the same thing. You will come across these different formats when analysing an organization's report and accounts in practice. In this section, you will be introduced to these different formats using a fictitious company, SCT plc, as well as three examples taken from practice illustrating the three BS styles. The plan is to look at the BS as a whole in this section and then deconstruct it and explore its component parts in detail in subsequent sections of this chapter using examples taken from practice to support theory.

Typically, the three formats of the BS you will come into contact with will balance at different points; I will refer to them as:

- type 1: total assets = equity and liabilities;
- type 2: total assets – current liabilities = capital employed;
- type 3: net assets = equity.

In Table 3.7 each BS type is illustrated as its accounting equation and is broken down into its constituent parts.

Table 3.7 Balance sheet formats: type 1 to 3

Type 1: total assets = equity and liabilities									
Total assets £m			**=**	**Total equity and liabilities £m**					
NCA	+ CA	= TA	=	EQ	+	NCL	+ CL	=	TEL
Type 2: total assets – current liabilities = capital employed									
Total assets – current liabilities £m			**=**	**Capital employed £m**					
NCA	+ CA	– CL	= TA – CL	=	EQ	+ NCL	=	CE	
Type 3: net assets = equity									
Net assets £m					**=**	**Equity £m**			
NCA +	CA –	CL –	NCL	=	NA	= EQ			

- NCA = non-current assets;
- CA = current assets;
- TA = total assets;
- TA – CL = total assets – current liabilities;
- CL = current liabilities;
- NCL = non-current liabilities;
- NA = net assets;
- EQ = equity;
- TEL = total equity & liabilities.

A fictitious company SCT PLC will be used as the instrument to compare the three BS types and for each type an example from practice will also be used to illustrate the different BS formats. For each BS type the accounting equation for SCT PLC will be illustrated, then the BS for SCT PLC will be presented.

Marks and Spencer Group PLC is a retailer. The organization has adopted the Type 3 BS format and their BS for 2018 and 2017 (Figure 3.6). To illustrate the different BS formats, Marks and Spencer Group PLC figures has been extracted from their 2018 annual report (2018:78) and adapted to depict the three formats and are presented in figures 3.2, 3.4 and 3.6.

Balance sheet type 1: total assets = equity and liabilities

The accounting equation for SCT plc is illustrated in Table 3.8 for BS type 1.

Table 3.8   SCT plc, total assets = total equity and liabilities

Total assets £m				=	Total equity and liabilities £m					
NCA	+	CA	=	TA	=	EQ	+	NCL	+	CL	=	TEL
62	+	38	=	100	=	55	+	25	+	20	=	100

Figure 3.1 illustrates the type 1 BS for SCT plc, which balances at £100m.

Figure 3.1   SCT plc balance sheet, total assets = total equity and liabilities

SCT plc Balance Sheet as at 31 March 20XX	
Non-current assets	**£m**
Land and buildings	35
Fixtures and fittings	12
Plant and machinery	10
Motor vehicles	5
	62
Current assets	
Inventories	15
Accounts receivables	22
Cash	1
	38
Total assets	**100**
Equity	
£1 ordinary shares	35
Retained earnings	20
	55
Non-current liabilities	
Long-term loan	25
Current liabilities	
Accounts payable	19
Taxation	1
	20
Total equity and liabilities	**100**

Deutsche Post DHL Group, the global mail and logistics organization, has adopted the type 1 BS format. Their BS for 2016 and 2017 has been extracted from their annual report (2017:104) and is illustrated in Figure 3.2.

Figure 3.2 Type 1 balance sheet Marks and Spencer Group PLC 2018 and 2017

CONSOLIDATED STATEMENT OF FINANCIAL POSITION	As at 31st March 2018 £m	As at 1st April 2017 £m
Non-current assets		
Intangible assets	599.2	709.0
Property, plant and equipment	4,393.9	4,837.8
Investment property	15.5	15.5
Investment in joint ventures	7.0	7.0
Other financial assets	9.9	3.0
Retirement benefit asset	970.7	706.0
Trade and other receivables	209.0	234.1
Derivative financial instruments	27.1	56.8
Deferred tax assets	–	–
	6,232.3	6,569.2
Current assets		
Inventories	781.0	758.5
Other financial assets	13.7	14.5
Trade and other receivables	308.4	318.6
Derivative financial instruments	7.1	163.1
Current tax assets	–	–
Cash and cash equivalents	207.7	468.6
	1,317.9	1,723.3
TOTAL ASSETS	**7,550.2**	**8,292.5**
EQUITY AND LIABILITIES		
Issued share capital	406.2	406.2
Share premium account	416.4	416.4
Capital redemption reserve	2,210.5	2,210.5
Hedging reserve	(65.3)	17.3
Other reserve	(6,542.2)	(6,542.2)
Retained earnings	6,531.1	6,648.1
Total shareholders' equity	**2,956.7**	**3,156.3**

(continued)

Figure 3.2 *(Continued)*

CONSOLIDATED STATEMENT OF FINANCIAL POSITION	As at 31st March 2018 £m	As at 1st April 2017 £m
Non-controlling interests in equity	(2.5)	(5.9)
Total equity	**2,954.2**	**3,150.4**
Non-current liabilities		
Retirement benefit deficit	22.5	13.2
Trade and other payables	333.8	328.5
Partnership liability to the Marks & Spencer UK Pension Scheme	263.6	324.6
Borrowings and other financial liabilities	1,670.6	1,711.7
Derivative financial instruments	30.7	0.8
Provisions	193.1	113.5
Deferred tax liabilities	255.7	281.8
	2,770.0	**2,774.1**
Current liabilities		
Trade and other payables	1,405.9	1,553.8
Partnership liability to the Marks & Spencer UK Pension Scheme	71.9	71.9
Borrowings and other financial liabilities	125.6	518.0
Derivative financial instruments	73.8	10.5
Provisions	98.8	147.2
Current tax liabilities	50.0	66.6
	1,826.0	**2,368.0**
TOTAL EQUITY AND LIABILITIES	**7,550.2**	**8,292.5**

Table 3.9 simplifies Marks and Spencer Group PLC BS into its accounting equation and broken-down into its account types to illustrate the point where the statement balances. The BS for 31 December 2018 balances at total assets = total equity and liabilities (TEL), which is €38,672m.

Table 3.9   Accounting equation (Type 1) Marks and Spencer Group PLC 2018

Total assets £m			=	Total equity and liabilities £m					
NCA	+	CA	=	TA	=	EQ	+	NCL	+	CL	=	TEL
6,232.3	+	1,317.9	=	7,550.2	=	2,954.2	+	2,770.0	+	1,826.0	=	7,550.2

Balance sheet type 2: total assets less current liabilities = capital employed

The accounting equation for SCT plc is illustrated in Table 3.10 for BS type 2.

The type 2 BS for SCT plc is illustrated in Figure 3.3, which balances at £80m.

Table 3.10   SCT plc, total assets – current liabilities = capital employed

Total assets – current liabilities £m					=	Capital employed £m				
NCA	+	CA	–	CL	=	TA – CL	=	EQ	+	NCL	=	CE
62	+	38	–	20	=	80	=	55	+	25	=	80

Figure 3.3   SCT plc balance sheet, total assets – current liabilities = capital employed

SCT plc Balance Sheet as at 31 March 20XX	
Non-current assets	**£m**
Land and buildings	35
Fixtures and fittings	12
Plant and machinery	10
Motor vehicles	5
	62
Current assets	
Inventories	15
Accounts receivables	22
Cash	1
	38
Current liabilities	
Accounts payables	19
Taxation	1
	20
Net current assets	**18**
Total assets less current liabilities	**80**

(continued)

Figure 3.3 (*Continued*)

SCT plc Balance Sheet as at 31 March 20XX	
Financed by	
Equity	
£1 ordinary shares	35
Retained earnings	20
	55
Non-current liabilities	
Long-term loan	25
Total equity and non-current liabilities	**80**

Figure 3.4 illustrates Marks and Spencer Group PLC BS in the Type 2 BS format and their BS for 2018 and 2017 has been extracted and adapted from their 2018 annual report (2018:78).

Figure 3.4 Type 2 balance sheet Marks and Spencer Group PLC 2018 and 2017

CONSOLIDATED STATEMENT OF FINANCIAL POSITION	As at 31st March 2018 £m	As at 1st April 2017 £m
Non-current assets		
Intangible assets	599.2	709.0
Property, plant and equipment	4,393.9	4,837.8
Investment property	15.5	15.5
Investment in joint ventures	7.0	7.0
Other financial assets	9.9	3.0
Retirement benefit asset	970.7	706.0
Trade and other receivables	209.0	234.1
Derivative financial instruments	27.1	56.8
Deferred tax assets	–	–
	6,232.3	**6,569.2**
Current assets		
Inventories	781.0	758.5
Other financial assets	13.7	14.5
Trade and other receivables	308.4	318.6
Derivative financial instruments	7.1	163.1
Current tax assets	–	–
Cash and cash equivalents	207.7	468.6
	1,317.9	**1,723.3**

(*continued*)

Figure 3.4   (*Continued*)

CONSOLIDATED STATEMENT OF FINANCIAL POSITION	As at 31st March 2018 £m	As at 1st April 2017 £m
Current liabilities		
Trade and other payables	1,405.9	1,553.8
Partnership liability to the Marks & Spencer UK Pension Scheme	71.9	71.9
Borrowings and other financial liabilities	125.6	518.0
Derivative financial instruments	73.8	10.5
Provisions	98.8	147.2
Current tax liabilities	50.0	66.6
	1,826.0	**2,368.0**
Net current liabilities	(508.1)	(644.7)
Total assets less current liabilities	**5,724.2**	**5,924.5**
Financed by:		
Equity		
Issued share capital	406.2	406.2
Share premium account	416.4	416.4
Capital redemption reserve	2,210.5	2,210.5
Hedging reserve	(65.3)	17.3
Other reserve	(6,542.2)	(6,542.2)
Retained earnings	6,531.1	6,648.1
Total shareholders' equity	**2,956.7**	**3,156.3**
Non-controlling interests in equity	(2.5)	(5.9)
Total equity	**2,954.2**	**3,150.4**
Non-current liabilities		
Retirement benefit deficit	22.5	13.2
Trade and other payables	333.8	328.5
Partnership liability to the Marks & Spencer UK Pension Scheme	263.6	324.6
Borrowings and other financial liabilities	1,670.6	1,711.7
Derivative financial instruments	30.7	0.8
Provisions	193.1	113.5
Deferred tax liabilities	255.7	281.8
	2,770.0	2,774.1
Equity and non-current liabilities	**5,724.2**	**5,924.5**

Table 3.11 illustrates the accounting equation for Marks and Spencer Group PLC 2018, with this BS format the statement balances when total assets less current liabilities is equal to capital employed (equity and non-current liabilities), which for 31 March 2018 is £5,724.2 million.

Table 3.11   Accounting equation (Type 2) Marks and Spencer Group PLC 2018

Total assets – current liabilities £m					= Capital employed £m				
NCA	+ CA	– CL	= TA – CL =		EQ	+ NCL	= CE		
6,232.3	+ 1,317.9	– 1,826.0	= 5,724.2	=	2,954.2	+ 2,770.0	= 5,724.2		

Balance sheet type 3: net assets = equity

The accounting equation for SCT plc is illustrated in Table 3.12 for BS type 3. The type 3 BS for SCT plc is illustrated in Figure 3.5, which balances at £55m.

Table 3.12   SCT plc balance sheet, net assets = equity

Net assets £m							=	Equity £m
NCA	+ CA	– CL	– NCL	= NA	=	EQ		
62	+ 38	– 20	– 25	= 55	=	55		

Figure 3.5   SCT plc balance sheet, net assets = equity

SCT plc Balance Sheet as at 31 March 20XX	
Non-current assets	**£m**
Land and buildings	35
Fixtures and fittings	12
Plant and machinery	10
Motor vehicles	5
	62
Current assets	
Inventories	15
Accounts receivable	22
Cash	1
	38
Total assets	**100**
Liabilities	
Current liabilities	
Accounts payable	19
Taxation	1
	20

(continued)

Figure 3.5 (*Continued*)

SCT plc Balance Sheet as at 31 March 20XX	
Non-current liabilities	
Long-term loan	25
Total liabilities	45
Net assets	**55**
Financed by	
Equity	
£1 ordinary shares	35
Retained earnings	20
Total equity	**55**

Marks & Spencer Group plc is a retailer; the organization has adopted the type 3 BS format. Their BS for 2018 and 2017 has been extracted from their 2018 annual report (2018:78) and is illustrated in Figure 3.6.

Figure 3.6 Type 3 balance sheet: Marks & Spencer Group plc 2018 and 2017

CONSOLIDATED STATEMENT OF FINANCIAL POSITION	As at 31 March 2018 £m	As at 1 April 2017 £m
Non-current assets		
Intangible assets	599.2	709.0
Property, plant and equipment	4,393.9	4,837.8
Investment property	15.5	15.5
Investment in joint ventures	7.0	7.0
Other financial assets	9.9	3.0
Retirement benefit asset	970.7	706.0
Trade and other receivables	209.0	234.1
Derivative financial instruments	27.1	56.8
Deferred tax assets	–	–
	6,232.3	6,569.2
Current assets		
Inventories	781.0	758.5
Other financial assets	13.7	14.5
Trade and other receivables	308.4	318.6
Derivative financial instruments	7.1	163.1
Current tax assets	–	–
Cash and cash equivalents	207.7	468.6
	1,317.9	1,723.3
Total assets	7,550.2	8,292.5

(*continued*)

Figure 3.6   (*Continued*)

CONSOLIDATED STATEMENT OF FINANCIAL POSITION	As at 31 March 2018 £m	As at 1 April 2017 £m
Liabilities		
Current liabilities		
Trade and other payables	1,405.9	1,553.8
Partnership liability to the Marks & Spencer UK Pension Scheme	71.9	71.9
Borrowings and other financial liabilities	125.6	518.0
Derivative financial instruments	73.8	10.5
Provisions	98.8	147.2
Current tax liabilities	50.0	66.6
	1,826.0	2,368.0
Non-current liabilities		
Retirement benefit deficit	22.5	13.2
Trade and other payables	333.8	328.5
Partnership liability to the Marks & Spencer UK Pension Scheme	263.6	324.6
Borrowings and other financial liabilities	1,670.6	1,711.7
Derivative financial instruments	30.7	0.8
Provisions	193.1	113.5
Deferred tax liabilities	255.7	281.8
	2,770.0	2,774.1
Total liabilities	4,596.0	5,142.1
Net assets	**2,954.2**	**3,150.4**
Equity		
Issued share capital	406.2	406.2
Share premium account	416.4	416.4
Capital redemption reserve	2,210.5	2,210.5
Hedging reserve	(65.3)	17.3
Other reserve	(6,542.2)	(6,542.2)
Retained earnings	6,531.1	6,648.1
Total shareholders' equity	**2,956.7**	**3,156.3**
Non-controlling interests in equity	(2.5)	(5.9)
Total equity	**2,954.2**	**3,150.4**

Table 3.13   Accounting equation (type 3), Marks & Spencer Group plc 2018

Net assets £m								=	Equity £m
NCA	+	CA	−	CL	−	NCL	=	NA	=	EQ
6,232.3	+	1,317.9	−	1,826.0	−	2,770.0	=	2,954.2	=	2,954.2

Table 3.13 illustrates the accounting equation for Marks & Spencer Group plc 2018. With this BS format the statement balances when net assets are equal to equity, which for 31 March 2018 is £2,954.2m.

Each of the BS formats contains the same information; however, they balance at various points depending on different financial perspectives.

Here are a couple of activities for you to have a go at which are designed to reinforce the learning from previous sections.

Activity 3.1 has been designed to develop your knowledge of the account types and their relevant account items. Have a go at Activity 3.1 now; when you have finished, compare your solution with the answer in section 3.14.

Activity 3.1

Complete Table 3.14 by allocating each account item to its relevant account type.

Table 3.14 Account item and type

Account item	Account type				
	NCA	CA	EQ	NCL	CL
Land and buildings					
Ordinary share capital					
Long-term loan					
Goodwill					
Retained earnings					
Accounts payables					
Plant and machinery					
Accounts receivables					
Fixtures and fittings					
Motor vehicles					
Finished goods					
Raw materials					
Dividends payable					
Taxation payable					
Bank overdraft					
Work in progress					
Cash					

Now have a go at Activity 3.2. The aim of this activity is to explore the components of the account equation, find the missing value enabling you to balance the equation, and finally construct a type 1 BS, therefore developing your knowledge of the key components and the format of a BS. When you have constructed your BS for Ultra plc, check out the solution in section 3.14.

Activity 3.2

The following information has been taken from the accounts of Ultra plc as at 31 December 20XX. Formulate the accounting equation to find the value of the company's long-term loan and then construct the type 1 balance sheet for the company.

Table 3.15   Ultra plc account items

Account item	£m
Accounts receivables	10
Cash	2
Accounts payable	7
Dividend payable	1
Inventories	4
Share capital	25
Retained earnings	7
Property, plant and equipment	32

In sections 3.5, 3.6, 3.7 and 3.8, the BS will be deconstructed into its significant components, which are:

- assets:
  - non-current assets:
    - intangible assets;
    - tangible assets;
  - current assets;
- liabilities:
  - non-current liabilities;
  - current liabilities;
- working capital;

- equity:
  - share capital;
  - retained earnings;
  - reserves.

In each section, relevant examples from practice will be included and the Deutsche Post DHL Group 2017 annual report will be used to draw on examples from logistics. I would like to thank and acknowledge Deutsche Post DHL Group for giving permission to use their accounts.

3.5 Assets

Assets are subdivided into two types: non-current assets (NCA) and current assets (CA). However, NCA is further classified into intangible and tangible assets. An asset is defined by CIMA (2005:59) as a: 'Resource controlled by the entity as a result of past events and from which future economic benefits are expected to flow to the entity.'

This definition is extremely important to SC practitioners and the SCM decisions they make with regard to the deployment of resources in their SC. Decisions to spend money on SC assets now, whether they are NCAs or CAs, are made with regard to earning future benefits. For instance, raw materials are purchased to be converted into finished goods using plant and machinery, which may have a useful life of 20 years; the former is a CA, the latter is an NCA. Here is a little task to get you thinking about the SC assets: the next time you purchase or consume any of the following goods or services, think of the different supply chain assets used in their production and delivery:

- railway ticket;
- double expresso;
- CT scan;
- theatre ticket;
- banana;
- boil a kettle.

Non-current assets

An NCA, according to CIMA (2005:74), is as follows: 'Tangible or intangible asset, acquired for retention by an entity for the purpose of providing a service to the entity and not held for resale in the normal course of trading.'

This definition refers to NCAs which are held by an organization but are not for resale; they are employed to facilitate a service for the organization. They can be intangible and tangible and typically will have a useful life of more than one year. Deutsche Post DHL Group (2017:104) NCAs for the financial years 2017 and 2016 are illustrated in Table 3.16.

Table 3.16   Deutsche Post DHL Group, non-current assets 2017 and 2016

Assets €m	31/12/2017	31/12/2016	% Change
Intangible assets	11,792	12,554	−6.07%
Property, plant and equipment	8,782	8,389	4.68%
Investment property	21	23	−8.70%
Investments accounted for using the equity method	85	97	−12.37%
Non-current financial assets	733	689	6.39%
Other non-current assets	231	222	4.05%
Deferred tax assets	2,272	2,192	3.65%
	23,916	24,166	−1.03%

The total value of Deutsche Post DHL Group's NCA on their 2017 annual report is €23,916m, of which intangible NCAs are €11,792m (43.31%) and tangible NCAs are €12,124m (50.69%), with property, plant and equipment accounting for 72.43% of tangible NCAs. These NCAs are held by the business for the purpose of providing a service to the organization, enabling them to deliver a global mail and logistics operation.

NCAs are classified into intangible and tangible. In the next sub-section the characteristics of each type of NCA will be explored, beginning with intangible NCAs.

Intangible non-current assets

The following definitions highlight the characteristics and introduces examples of intangible NCAs.

CIMA (2005:72) defines an intangible NCA as:

Identifiable non-monetary asset without physical substance which must be controlled by the entity as the result of past events and from which the entity expects a flow of future economic benefits.

Deutsche Post DHL Group (2017:114) defines intangible non-current assets as: 'Intangible assets, which comprise internally generated and purchased intangible assets and purchased goodwill, are measured at amortized cost.'

Intangible NCAs do not have a physical presence; however, they can be purchased, but also generated internally, and over time their value is amortized. The concept of amortization and depreciation will be discussed in greater depth in Chapter 5. There are processes that match a proportion of the value of the NCA against the revenue generated by the asset over its useful life, typically an equal amount – it is an apportionment.

Table 3.17   Deutsche Post DHL Group, intangible non-current assets 2017

Intangible assets	€m
Internally generated intangible assets	172
Purchased brand names	30
Purchased customer lists	29
Other purchased intangible assets	326
Goodwill	11,169
Advance payments and intangible assets under development	66
	11,792

Table 3.17 illustrates Deutsche Post DHL Group's (2017:130) NCAs for the financial year 2017.

Goodwill accounts for 94.72% of Deutsche Post DHL Group's intangible NCAs and 46.70% of the organization's total NCAs for the financial year 2017.

Tangible assets

Deutsche Post DHL Group's (2017:132) property, plant and equipment (PPE) assets account for 36.74% of total NCAs for the financial year 2017. A breakdown of these assets is illustrated in Table 3.18.

Table 3.18   Deutsche Post DHL Group, property, plant and equipment assets 2017

Property, plant and equipment	€m	%
Land and buildings	2,399	27%
Technical equipment and machinery	2,264	26%
Other equipment, operating and office equipment	641	7%
Aircraft	1,381	16%
Vehicle fleet and transport equipment	1,322	15%
Advance payments and assets under development	775	9%
	8,782	100%

Table 3.19 provides a framework to identify the different tangible NCA employed by activities. Why not take the framework and use it in your organization or if you are researching an end-to-end SC in a particular industrial sector use the table to capture the tangible NCAs?

Table 3.19   Supply chain activities and tangible NCA

Activity	Tangible NCA
Procurement	
Goods In	
Storage	
Picking	
Co packing	
Goods out	
Transport	
Quality control	
Production	
Returns management	

Table 3.20 focuses on the assets of a variety of international organizations operating in different industrial sectors.

Table 3.20   Total assets

Company	Financial Year	Intangible NCA	Tangible NCA	Current assets	Total assets
BASF Group €m	2017(170)	13,594.0	34,029.0	31,145.0	78,768.0
Deutsche Post DHL Group €m	2017(104)	12,554.0	11,612.0	14,756.0	38,922.0
Marks and Spencer Group PLC £m	2017(78)	709.0	5,860.2	1,723.3	8,292.5
Nestlé Group CHFm	2017(66)	20,615	77,575	32,190	130,380
The Procter & Gamble Company $m	2017(38)	68,886.0	25,026.0	26,494.0	120,406.0

Current assets

A current asset, according to CIMA (2005:65), is an:

Asset which satisfies any of the following criteria:

- is expected to be realized in, or is intended for sale or consumption in the entity's normal operating cycle;

- is held primarily for the purpose of being traded;

- is expected to be realized within twelve months of the balance sheet date;

- is cash or cash equivalent.

Deutsche Post DHL Group's (2017:104) current assets for the financial years 2017 and 2016 are illustrated in Table 3.21.

Table 3.21　Deutsche Post DHL Group, current assets 2017 and 2016

Current assets €m	31/12/17	31/12/16	% change
Inventories	327	275	18.91%
Current financial assets	652	374	74.33%
Trade receivables	8,218	7,965	3.18%
Other current assets	2,184	2,176	0.37%
Income tax assets	236	232	1.72%
Cash and cash equivalents	3,135	3,107	0.90%
Assets held for sale	4	0	
	14,756	14,129	4.44%

In Table 3.21 Deutsche Post DHL Group's trade receivables (the value of the money owed to the organization from its customers) accounts for 55.69% of CAs, while inventory is 2.2% of CAs. SC practitioners, therefore, need to be aware of the contextual factors of the industrial environment in which the organization operates.

However, inventory as a percentage of CA or TA is an extremely useful measure for SC practitioners. CIMA (2005:73) defines inventory as:

Assets held for sale in the ordinary course of business in the process of production for such a sale or in the form of materials or supplies to be consumed in the production process or in the rendering of services.

The next table illustrates the significance of point of industrial context using CA from the retailer Marks and Spencer Group PLC. The data has been extracted from their 2018 (78) annual report. Inventories as a percentage of current assets for Marks and Spencer Group PLC £m in 2018 are 59.3.% and inventories of TA are 10.3%. In the case of account receivables, they are 23.4% of CA and 4.1% of TA.

Tables 3.21 and 3.22 reinforce the importance for SC practitioners of understanding the contextual factors of the industrial environment their organization operates in.

Table 3.22   Marks and Spencer Group PLC current assets 2018

Current assets	£m	% of CA
Inventories	781.0	59.3
Other financial assets	13.7	1.0
Trade and other receivables	308.4	23.4
Derivative financial instruments	7.1	0.5
Cash and cash equivalents	207.7	15.8
Current assets	**1,317.9**	**100.0**

3.6 Liabilities

Liabilities, like assets, are subdivided into two types: non-current liabilities (NCLs) and current liabilities (CLs). A liability is defined by CIMA (2005:73) as a:

> Present obligation of the entity arising from past events, the settlement of which is expected to result in an outflow from the entity of resources embodying economic benefits.

Effectively a liability is an obligation to pay in the future an individual or an organization for goods or service supplied and finances extended to the business (short-term overdraft or a long-term loan).

Non-current liabilities

An NCL is typically a long-term obligation, which is classified as a liability falling due in more than one year's time. Typically, decisions relating to NCLs are generally outside of the remit of SC practitioners and are taken by other functions within an organization; however, indirectly, SC practitioners will provide information concerning the future funding relating to CAs and NCAs used in the SC. Table 3.23 illustrates Deutsche Post DHL Group's non-current provisions and liabilities for the financial years 2017 and 2016.

Non-current provisions and liabilities in 2017 accounts for 29.4% of the total equity and liabilities for Deutsche Post DHL Group.

Table 3.23 Deutsche Post DHL Group, non-current provisions and liabilities

Non-current provisions and liabilities €m	31/12/17	31/12/16
Provisions for pensions and similar obligations	4,450	5,580
Deferred tax liabilities	76	106
Other non-current provisions	1,421	1,498
Non-current provisions	**5,947**	**7,184**
Non-current financial liabilities	5,151	4,571
Other non-current financial liabilities	272	372
Non-current liabilities	**5,423**	**4,943**
Non-current provisions and liabilities	**11,370**	**12,127**

Current liabilities

CLs are typically obligations to pay that fall due in less than one year; they include accounts payable (monies owed to suppliers of goods and services to the business), dividends payable to shareholders and tax payable to government. CIMA (2005:65) defines a current liability as a:

Liability which satisfies any of the following criteria:

- is expected to be settled in the entity's normal operating cycle;
- is held primarily for the purpose of being traded;
- is due to be settled within twelve months of the balance sheet date.

Deutsche Post DHL Group's (2017:104) current liabilities for the financial years 2017 and 2016 are illustrated in Table 3.24. It can be seen from the table that trade payables is the largest component of the organization's CLs, which equates to 55.34% of total CLs in 2017 and 53.19% in 2016. CLs in 2017 account for 34.31% of the total equity and liabilities for Deutsche Post DHL Group.

Table 3.24 Deutsche Post DHL Group, current liabilities 2017 and 2016

Current liabilities €m	31/12/17	31/12/16	% change
Current financial liabilities	899	1,464	−38.59%
Trade payables	7,343	7,178	2.30%
Other current liabilities	4,402	4,292	2.56%
Income tax liabilities	624	561	11.23%
	13,268	**13,495**	**−1.68%**

3.7 Working capital

Typically working capital is calculated by subtracting CLs from CAs. Working capital is defined by CIMA (2005:82) as: 'Capital available for conducting the day-to-day operations of an entity, normally the excess of current assets over current liabilities.'

You may have also come across the terms 'net current assets' and 'net current liabilities', which refer to working capital. When the value of current assets exceeds the amount of current liabilities, working capital is referred to as net current assets; when current liabilities are greater than current assets, net current liabilities will be adopted. Table 3.25 illustrates the working capital calculation for five international companies operating in different industrial sectors and based in various geographical regions. The data has been extracted from the BS in their annual reports and accounts for 2017, Marks and Spencer Group PLC and Nestlé Group are organizations that have net current liabilities while the others have net current assets.

Table 3.25   Working capital calculation

Company	Financial Year	Current assets	Current liabilities	Working capital
BASF Group €m	2017 (170)	31,145	14,880	16,265
Deutsche Post DHL Group €m	2017 (104)	14,756	13,268	1,488
Marks and Spencer Group PLC £m	2017 (78)	1,723.3	2,368.0	−644.7
Nestlé Group CHFm	2017 (66 & 67)	32,190	36,054	−3,864
The Procter & Gamble Company $m	2017 (38)	26,494	30,210	−3716

Remember when comparing organizations, it is important that you compare like with like, ie within industrial sector and same financial year. The next table illustrates the working capital calculation for organizations operating within the retail sector, using the current ratio as a measurement of working capital. The current ratio takes current assets as a ratio of current liabilities. If the ratio is greater than 1 the company has net current assets; if less than 1 they have net current liabilities.

All of the retailers in table 3.26 have non-current liabilities. Is this by chance or is it the case within the retailing sector?

Table 3.26   Working capital calculation retail sector

Company	Financial Year	Current Ratio
Marks and Spencer Group PLC	2018	0.72:1.00
Wm Morrison Supermarkets PLC	2018	0.42:1.00
J Sainsbury PLC	2018	0.76:1.00
Tesco PLC	2018	0.71:1.00

SOURCE *Fame* (Bureau van Dijk, 2019)

3.8 Equity

Equity represents the owner's stake in the organization, which includes the share capital and the reserves of the organization. CIMA (2005:68) defines equity as:

> Residual interest in the assets of the entity after deducting all its liabilities. It is comprised of share capital, retained earnings and other reserves of a single entity, plus minority interests in a group, representing the investment made in the entity by its owners.

In section 3.4 the three types of BS were introduced to you; type 3 balances at the value of the organization's equity, as illustrated by the accounting equation for Marks & Spencer Group plc 2018 in Table 3.27. The BS balances when net assets are equal to equity, which for 31 March 2018 is £2,954.2m.

Table 3.27   Accounting equation (type 3), Marks & Spencer Group plc 2018

Net assets £m								=	Equity £m
NCA	+	CA	–	CL	–	NCL	=	NA	= EQ
6,232.3	+	1,317.9	–	1,826.0	–	2,770.0	=	2,954.2	= 2,954.2

Deutsche Post DHL Group's equity accounts for 33.37% of total equity and liabilities for 2017, as illustrated in Figure 3.2.

3.9 Financial ratios and the balance sheet

This section will focus on the financial ratios that are relevant to the BS only, and are derived by data contained only in the balance sheet. Chapter 5 will explore the use of financial ratios from a holistic perspective, including IS, BS and ratios which combine data from both the IS and the BS. Typical BS financial ratios that would be of interest to SC practitioners and other functions, along with their calculation method, are illustrated in Table 3.28.

Table 3.28   Balance sheet financial ratios

Financial ratio	Calculation
Current ratio (current assets:current liabilities)	CA:CL
Acid test/quick ratio (current assets – inventory;current liabilities)	(CA–INV):CL
Long-term loans (LTL) as a percentage of capital employed	(LTL/CE) *100
Long-term loans (LTL) plus short-term loans (STL) as a percentage of capital employed	[(LTL+STL)/CE] *100
Inventory (INV) as a percentage of current assets (CA)	(INV/CA) *100
Inventory (INV) as a percentage of total assets	(INV/TA) *100
Accounts receivables (AR) as a percentage of current assets (CA)	(AR/CA) *100
Accounts payables (AP) as a percentage of current liabilities (CL)	(AP/CL) *100
Non-current assets (NCA) as a percentage of total assets (TA)	(NCA/TA) *100
Current assets (CA) as a percentage of total assets (TA)	(CA/TA) *100
Non-current liabilities (NCL) as a percentage of total equity and liabilities (TEL)	(NCL/TEL) *100
Current liabilities (CL) as a percentage of total equity and liabilities (TEL)	(CL/TEL) *100
Equity (EQ) as a percentage of total equity and liabilities (TEL)	(EQ/TEL) *100

Table 3.29 illustrates the current and acid test ratios for a selection of international organizations operating in different industrial sectors.

Table 3.29   Liquidity ratios

Company	Financial Year	Current Assets	Current liabilities	Current Inventory	Current Ratio	Acid test
BASF Group €m	2017(170)	31,145.0	14,880.0	10,303.0	2.093	1.401
Deutsche Post DHL Group €m	2017(104)	14,756.0	13,268.0	327.0	1.112	1.088
Marks and Spencer Group PLC £m	2017(78)	1,723.3	2,368.0	758.5	0.728	0.407
Nestlé Group CHFm	2017(66 & 67)	32,190	36,054	9,061	0.913	0.642
The Procter & Gamble Company $m	2017(38)	26,494.0	30,210	4,624.0	0.877	0.724

In Table 3.29 the current ratio has a range of 1.365 between the highest and lowest values and the acid test ratio has a range of 0.994. Table 3.29 contains information from organizations operating in different industrial sectors, which provides different perspectives, but when analysing a single sector it is important to compare like with like as depicted in Table 3.29, which compares four organizations in the retail sector using data extracted from their annual report and accounts.

Table 3.30 illustrates that the average current ratio for these four retailers is 0.6.5, however the range is £0.34. Therefore, for every £1 of current liabilities there is only £0.65 current assets available. If we now focus on the average acid test ratio, which takes inventory out of the liquidity equation, the average figure is now £0.42 of current assets for every £1 of current liabilities and the range is £0.41. When focusing on inventory as a percentage of current assets the average for the four retailers is 38.07%, but the range is 43, with Marks and Spencer PLC on 59% and Tesco PLC on 16%.

Table 3.30   Liquidity ratios retail sector

Company	Financial Year	Current ratio	Acid test ratio	Inventory as a % of current assets	Inventory turnover * pa
Marks and Spencer Group PLC	2018	0.72	0.29	59.26	13.70
Wm Morrison Supermarkets PLC	2018	0.42	0.19	53.51	25.16
J Sainsbury PLC	2018	0.76	0.59	23.01	15.72
Tesco PLC	2018	0.71	0.60	16.49	25.40
Average	**2018**	**0.65**	**0.41**	**38.07**	**20.00**

Adapted: *Fame* (Bureau van Dijk, 2019)

Activity 3.3

The following information in Table 3.31 has been extracted from the accounts of FMCG plc for the financial year as at 31 March 20XX.

Table 3.31   Accounting items FMCG plc as at 31 March 20XX.

Account	£m
Accounts payables	370
Accounts receivables	420
Cash	60
Dividend payable	30
Finished goods	160
Raw materials	320
Tax payable	80
Work in progress	240

Calculate the following:

1 the company's current assets;
2 the company's current liabilities;
3 the value of the company's working capital;
4 the current ratio;
5 the quick/acid test ratio;
6 inventory as a percentage of current assets.

3.10 Supply chain decisions on the balance sheet

This section will focus on the impact of SC initiatives on the balance sheet, focusing on two particular areas: reducing both inventories and tangible non-current assets. Other SC initiatives will be explored in subsequent sections of the book.

Tangible non-current assets

There are many financial ratios that measure asset turnover. Total asset turnover is one such ratio and is calculated by dividing revenue by the value of total assets. If an organization has revenue of £10m and total assets (NCA + CA) of £5m, its total asset turnover ratio will be 2. If tangible non-current assets are 40% of TA, that is, £2m, and it was possible to adopt an SC initiative that would reduce these assets by 40%, all other variables remaining constant, the total assets of the organization will reduce to £4.2m and the asset turnover ratio would increase to 2.38.

Typical supply chain initiatives targeted at reducing tangible non-current assets are illustrated in Table 3.32.

Table 3.32 Tangible NCA reduction initiatives

Initiative	Description
Outsourcing	Outsourcing SC activities including inbound logistics, manufacturing and outbound logistics to third-party providers. Non-SC activities such as HR, catering, accounting and facilities management are further examples of outsourcing.
Shared services	Working with other organizations, often in the same sector, to reduce non-tangible assets and operating costs; examples include sharing call centres in the case of emergency services.
Collaboration	Collaboration with customers, suppliers and even competitors to improve asset utilization, for example sharing capacity on transport assets including trucks and rail wagons.
Productivity	Network redesign to improve vehicles' utilization.
Asset disposals	Identifying redundant SC assets that are still on the balance sheet and disposal of them.
Renting assets	Renting tangible non-current assets instead of owning them; there are implications for the IS.
Invest in new non-current assets	Replace older non-current assets with new, more efficient non-current assets, for example new aircraft purchases by airlines and disposal of their older aircraft.

Inventories

The typical cost of holding a unit of inventory can be 25% (Christopher, 2011) of its cost for a year, and that cost includes the opportunity cost of the cash tied up in the inventory, insurance, the costs associated with storing and handling, obsolescence and shrinkage costs. These costs will have an impact on the profitability of the organization via the IS.

However, unsold inventory is a current asset on the BS and high levels of inventories trap cash, which could be used elsewhere in the company. Inventory also impacts on efficiency and performance measures that focus on the ability of the organization to generate sales from its total assets.

Using the previous example again, the company has revenue of £10m and their total assets are £5m; therefore, the total asset turnover ratio will be 2. The organization's inventories account for 20% of their TAs, that is, £1m. If the business decides to implement an SC initiative that would reduce inventories by 50%, the total asset turnover ratio would increase to 2.22.

SC initiatives identified by Templar *et al* (2016:58), which focus on reducing inventories, are illustrated in Table 3.33.

Table 3.33   Inventory reduction initiatives

Initiative	Description
Postponement	Delaying the conversion of raw materials or WIP into finished goods until the last possible moment to avoid holding excessive finished goods inventories and therefore enhancing agility to react to changes in consumer demand. An everyday example is the way DIY stores are able to mix a specific colour of paint for a customer without the need to hold inventory of that colour, only the raw materials component, which can also be configured into a variety of different colours.
Electronic data interchange (EDI)	The use of information technology to communicate customer demand data throughout the supply chain will provide opportunities to improve inventory management and therefore reduce inventory levels, costs and risk. Often the axiom 'replacing inventory with information' is recited when referring to the use of EDI.
Centralize inventory holding	Holding inventory centrally an organization can benefit from economies of scale, optimizing inventory and distribution costs, but also enhancing product availability and improving customer service levels.

(continued)

Table 3.33   *(Continued)*

Initiative	Description
Just in time	The delivery of a specified SKU by a supplier to a customer at the agreed time and location that will synchronize with the business process of the customer and therefore reduce the likelihood of holding inventory at the location.
Cross-docking	Avoid holding inventory at transhipment centres and the associated inventory storage cost, as goods are typically cross-docked from larger inbound deliveries for onward delivery in smaller shipments. A UK retailer is currently using an intermodal rail service to move containers of groceries from its rail-connected central distribution centre to a rail terminal over a hundred miles away, where the containers are then delivered by road to their various stores.
Vendor-managed Inventory	Typically, inventory is managed, often electronically, and maybe owned by the supplier at the customer's premises and then replenished when required. A typical example is flour and sugar in silos at bakeries and food manufacturers.
Standardized components	The use of standardized components within more than one finished product, for example automobiles and computers. The aim is to reduce the variety and complexity of inventory management and therefore reduce costs and improve financial performance.

Marks & Spencer plc's chairman Archie Norman (2018:22) highlighted the important relationship between supply chain management and inventory holding:

> Our supply chains in both Clothing & Home and in Food require significant re-engineering. In fast-moving fashion this means we are slower than most of our major competitors to market and carry high levels of stock.

3.11 Balance sheet case study

This case study has been designed to explore the content of this chapter and the accompanying solution will guide you through the process. Additional study questions can be found in section 3.15.

SCC plc has supplied you with the following information in Table 3.34 for their financial year ending 31 March 20XX.

1 Prepare SCC plc's trial balance as at 31 March 20XX.

2 Construct SCC's balance sheet as at 31 March 20XX.

3 Comment on the liquidity, working capital and gearing position of SCC plc.

Table 3.34   SCC plc, financial data for the financial year ending 31 March 20XX

Account Item	£
Accounts payable	1,100,000
Accounts receivable	750,000
Bank overdraft	250,000
Cash	50,000
Dividends payable	350,000
Finished goods	500,000
Fixtures and fittings	700,000
Intangible assets	3,000,000
Land and buildings	10,000,000
Long-term loan	5,000,000
Motor vehicles	600,000
Ordinary share capital	7,000,000
Plant and machinery	800,000
Raw materials	400,000
Retained earnings	3,000,000
Taxation payable	300,000
Work in progress	200,000

Solution Case study

Step 1: sort the account items into their account type. Table 3.35 illustrates the five account types that you will typically find in a BS, an example, and whether the item is a debit or credit balance.

Table 3.35 Account and balance type

Account type	Example	Balance type
Non-current asset (NCA)	Intangible	Debit
Current asset (CA)	Cash	Debit
Non-current liability (NCL)	Long-term loan	Credit
Current liability (CL)	Accounts payable	Credit
Equity (EQ)	Retained earnings	Credit

Step 2: now sort every account item and its corresponding value into the appropriate account type, as illustrated in Table 3.36. Add up all the debit balances and then do the same for the credit balances; they should be equal. The role of a trial balance is to check that the double-entry transactions have been completed correctly; in the case of SCC plc, the total debit and credit balances equal £17m.

Table 3.36 SCC plc, trial balance as at 31 March 20XX

SCC plc trial balance as at 31 March 20XX				
Account item	Account type	£k	Debit £k	Credit £k
Accounts payable	CL	1,100		1,100
Accounts receivable	CA	750	750	
Bank overdraft	CL	250		250
Cash	CA	50	50	
Dividends payable	CL	350		350
Finished goods	CA	500	500	
Fixtures and fittings	NCA	700	700	
Intangible assets	NCA	3,000	3,000	
Land and buildings	NCA	10,000	10,000	
Long-term loan	NCL	5,000		5,000
Motor vehicles	NCA	600	600	
Ordinary share capital	EQ	7,000		7,000
Plant and machinery	NCA	800	800	
Raw materials	CA	400	400	
Retained earnings	EQ	3,000		3,000
Taxation payable	CL	300		300
Work in progress	CA	200	200	
		34,000	**17,000**	**17,000**

Step 3: now formulate the accounting equation by adding up each of the account types, as depicted in Table 3.37.

Table 3.37   SCC plc, accounting equation as at 31 March 20XX

Total assets £m				=	Total equity and liabilities £m					
NCA	+	CA	=	TA	=	EQ	+	NCL	+	CL	=	TEL
15.1	+	1.9	=	17	=	10	+	5	+	2	=	17

Step 4: construct the organization's balance sheet, as illustrated in Figure 3.7.

Figure 3.7   SCC plc balance sheet as at 31 March 20XX

SCC plc balance sheet as at 31 March 20XX		
	£k	£k
Assets		
Non-current assets		
Land and buildings	10,000	
Fixtures and fittings	700	
Plant and machinery	800	
Motor vehicles	600	12,100
Intangible assets		3,000
Current assets		
Raw materials	400	
Work in progress	200	
Finished goods	500	
Accounts receivable	750	
Cash	50	1,900
Total assets		**17,000**
Equity		
Ordinary share capital	7,000	
Retained earnings	3,000	
Total equity		**10,000**

(continued)

Figure 3.7 (*Continued*)

SCC plc balance sheet as at 31 March 20XX		
	£k	**£k**
Non-current liabilities		
Long-term loan		5,000
Current liabilities		
Accounts payable	1,100	
Bank overdraft	250	
Dividends payable	350	
Taxation payable	300	2,000
Total equity and liabilities		**17,000**

Tables 3.38 and 3.39 illustrate the organization's accounting equation for the type 2 and type 3 BS formats.

Table 3.38   SCC plc, balance sheet total assets = capital employed

Total assets – current liabilities £m						**=**	**Capital employed £m**				
NCA	+	CA	–	CL	=	TA – CL =	EQ	+	NCL	=	CE
15.1	+	1.9	–	2.0	=	15	=	10	+	5	=	15

Table 3.39   SCC plc, balance sheet net assets = equity

Net assets £m								**=**	**Equity £m**
NCA	+	CA	–	CL	–	NCL	=	TNA	=	EQ
15.1	+	1.9	–	2	–	5	=	55	=	10

The company has current net liabilities, which means that they have greater short-term liabilities than current assets. This is supported by both the company's current and quick ratios, which are less than their respective benchmarks, as illustrated in Table 3.40.

According to the company's gearing ratio, the company is funded 33.33% by loan capital.

Table 3.40 SCC plc, liquidity and gearing ratios

Liquidity and gearing ratios	Actual	Benchmark
Current ratio	0.95:1	2:1
Quick ratio	0.40:1	1:1
Gearing %	33.33%	

3.12 Summary

In this chapter you were introduced to the balance sheet (BS) of an organization and its structure using numerous examples taken from practice supported by a set of activities. The BS is basically an accounting equation which illustrates where an organization has raised its funds from and then where these funds have been invested in the business. You were also introduced to the three BS formats that are typically used in practice. You can now recognize and explain the impact of supply chain management decisions on the elements (assets, liabilities and capital) that make up the BS of an organization. You can explain the effect of an SCM decision on the financial ratios that are used to evaluate the BS.

3.13 References

BASF Group (2017) *Report,* http://report.basf.com/2017/en/ (accessed 15 December 2018)

Bureau van Dijk (2018) www.bvdinfo.com (accessed 18 November 2018)

Christopher, M (2011) *Logistics and Supply Chain Management: Creating value-adding networks,* 4th edn, Pearson Education, Harlow

CIMA (2005) *CIMA Official Terminology,* CIMA Publishing, Oxford

Deutsche Post DHL Group (2017) *Annual Report,* https://annualreport2017.dpdhl.com/downloads-ext/en/documents/DPDHL_2017_Annual_Report.pdf (accessed 15 December 2018)

Marks & Spencer Group Plc (2017) *Annual Report and Financial Statements,* https://corporate.marksandspencer.com/documents/reports-results-and-publications/annual-report-2017.pdf (accessed 15 December 2018)

Marks & Spencer Group Plc (2018) *Annual Report and Financial Statements,* https://corporate.marksandspencer.com/annualreport (accessed 15 December 2018)

Nestlé (2017) *Annual Review*, www.nestle.com/investors/publications#tab-2017 (accessed 15 December 2018)

Procter & Gamble Company (2017) *Form 10-K*, www.annualreports.com/Hosted-Data/AnnualReports/PDF/NYSE_PG_2017.pdf (accessed 15 December 2018)

Templar, S, Findlay, C and Hofmann, E (2016) *Financing the End to End Supply Chain: A reference guide to supply chain finance*, 1st edn, Kogan Page, London

3.14 Solutions to the activities

Activity 3.1 solution

Table 3.41 illustrates the account items by the five account types.

Table 3.41   Account item and type

Account item	Account type				
	NCA	CA	EQ	NCL	CL
Land and buildings	✓				
Ordinary share capital			✓		
Long-term loan				✓	
Goodwill	✓				
Retained earnings			✓		
Accounts payable					✓
Plant and machinery	✓				
Accounts receivable		✓			
Fixtures and fittings	✓				
Motor vehicles	✓				
Finished goods		✓			
Raw materials		✓			
Dividends payable					✓
Taxation payable					✓
Bank overdraft					✓
Work in progress		✓			
Cash		✓			

Activity 3.2 solution

The accounting equation for Ultra plc is illustrated in Table 3.42.

The BS for Ultra plc is illustrated in Figure 3.8.

Table 3.42 Ultra plc, accounting equation

NCA	CA		CL		EQ		NCL	
PPE 32	Inventories	4	Accounts payable	7	Share capital	25	Non-current assets	8
	Accounts receivable	10	Dividend payable	1	Reserves	7		
	Cash	2						
32		16		8		32		8

Figure 3.8 Ultra plc balance sheet as at 31 December 20XX

ASSETS	£m
Property, plant and equipment	32
Non-current assets	**32**
Inventories	4
Accounts receivable	10
Cash	2
Current assets	**16**
Total assets	**48**
EQUITY AND LIABILITIES	
Share capital	25
Reserves	7
Equity	**32**
Long-term loan	8
Non-current liabilities	**8**
Accounts payable	7
Dividend payable	1
Current liabilities	**8**
Total equity and liabilities	**48**

Activity 3.3 solution

Table 3.43 illustrates the solution to Activity 3.3.

Table 3.43   Current assets and current liabilities

Current assets	£m	Current liabilities	£m
Raw materials	320	Accounts payable	370
Work in progress	240	Dividend payable	30
Finished goods	160	Tax payable	80
Accounts receivable	420		
Cash	60		
Total	**1,200**	**Total**	**480**

The company's working capital is calculated by subtracting the current liabilities from the current assets. The company's current assets are £1,200m; subtracting their current liabilities of £480m produces a working capital or net current assets of £720m.

The current ratio is derived by dividing the company's current assets of £1,200m by its current liabilities, £480m, and then expressing it as a ratio, which is 2.5:1.0. Therefore, every £1.00 of current liabilities, the organization has £2.50 of current assets to cover their short-term obligations if their creditors seek payment.

The quick/acid test ratio is calculated by taking the company's current assets (£1,200m), subtracting the value of their inventories (£720m), and then dividing by their current liabilities (£480m) and finally expressing it as a ratio. The company's acid test ratio is 1.00:1:00; after taking away the value of the organization's inventories, the company has £1 of current assets for every £1 of current liabilities.

The company's inventory as a percentage of current assets is 60% (£720m/£1,200m).

3.15 Study questions

Study question 3.1

MakeCo plc has supplied the information in Table 3.44 for the financial year ending 31 December 20XX.

Sales revenue for the year ending 31 December 20XX was £8,000,000 and their earnings before tax and interest were £800,000:

a You are required to prepare a balance sheet for MakeCo plc.

b Comment on the profitability, liquidity and gearing position of MakeCo plc, and support your findings by calculating the following financial ratios:

    1 earnings before tax and interest percentage;

    2 return on capital employed percentage;

    3 current ratio;

Table 3.44 MakeCo plc, financial data

Account item	£k
Land and buildings	8,000
Ordinary share capital	7,500
Long-term loan	3,000
Intangible assets	2,000
Retained earnings	2,600
Accounts payable	800
Plant and machinery	900
Accounts receivable	650
Fixtures and fittings	550
Motor vehicles	450
Finished goods	350
Raw materials	250
Dividends payable	200
Taxation payable	320
Bank overdraft	180
Work in progress	200
Cash	50

4 acid test ratio;

5 the value of the organization's working capital;

6 gearing percentage.

Study question 3.2

The current asset and current liability information illustrated in Table 3.45 has been extracted from the annual report and accounts of four fast-moving consumer goods (FMCG) companies for their financial year ending on 31 December 20XX.

Table 3.45   Current asset and current liability information, 31 December 20XX

Account item £m	Alpha	Beta	Gamma	Delta
Accounts payable	380	805	620	360
Accounts receivable	600	400	275	430
Cash	20	15	25	40
Dividend payable	10	80	50	40
Finished goods	100	150	90	70
Raw materials	400	300	80	240
Tax payable	90	130	80	70
Work in progress	200	150	100	160

For each FMCG company, calculate the following:

1 the value of their working capital;

2 their current ratio;

3 their quick/acid ratio;

4 inventory as percentage of current assets.

Study question 3.3

The information in Table 3.46 has been taken from the accounts of OTIF plc for the financial year ending 31 December 20XX. Formulate the accounting equation to find the value of the company's share capital, which has been omitted from Table 3.46, and then construct the balance sheet for OTIF plc.

Table 3.46   OTIF plc, balance sheet data as at 31 December 20XX

Account item	£m
Accounts payable	28
Accounts receivable	45
Cash	5
Dividend payable	4
Finished goods	5
Fixtures and fittings	10
Goodwill	10
Land and buildings	100
Long-term loan	50
Motor vehicles	30
Plant and machinery	60
Raw materials	15
Reserves	60
Share capital	?
Tax payable	8
Work in progress	10

The company's preferred BS format is total assets equals total equity and liabilities.

3.16 Study question solutions

Study question 3.1 solution

Figure 3.9 depicts the BS for MakeCo plc as at 31 December 20XX.

Figure 3.9   MakeCo plc balance sheet as at 31 December 20XX

MakeCo plc balance sheet as at 31 December 20XX		
	£k	£k
Assets		
Non-current assets		
Intangible assets		2,600
Land and buildings	8,000	
Fixtures and fittings	550	
Plant and machinery	900	
Motor vehicles	450	9,900
Current assets		
Raw materials	250	
Work in progress	200	
Finished goods	350	
Accounts receivable	650	
Cash	50	1,500
Total assets		**14,000**
Equity		
Ordinary share capital	7,500	
Retained earnings	2,000	
Total equity		**9,500**
Non-current liabilities		
Long-term loan		3,000
Current liabilities		
Accounts payable	800	
Bank overdraft	180	
Dividends payable	200	
Taxation payable	320	1,500
Total equity and liabilities		**14,000**

1. The earnings before tax and interest (EBIT) percentage is calculated by dividing EBIT/revenue and multiplying by 100; MakeCo plc's EBIT percentage is 10%. EBIT/revenue and multiplying by 100 = £800,000/£8,000,000 *100 = 10%

2. The return on capital employed (ROCE) percentage is calculated by dividing EBIT/capital employed and multiplying by 100; MakeCo plc's ROCE percentage is 6.4%.

    EBIT/capital employed and multiplying by 100 = £800,000/£12,500,000 *100
    = 6.4%

3. The current ratio is the ratio between the organization's current assets and current liabilities; in the case of MakeCo plc, its current ratio is 1:1.

    Current assets: Current liabilities = £1,500,000: £1,500,000 = 1:1

4. The acid test ratio is the ratio between the organization's current assets minus its inventories and current liabilities; in the case of MakeCo plc, its acid test ratio is 0.47:1.00.

    Current assets – inventories:Current liabilities = £700,000:£1,500,000
    = 0.47:1.00

5. The value of the organization's working capital is zero; it is calculated by subtracting current liabilities from current assets.

    Current assets – Current liabilities = £1,500,000 – £1,500,000 = 0

6. The gearing percentage is calculated by dividing the non-current liabilities by the organization's capital employed, then multiplying by 100 to give a percentage. MakeCo plc's gearing percentage is 24%.

    (non-current liabilities/capital employed) *100 = (£3,000,000/£12,500,000) *100
    = 24%

The company has no working capital at all, as their current assets equal their current liabilities. This is supported by both the company's current (1:1) and acid test ratios (0.47:1), which are less than their respective benchmarks of 2:1 and 1:1.

According to the company's gearing ratio, the company is funded 24% by loan capital. However, the company is profitable with an EBIT % of 10% and an ROCE % of 6.4%.

Study question 3.2 solution

Table 3.47 illustrates the working capital analysis for the four FMCG companies.

Table 3.47 FMCG companies' working capital analysis 31 December 20XX

Company	Current assets	Current liabilities	Working capital	Current ratio	Acid test ratio	Inventory %
Alpha	1,320	480	840	2.75:1.00	1.29:1.00	53.0
Beta	1,015	1,015	0	1.00:1.00	0.41:1.00	59.1
Gamma	570	750	−180	0.76:1.00	0.40:1.00	47.4
Delta	940	470	470	2.00:1.00	1.00:1.00	50.0

Alpha has the greatest working capital figure of £840m, the highest current and acid test ratios of 2.75:1 and 1.29:1, and its inventories represent 53% of the value of its current assets. Beta has zero working capital, a current ratio of 1 and an acid test ratio of 0.41, with inventories accounting for 59.1% of total current assets. Beta has a potential liquidity issue if their suppliers require payment. Gamma has the lowest inventory percentage, with 47.4% of its current assets represented by inventories. However, it has net current liabilities, with its current liabilities exceeding its current assets by £180m; this is also reflected in its liquidity ratios of 0.76 and 0.40 respectively. There is a probable liquidity issue here; however, if the organization has excellent cash flow this could be mitigated, but we don't have the data to confirm this. Finally, Delta has liquidity ratios which are typically associated with a manufacturing organization: a current ratio of 2 and an acid test ratio of 1. Inventories represent 50% of current assets and the company has net current assets of £470m.

Workings

I have included the workings in Table 3.48 for the Delta solution, which will be the same approach for the other three companies.

Table 3.48   Delta workings

Step 1	Identify all the current asset items for Delta.	
		£m
	Raw materials	240
	Work in progress	160
	Finished goods	70
	Accounts receivable	430
	Cash	40
	Current assets	940
Step 2	Identify all the current liability items for Delta.	
		£m
	Accounts payable	360
	Dividend payable	40
	Tax payable	70
	Current liabilities	470
Step 3	Calculate Delta's working capital (WC) by subtracting current liabilities (CL) from the company' current assets (CA). WC = CA − CL = £940m − £470m = £470m Delta has £470m working capital, or net current assets of £470m.	
Step 4	Calculate the current ratio, which is derived by taking the ratio of current assets to current liabilities. CA:CL = £940m:£470m = 2.0:1.0 Delta has £2 of CA for every £1 of CL.	
Step 5	Calculate the acid test ratio, which is calculated by subtracting the value of the company's inventory from its current assets, as a ratio of its current liabilities. (CA − IN):CL = (£940m − £470m):£470m = 1.0:1.0 Delta has £1 of CA for every £1 of CL.	
Step 6	To calculate inventory as a percentage of current assets, take the value of Delta's inventory and divide by the value of its current assets, then multiply by 100 to derive the percentage. (IN/CA) * 100 = (£470m/£940m) *100 = 50%	

Study question 3.3 solution

Step 1: match every account item to their relevant account type, as illustrated in the Table 3.49.

Table 3.49 OTIF plc, account items by account type

Non-current assets (NCA)	Current assets (CA)	Current liabilities (CL)	Equity (EQ)	Non-current liabilities (NCL)
Land and buildings	Accounts receivable	Accounts payable	Reserves	Long-term loan
Fixtures and fittings	Cash	Dividend payable	Share capital	
Goodwill	Finished goods	Tax payable		
Motor vehicles	Raw materials			
Plant and machinery	Work in progress			
210	**80**	**40**	**60 +?**	**50**

Step 2: taking the total of each account type, insert them into the accounting equation to find the value of the company's total assets (see Table 3.50).

Table 3.50 Accounting equation (type 1) OTIF plc 20XX

Total assets £m			=	Total equity and liabilities £m				
NCA	+ CA	= TA	=	EQ	+ NCL	+ CL	=	TEL
210	+ 80	= 290	=	?	+ 50	+ 40	=	290

Step 3: using the type 1 BS, we know that the total assets will equal the total equity and liabilities. OTIF plc has total assets of £290m; therefore its total equity and liabilities should also be £290m.

Step 4: the share capital has been omitted by mistake; however, it is possible to find the value of the share capital by changing the subject of the formula to:

share capital = (total equity + liabilities) – non-current liabilities – current liabilities – reserves

Share capital = 290 – 50 – 40 – 60 = 140.

Step 5: it is now possible to build the BS for OTIF plc, as illustrated in Figure 3.10.

Figure 3.10   OTIF plc balance sheet as at 31 December 20XX

OTIF plc Balance sheet as at 31 December 20XX	
ASSETS	**£m**
Intangible	10
Property, plant and equipment	200
Non-current assets	**210**
Inventories	30
Accounts receivable	45
Cash	5
Current assets	**80**
Total assets	**290**
EQUITY AND LIABILITIES	
Share capital	140
Reserves	60
Equity	**200**
Long-term loan	50
Non-current liabilities	**50**
Accounts payable	28
Dividend payable	4
Tax payable	8
Current liabilities	**40**
Total equity and liabilities	**290**

Cash and working capital management

04

In Chapters 2 and 3, we concentrated on the income statement (IS) and the balance sheet (BS), focusing on the relationship between supply chain decisions and their impact on revenue generation and expenditure in the case of the IS, and their relationship with assets, liabilities and equity in respect of the BS. In this chapter we are going to focus on the significant relationship between supply chain management (SCM) decisions and an organization's cash flow. There are many metaphors that have been used in the past to describe how cash flows in business. Two graphic examples that come to mind: when I was studying accountancy many years ago, they were (1) the 'in and out doors' in a restaurant, and (2) the bath tub with the taps full on representing cash coming into the business and, as the bath had no plug fitted, the water gushing out represented cash leaving the business. There is also an expression often used to highlight the importance of cash – you have probably come across it before – it is the old adage 'cash is king'. But cash flow is incredibly significant not only for business, but for governments, charities, non-governmental organizations (NGOs) and, yes, individuals like us. We can all relate to an unexpected incident that occurred which has impacted on our cash flow and where we have had to find additional sources of finance to fill a liquidity gap. This is also the case for organizations.

I remember many years ago having a conversation with a colleague at Cranfield University, who described cash as the 'stem cell of business'. At the time I didn't realize how profound this description was. Stem cells have the potential to change into any other type of cell within our body. Cash also has the ability to change its form in business, including converting into different other assets (NCA and CA), paying off short-term and long-term debt (NCL and CL), repaying equity and paying expenses (materials, wages and overheads). Hence, cash is the most important asset in business.

4.1 Aim and objectives

The aim of this chapter is to introduce you to the importance of managing cash flow, no matter which type of organization you own, manage or work for.

At the end of this chapter you will be able to:

- explain the importance of cash in business;
- construct a cash flow forecast;
- identify the different components of the cash-to-cash cycle;
- identify the impact of supply chain decisions on cash flow;
- explain the relationship between supply chain management and supply chain finance;
- explore the relationship between liquidity and cash flow;
- calculate financial ratios that are relevant to evaluating cash flow.

4.2 The importance of cash in business

The importance of cash flow in business is highlighted by Christopher (2011:58), who considers the strategic role of cash management equivalent with profit-generation: 'Strong positive cash flow has become as much a desired goal of management as profit.'

Often, we come across numerous metaphors in life which are then used as enablers to explain different concepts. For me, the most powerful image that represents cash in a business is the level of oil in the internal combustion engine that powers my car. If there is no oil in the engine, it will seize up and will not work. If a business runs out of cash and there is no financing alternative, the business will cease to function. If you are a manufacturing company and your customers have long payment terms that have a negative impact on your cash flow, how do you then buy raw materials, convert them into finished goods and distribute them to your customers if you have no cash?

Recognizing that cash flows in and out of a business at different times and speeds is essential to the success and survival of any business. Christopher (2011) stresses the importance of cash flow, and the ability to manage cash is a key concept that supply chain practitioners need to be aware of, but also master.

Have a go at Activity 4.1, which relates to a typical road freight haulage operation.

Activity 4.1

List as many different cash receipts and payments as you can think of that a road haulage company will have in its annual operation.

Cash receipts	Cash expenditures

Now I would like you to think about the different cash receipts and payments that your business, or a university, will have in a typical year.

Cash flow statement

An organization's annual report includes a cash flow statement (CFS), which details the cash generated and consumed within the last financial year. The CFS starts with the cash generated from operations taking the operating profit for the business from the Income Statement, which is then adjusted for non-cash items such as depreciation and amortization and other items such as profit or loss on disposals of assets to generate the operating cash flows before any changes in working capital. The changes in the organization's working capital are then taken into consideration to derive the cash generated from operations. Table 4.1 illustrates the cash generated from operations calculation which has been extracted from the 2018 Financial Statements of Marks and Spencer Group PLC (2018:80).

An important question to explore is how do we as supply chain practitioners' impact on the cash generated from operations? Supply chain practitioners take decisions with regard to purchasing and disposing of non-current assets, procurement and supplier relationship management, inventory management, revenue generation and customer relationship management and expenditure decisions relating to operations, warehousing and distribution.

Table 4.1   Consolidated statement of cash flows Marks and Spencer Group PLC 2018 and 2017

	52 weeks ended 31 March 2018	52 weeks ended 1 April 2017
	£m	£m
Cash flows from operating activities		
Cash generated from operations	944.1	1,165.7
Income tax paid	(94.3)	(98.0)
Net cash inflow from operating activities	**849.8**	**1,067.7**
Cash flows from investing activities		
Proceeds on property disposals	3.2	27.0
Purchase of property, plant and equipment	(274.9)	(309.1)
Proceeds on disposal of Hong Kong business	22.9	–
Purchase of intangible assets	(74.3)	(101.1)
Reduction of current financial assets	0.8	4.6
Interest received	6.0	6.6
Net cash used in investing activities	**(316.3)**	**(372.0)**
Cash flows from financing activities		
Interest paid	(112.2)	(111.2)
Cash inflow/(outflow) from borrowings	43.8	(32.7)
Repayment of syndicated loan	–	(215.3)
Decrease in obligations under finance leases	(2.6)	(2.0)
Payment of liability to the Marks & Spencer UK Pension Scheme	(59.6)	(57.9)
Equity dividends paid	(303.4)	(377.5)
Shares issued on exercise of employee share options	0.1	5.5
Purchase of own shares by employee trust	(3.1)	–
(Redemption)/issuance of medium-term notes	(328.2)	300.0
Net cash used in financing activities	**(765.2)**	**(491.1)**
Net cash (outflow)/inflow from activities	(231.7)	204.6
Effects of exchange rate changes	(3.5)	5.6
Opening net cash	406.2	196.0
Closing net cash	**171.0**	**406.2**

However, cash can also be generated and consumed by numerous other factors. Table 4.2 illustrates the typical cash generators and consumers to be found in an organization's cash flow statement. The list of typical cash generators and consumers is not exhaustive, but provides you with an interesting insight into the range of cash generators and consumers typically to be discovered in business. Hence, supply chain practitioners need to be aware of the impact their decisions have on these cash generators and consumers and the consequences for the overall cash flow position of their organization.

Table 4.2   Typical Cash generators and consumers

Cash generators	Cash consumers
• Cash generated from operations • Proceeds from the sale of property, plant and equipment • Reduction of current financial assets • Proceeds on disposal a part of the business • Interest received • Cash inflow from borrowings • Shares issued on exercise of employee share options • Issuance of medium-term notes • Effects of exchange rate changes • Dividends received • Proceeds from the sale of investments • Proceeds on settlement of derivative financial instruments • Proceeds from issuance of ordinary shares • Tax received	• Taxation paid • Purchase of property, plant and equipment, investment property and assets classified as held-for-sale. • Purchase of intangible assets • Repayment of syndicated loan • Interest paid • Payment of liability to the pension scheme • Dividends paid • Effects of exchange rate changes • Purchase of own shares for trust • Repayment of obligations under finance leases • Redemption of medium-term notes • Effects of exchange rate changes • Costs incurred on repayment of borrowings • Settlements of employee tax liability for share awards • Acquisition of subsidiaries, net of cash acquired

4.3 The cash flow forecast

This section will introduce you to the cash flow forecast (CFF), in my opinion the most important financial planning document in business, but also in life – as my children have found as I have continually stated over the years to help them with their finances. It is important to highlight the emphasis of the CFF and the CFS; typically the CFF is just to forecast future cash flows, for example for a new business venture or introducing a new product, while a CFS illustrates what has happened in the past related to cash generated and consumed. The following fictitious case study, MakeCo plc, has been designed to highlight to you the importance of the CFF and also to explore the linkages between the three financial documents: the CFF, the IS and the BS. MakeCo plc, a new business venture, is being planned and its future financing is explored by first constructing the CFF, then the IS and finally the BS.

Case study: MakeCo plc

Three designers are planning to form a new company to assemble a unique furniture system that they have invented. The unique design uses a kit of standard components that enables customers to create their own design, or they can use a range of designs that can be downloaded for a fee over the internet. A comprehensive marketing study has been conducted and a preliminary sales forecast has been produced. An initial investment of £250k of capital can be raised by a share issue to family and friends. However, it is likely that additional funding will be required if the forecast demand for the furniture system materializes. Therefore, another cash injection will be required fairly soon; it is likely that this new funding will be a long-term loan, hence a business case will need to be prepared to support the application for additional financing.

They plan to purchase components from five suppliers and these components are then delivered by each supplier to a distributed centre operated by a third-party logistics provider (3PL). The 3PL provides a vendor-managed inventory (VMI) solution to the company's rental factory; a fixed monthly management fee has been arranged for the VMI service. The company operates an assemble-to-order process and the kits are assembled by the workforce in the factory. There is no inventory of assembled kits as the company has adopted a pick to zero and postponement strategy with regard to their finished goods inventories; however, there will be raw materials inventories held at the distribution centre at the year end. The kits are dispatched to five retail customers who have been licensed to distribute and sell them by a second 3PL to their customers' distribution centres. MakeCo plc's supply chain operation is illustrated in Figure 4.1.

Figure 4.1 MakeCo plc supply chain operation

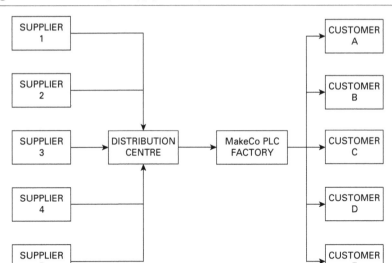

The following forecast information has been provided by the designers and they need your help to build their business plan:

- initial share capital £250k;

- on 1 January £140k is required to purchase supply chain non-current assets;

- the non-current assets have a life of 10 years and no residual value;

- the straight-line method of depreciation has been chosen by the company, depreciation costs are £14k per annum;

- revenue for the year is forecast to be £2,400k;

- there is no opening inventory of components on 1 January 20XX, but the material cost of components per kit is estimated to be 35% of revenue;

- factory rent of £50k per quarter paid in advance;

- factory labour costs for January to June £20k per month, from July onwards £30k per month;

- sales and general administration costs £10k per month;

- factory overheads are estimated to be £20k per month;

- inbound 3PL distribution costs £8K per month;

- outbound 3PL distribution costs are £14k paid quarterly in arrears;

- a dividend of £48k is planned to be paid in December;

- total components purchased for the year are £1,000k;
- corporation tax for the year is estimated to be £116k and will be paid on 31 March 20X9.

The forecast cash receipts from customers and cash payments to component suppliers are itemized in Table 4.3.

Table 4.3 Forecast cash receipts and payments

Forecast £k	JAN	FEB	MAR	APR	MAY	JUN	JUL	AUG	SPT	OCT	NOV	DEC
Receipts from customers	0	0	20	35	50	75	90	120	150	200	280	300
Payment to suppliers	30	30	30	50	50	50	50	70	70	70	70	70

Typically, a business plan should include the following statements:

1 a monthly cash flow forecast (CFF) for the year ending 31 December 20X8;

2 a forecast income statement (IS) for the year ending 31 December 20X8.

3 a balance sheet (BS) as at 31 December 20X8.

MakeCo plc cash flow forecast

The first step when constructing a cash flow forecast is to identify all the relevant cash flows from the information supplied by the designers that will occur in the financial year, which are illustrated in Table 4.4.

Table 4.4 Relevant cash flows

Cash In	Cash out
Share capital	Purchasing non-current assets
Cash receipts from customers	Cash payments to component suppliers
	Direct labour cost
	Sales and general administration costs
	Factory rent
	Inbound 3PL distribution costs
	Outbound 3PL distribution costs
	Dividend payment

The following were not cash receipts or payments, or the cash flow did not occur within the time period and therefore are not included in the CFF, but are relevant to the IS and the BS:

- Revenue for the year is forecast to be £2,400k.
- Depreciation costs are £14k per annum.
- Total components purchased for the year is £1,000k.
- Corporation tax for the year is estimated to be £116k.
- Material cost of components per kit is estimated to be 35% of revenue.

The question you are about to pose is, why aren't they included? Here is the explanation for each point.

Revenue is the value of invoices raised to customers within the financial year; it is the top line on the income statement, but it is not the cash received in the financial year. However, if every sale was a cash transaction it would be the total cash receipts for the period, but not all customers pay straight away: some are given credit and some customers will default and not pay. Therefore, revenue will be a variable used to calculate the value of accounts receivable on the BS at the end of the financial year, but will not be included in the cash flow forecast.

Depreciation is an accounting adjustment to reflect the consumption of a non-current asset in generating revenue for the period; it is not a cash flow. However, the purchase and sale of non-current assets are cash flows; therefore the purchase of £140k of non-current assets is a cash flow. It is a very important point to remember that depreciation is not a cash flow; it is an accounting adjustment which is an expense in the IS and reduces the value of assets on the BS. It is an important area that SC practitioners need to be aware of and is the subject of Chapter 5.

Total components purchased for the year are the value of the total purchases made in the year with suppliers (the sum of the purchase orders issued for the accounting period); they are not the value of cash payments to suppliers. The components purchased for the year will be used in the cost of goods sold calculation in the IS and will also be used to calculate the accounts payable figure on the BS.

If the corporation tax was paid in the financial year, it would be included in the cash flow forecast. However, the tax payment is due in the next financial year, hence it is relevant to the IS as an expense in this financial year, but the payment will be made next year; therefore it is charged as an expense this year and shown as a current liability on the BS. It is an accrual, which meets the matching concept introduced in Chapter 2. CIMA (1989:5) defines the matching concept as:

Revenues and costs are matched one with the other and dealt with in the profit and loss account of the period to which they relate irrespective of the period of receipt or payment (SSAP2).

Finally, the material cost per kit is an estimate; it is not a cash flow.

Now that the relevant cash flows have been identified, the next stage is to focus on their timing: when do they occur in the accounting period? Using the information supplied, we can now construct the most important financial statement in business, which I stressed earlier: the cash flow forecast (CFF). It is a very significant document because the CFF provides the business with five important figures. It records:

- cash received by the organization in the accounting period;
- cash paid out by the organization in the accounting period;
- the net monthly cash position;
- the cumulative cash position during the accounting period;
- the opening and closing cash balance – the latter is the cash position disclosed on the BS at the end of the financial year.

Table 4.5 illustrates the CFF for MakeCo plc for the year ending 31 December 20X8.

The total cash inflow received by MakeCo for the financial year 20X8 is forecasted to be £1,570, which was made up of £250k from selling shares and the rest received from customers that have purchased the kits. The cash received from customers has a positive trend, with cash received in December of £300k, which is 15 times greater than the cash received in March.

The forecast total cash outflow for the accounting period is £1,840k, with the largest item of expenditure being the purchase of components from suppliers, which equates to 35% of the total expenditure for the year.

Let us now focus on the organization's monthly net cash flow position. The cash flow forecast highlights that the three months of the last financial quarter all have positive cash balances, with the other previous months having negative cash balances and with April having the largest deficit of £123k. The importance of the CFF as a planning tool cannot be overstated, especially with regard to taking a holistic perspective of the year, but also in its usefulness in highlighting trends, especially when combined with a user-friendly graphical interface, as illustrated in Figure 4.2. The figure illustrates two trends for the year: the first is that the monthly net cash flow is moving from negative to positive, but as you would also expect, this trend is reflected in a negative cumulative cash flow position as it is improving from the lowest

Table 4.5 MakeCo plc cash flow forecast for the year ending 30 December 20X8

Receipts £ 000	JAN	FEB	MAR	APR	MAY	JUN	JUL	AUG	SPT	OCT	NOV	DEC	TOTAL
Share capital	250	0	0	0	0	0	0	0	0	0	0	0	250
Sales	0	0	20	35	50	75	90	120	150	200	280	300	1,320
Total	250	0	20	35	50	75	90	120	150	200	280	300	1,570

Payments £ 000	JAN	FEB	MAR	APR	MAY	JUN	JUL	AUG	SPT	OCT	NOV	DEC	TOTAL
Non-current assets	140	0	0	0	0	0	0	0	0	0	0	0	140
Component suppliers	30	30	30	50	50	50	50	70	70	70	70	70	640
Factory labour	20	20	20	20	20	20	30	30	30	30	30	30	300
Factory rent	50	0	0	50	0	0	50	0	0	50	0	0	200
Sales & general administration	10	10	10	10	10	10	10	10	10	10	10	10	120
Inbound distribution	8	8	8	8	8	8	8	8	8	8	8	8	96
Outbound distribution	0	0	14	0	0	14	0	0	14	0	0	14	56
Dividend	0	0	0	0	0	0	0	0	0	0	0	48	48
Factory overheads	20	20	20	20	20	20	20	20	20	20	20	20	240
Total	278	88	102	158	108	122	168	138	152	188	138	200	1840

	JAN	FEB	MAR	APR	MAY	JUN	JUL	AUG	SPT	OCT	NOV	DEC	
Net cash flow £ 000	-28	-88	-82	-123	-58	-47	-78	-18	-2	12	142	100	-270
Bal. brought forward	0	-28	-116	-198	-321	-379	-426	-504	-522	-524	-512	-370	
Bal. carried forward	-28	-116	-198	-321	-379	-426	-504	-522	-524	-512	-370	-270	

Figure 4.2   MakeCo plc monthly net cash flow and cumulative cash flow 20X8

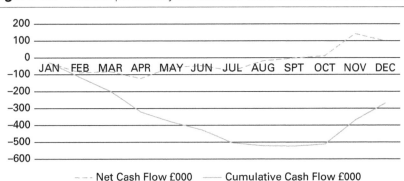

negative cash position in September of £524k to negative £270k at the year-end. Thus, based on the cash flow forecast, MakeCo plc would have a negative position at the year end of £270k, but would require a facility to borrow up to £524k to cover the cumulative cash deficit in September. MakeCo plc has a potential liquidity issue, which will need to be addressed; however, at this point we don't know if the company is profitable until we derive the IS.

MakeCo plc cash flow forecast

Now let us consider if MakeCo plc is going to make a profit or loss in their first year of trading by constructing their income statement. The first step is to calculate the gross margin for the organization. The company's forecast sales for the year-end were £2.4m, they plan to have zero component inventories at the beginning of the financial year, their purchases for the year are forecast to be £1.0m and they have estimated their cost of sales to be £0.84m (35% of revenue).

Table 4.6   MakeCo plc forecast gross profit for the year ending 31 December 20X8

	£k	£k
Revenue		2,400
Less cost of goods sold		
Opening inventory	0	
Plus purchasing	1,000	
Minus closing inventory	160	840
Gross profit		1,560

Changing the subject of the cost of goods sold equation, the components closing inventory can be derived as follows:

closing inventory = opening inventory + purchases − cost of goods sold.
closing inventory = 0 + £1.0m − £0.84m = £0.16m

MakeCo plc has decided to include their factory labour costs as operating expenses. MakeCo plc forecast gross profit for the year is £1.56m, which is a margin of 65%.

Forecast operating expenses for the year include the following:

- factory labour costs (£300k);

- sales and general administration costs (£120k);

- factory rent (£200k);

- inbound 3PL distribution costs (£96k);

- outbound 3PL distribution costs (£56k);

- depreciation (£14k)*;

- factory overheads (£240k).

*The depreciation for the non-current assets for year is calculated using the company's chosen method: 'straight-line'. The total cost of the non-current assets is divided by the useful life to give the annual depreciation cost. The depreciation charge for MakeCo plc will be £140k divided by 10 = £14k per annum.

The company forecast earnings before tax will be gross profit minus operating expenses, which is £1,560k − £1,026k = £534k. The company's forecast tax liability is £116k and they plan to pay a dividend to their shareholders of £48k; therefore retained earnings will be £370k. The forecast IS for MakeCo plc for the year ending 31 December 20X8 is illustrated in Figure 4.3.

Figure 4.3   MakeCo plc forecast income statement 20X8

MakeCo plc Forecast income statement for the year ending 31 December 20X8		
	£ 000	£ 000
Sales		2,400
Less cost of goods sold:		
Opening inventory	0	
Plus purchases	1,000	
Minus closing inventory	160	840
Gross profit		1,560

(continued)

Figure 4.3   *(Continued)*

MakeCo plc Forecast income statement for the year ending 31 December 20X8		
	£ 000	£ 000
Less other expenses		
Factory labour	300	
Factory rent	200	
Sales & general	120	
administration	96	
Inbound distribution	56	
Outbound distribution	240	
Factory overheads	14	1,026
Depreciation		
Earning before taxation		534
Taxation		116
Earnings after taxation		418
Dividend paid		48
Retained earnings		370

In Chapter 2 (Table 2.1) you were introduced to a set of profitability ratios. These ratios have been used to analyse MakeCo plc's income statement and profitability; they are presented in Table 4.7.

Table 4.7   MakeCo plc forecast profitability ratios

Ratio	Formula	Calculation
Gross margin	(Gross profit/ Revenue) *100	(£1,560k/£2,400k) *100 = 65.0%
Earnings before tax	(Earnings before tax/ Revenue) *100	(£534k/£2,400k) *100 = 22.25%
Earnings after tax	(Earnings after tax/ Revenue) *100	(£418k/£2,400k) *100 = 17.42%
Retained earnings	(Retained earnings/ Revenue) *100	(£370k/£2,400k) *100 = 15.42%

MakeCo plc makes forecast earnings before tax of 22.25% for the year and the company's retained earnings (bottom line) are £370k, which equates to 15.42% of revenue (top line). When building the business case for MakeCo plc, it is important that the forecast financial statements are produced in the following order: first the CFF, as this statement provides the cash figure (positive or negative) in the BS for financial year end; second the IS, as it derives the retained earnings for the accounting period, which is also included in the balance sheet; finally, the balance sheet can be drawn up, which takes into consideration all the timing differences between the IS and CFF. Here is a simplistic example: from the IS the sales revenue (£2,400k) for the year can be found; subtracting the cash received (£1,320) from customers recorded in the CFF produces the accounts receivable (£1,080) on the BS; another example is the accounts payable calculation.

MakeCo plc balance sheet

In the previous chapter on the BS you were introduced to three types of BS formats used in business; Figures 4.4 and 4.5 illustrate the type 1 and type 2 formats for MakeCo plc as at 31 December 20X8. Using the type 1 BS format, let us examine and analyse each key section of the company's BS.

Figure 4.4   MakeCo plc forecast balance sheet (type 1) 20X8

MakeCo plc forecast balance sheet as at 31 December 20X8	
Assets	**£,000**
Non-current assets	
Property, plant and equipment	<u>126</u>
Current assets	
Inventory	160
Accounts receivable	1,080
Cash and cash equivalents	<u>0</u>
Total assets	<u>**1,366**</u>
Equity	
Ordinary shares	250
Retained profit	<u>370</u>
Total equity	**620**
Liabilities	
Current liabilities	
Accounts payable	360
Taxation	116
Borrowings (bank overdraft)	<u>270</u>
	<u>746</u>
Total equity and liabilities	<u>**1,366**</u>

Figure 4.5   MakeCo plc forecast balance sheet (type 2) 20X8

MakeCo plc forecast balance sheet as at 31 December 20X8			
	£,000	£,000	£,000
Assets			
Non-current assets			
Property, plant and equipment			<u>126</u>
Current assets			
Inventory	160		
Accounts receivable	1,080		
Cash and cash equivalents	<u>0</u>	1,240	
Current liabilities			
Accounts payable	<u>360</u>		
Taxation	<u>116</u>		
Borrowings (bank overdraft)	<u>270</u>	<u>746</u>	
Net current assets			<u>494</u>
Total assets minus current liabilities			<u>620</u>
Financed by:			
Equity			
Ordinary shares		<u>250</u>	
Retained profit		<u>370</u>	
Capital employed			<u>620</u>

The company purchases non-current assets (NCAs) on 1 January 20X8 that cost £140k; these NCAs have been used throughout the year to generate sales of £2,400k; therefore, under the matching concept, a proportion of the NCA costs will be charged to the products cost in the form of depreciation (£14k as an operating expense in the IS). The value of the NCA on the BS will be reduced by the cumulative depreciation at the end of the financial year, from £140k minus £14k depreciation to £126k. NCAs are typically valued on the BS using their historical cost (£140k) minus cumulative depreciation (£14k) to produce their net book value on the BS (£126k).

The company's current assets (CAs) total £1,240k and comprise inventories (£160k) and accounts receivable (£1,080k); the company has no cash (see CFF). MakeCo plc has total assets (TA) of £1,366, which have been financed by equity (EQ) of £620k and current liabilities (CL) of £746k. The EQ includes the share capital and retained earnings from the IS. The CL includes the amounts owed to their suppliers, the tax payable to the government and finally the overdraft of £270k to the bank.

In summarizing MakeCo plc's forecast financial position, they are profit-able, and they have grown their shareholders' equity from £250k to £620k in the year; however, they have a liquidity issue with regard to cash flow from January to September, which needs to be addressed. The aim of the forecasting process is to develop a number of scenarios before establishing the final business case to the bank. Have a go at the next activity.

In my opinion, the most significant financial ratio in business that supply chain practitioners need to be aware of is the return on capital employed (ROCE). The ratio takes the earnings before interest and tax (EBIT) from the IS and then divides EBIT by the capital employed (CE) from the BS to calcu-late the ROCE for the organization. Alternatively, it can be derived by taking EBIT and dividing by non-current assets (NCA) plus working capital (CA – CL), multiplied by 100 to give a percentage. ROCE, according to Brookson (2001:43), 'reveals how much profit is being made on the money invested in the business and is a key measure of how well management is doing its job'.

The ROCE for MakeCo plc is 86.13%, the company's EBIT £534k, and its CE is £620k, or NCA + working capital. Inserting these figures into the ROCE calculation (£534k/£620k) *100 derives 86.13%. This ratio is important for supply chain practitioners as the decisions taken by them impact on sales, expenditure, NCAs and working capital. In Chapter 6 we will explore further the impact of supply chain decisions on the financial performance of the firm.

Now have a go at the next activity.

Activity 4.2

Your task is to identify 10 initiatives that the owners of MakeCo plc could implement to improve their current cash flow situation.

1
2
3
4
5
6
7
8
9
10

4.4 The cash-to-cash cycle

The cash-to-cash cycle (working capital cycle) is defined by CIMA (2005:98) as:

> The period of time which elapses between the point at which cash begins to be expended on the production of a product and the collection of cash from the purchaser.

The cash-to-cash cycle time is usually calculated in days; it is derived by taking the average number of inventory days plus the average number of receivable days, then subtracting the average number of payable days. Table 4.8 illustrates the formula for each of the components of the cash-to-cash cycle calculation.

Table 4.8 Cash-to-cash cycle components

Average number of inventory days	Average inventory/Average daily cost of sales in period (CIMA Official Terminology 2005:23)
Average number of receivable days	Average trade receivables/Average daily revenue on credit terms (CIMA Official Terminology (2005:24)
Average number of payable days	Average trade payables/Average daily purchases on credit terms (CIMA Official Terminology (2005:24)

Now have go at the following activity.

Activity 4.3

The information in Table 4.9 has been extracted from the report and accounts of four of your major competitors for the financial year ending 31 December 20XX. However, the management accountant has been taken ill.

Table 4.9 Cash-to-cash ratios

Company	Alpha	Beta	Delta	Gamma
Inventory days	60	45	30	
Accounts receivable days	45	75		60
Accounts payable days	75		45	90
Cash-to-cash cycle days		60	75	45

You are required to complete Table 4.9 and then use the information to answer the following questions.

1 Which company has the shortest cash-to-cash cycle time?

2 Which company's customers take the longest time to pay them?

3 Which company has the largest number of days' inventory?

4 Which company is quickest to pay its suppliers?

5 Which company has the lowest inventory days?

6 Which company has the longest cash-to-cash cycle time?

7 Which company is slowest to pay its suppliers?

8 Which company's customers take the shortest time to pay them?

When looking at financial ratios over a number of years it is possible to iden-tify trends, as the ratios are calculated using source data from the company's reports and accounts, which are also derived by the decisions taken by the company's employees. Table 4.10 illustrates the following working capital ratios for Marks & Spencer Group plc from 2002 to 2018:

- inventory days;
- accounts receivable days;
- accounts payable days;
- cash-to-cash cycle days.

Over the period of 17 years it can be seen that inventory days have increased from 14.59 days in 2002 to 26.65 days in 2018, an increase of 82.7%. A While accounts receivable days have also increased from 0.98 days in 2002 to 3.89 days in 2018, which equates to an increase of 297% over the same period. The company's accounts payable have gone from 8.96 days in 2002 to 29.78 days, an increase of 232.4%. These changes appears to have had a positive impact on the company's cash-to-cash cycle, as it has reduced from 6.62 days in 2002 to 0.75 days, as illustrated in Figure 4.6.

From 2010 to 2017 the company's cash-to-cash cycle was negative and therefore the company had no liquidity gap. However, in 2008 the company had a cash-to-cash cycle time of 14.02. A positive number indicates a liquid-ity gap, which means that the company has to find alternative finance to fund its working capital, because there is an average waiting time of 14.02 days before they receive their cash.

Table 4.10 Working capital ratios for Marks & Spencer Group plc 2002–2018

Year	2018	2017	2016	2015	2014	2013	2012	2011	2010	2009	2008	2007	2006	2005	2004	2003	2002
In days	26.65	26.06	27.66	28.24	29.93	27.93	25.05	25.68	23.47	21.59	19.78	17.69	17.52	15.61	17.50	16.35	14.59
AR days	3.89	3.76	4.00	4.38	4.49	3.94	4.21	3.68	3.39	3.36	3.42	2.89	1.97	1.28	1.34	1.45	0.98
AP days	29.78	33.25	35.34	34.25	40.50	35.41	36.32	34.45	30.32	14.38	9.18	11.04	11.36	8.98	9.24	9.11	8.96
C2C days	0.75	−3.43	−3.67	−1.63	−6.08	−3.53	−7.06	−5.08	−3.46	10.57	14.02	9.54	8.13	7.91	9.60	8.69	6.62

Adapted from: Fame, published by Bureau van Dijk (2018)

Figure 4.6   Cash-to-cash cycle time (days) Marks & Spencer Group plc 2002–2018

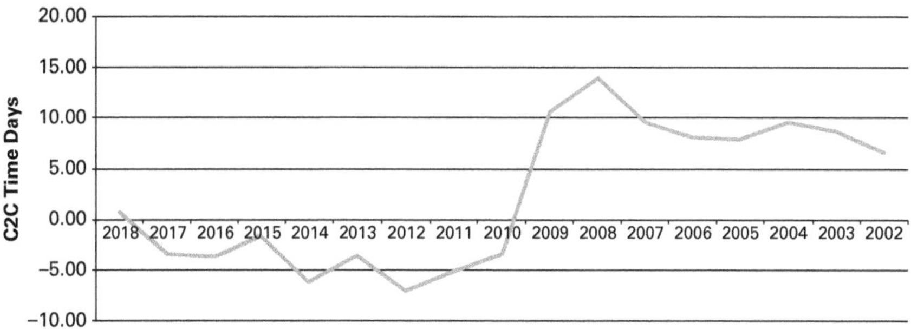

Adapted from: Fame, published by Bureau van Dijk (2018)

Table 4.11 illustrates the cash-to-cash cycle along a confectionery supply chain and introduces the premise that different industry sectors have fundamentally different cycle times due to contextual factors related to the sector in which they operate. Hence within an end-to-end supply chain, its organizations may have positive and negative cash-to-cash cycles. In Table 4.11 the cash-to-cash cycle times range from –8 days for the retail multiple to 42 days for the raw material supplier.

Table 4.11   Confectionery supply chain working capital ratios

Cash-to-cash cycle ratios	Retail multiple	Food processor	Raw material
Average number of inventory days	16	34	35
+ Average number of receivable days	2	29	30
− Average number of payable days	26	34	23
= Cash-to-cash cycle days	−8	29	42

Figure 4.7 illustrates the four working capital ratios for Unilever from 1998 to 2017; the figure charts the improvement on the cash-to-cash cycle time from 47.35 days in 1998 to –5.55 days in 2017. The improvement in the ratio has been influenced by a reduction in the accounts receivable days over the period; also, the company has reduced the number of days' inventory and there has been a significant increase in the accounts payable days from 2007; previously the accounts payable ratio was fairly constant from 1998.

Figure 4.7   Unilever plc working capital ratios

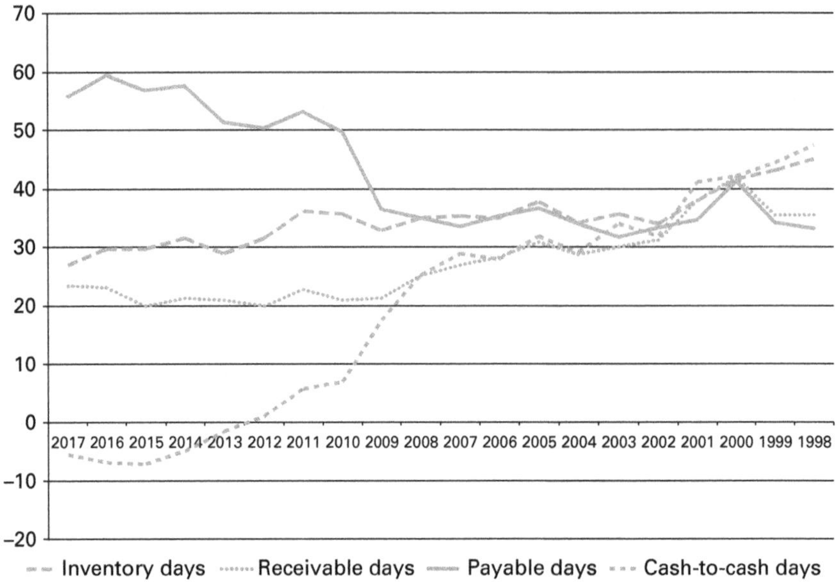

Adapted from: Fame, published by Bureau van Dijk (2018)

Using the working capital ratio formulas in Table 4.8, have go at the following activity.

Activity 4.4

You have been supplied in Table 4.12 with data for three companies from the same industrial sector.

Table 4.12   Cash-to-cash cycle ratios

Company	Red	Yellow	Green
Average inventory £k	15,000	12,000	8,000
Cost of sales £k	60,000	64,000	52,000
Average accounts payable £k	20,000	15,000	16,000
Average accounts receivable £k	25,000	28,000	32,000
Sales (credit) £k	100,000	120,000	80,000
Purchases (credit) £k	48,000	64,000	48,000

Calculate the following ratios for each company and comment on your findings.

1 inventory holding days;

2 accounts receivable days;

3 accounts payable days;

4 cash-to-cash cycle.

4.5 The relationship between liquidity and cash flow

According to the CIMA terminology (2005:92), liquidity is defined as the 'availability of sufficient funds to meet financial commitments as they fall due'. Typically, two financial ratios are used by accountants to measure the liquidity of a business: the current ratio and the acid-test ratio. The latter is also known as the quick or liquidity ratio. The current ratio compares the ratio of current assets to current liabilities; for instance, if an organization has current assets of £10m and current liabilities of £2.5m, the current ratio is 4:1. Therefore, the business has £4 of current assets available for every £1 of short-term liabilities if they fall due. The acid-test ratio compares current assets minus inventories against the value of current liabilities; it is considered to be a stronger measure of liquidity. In the previous calculation, let's assume that £2.5m of the £10m current assets is inventory; the acid-test ratio is then calculated as follows:

currents assets – inventory: current liabilities = £10m – £2.5m: £2.5m = 3:1

Figure 4.8 illustrates the current and liquidity ratios for the fast-moving consumer goods (FMCG) company Unilever plc from 1998 to 2017.

Typically, accounting text books advocate in the case of manufacturing companies that the current ratio should be around 2:1 and the acid-test ratio 1:1. However, it will depend on the contextual factors relating to the industrial sector and the organization's ability to generate cash flow.

Figure 4.8   Unilever plc current and liquidity ratios 1998 to 2017

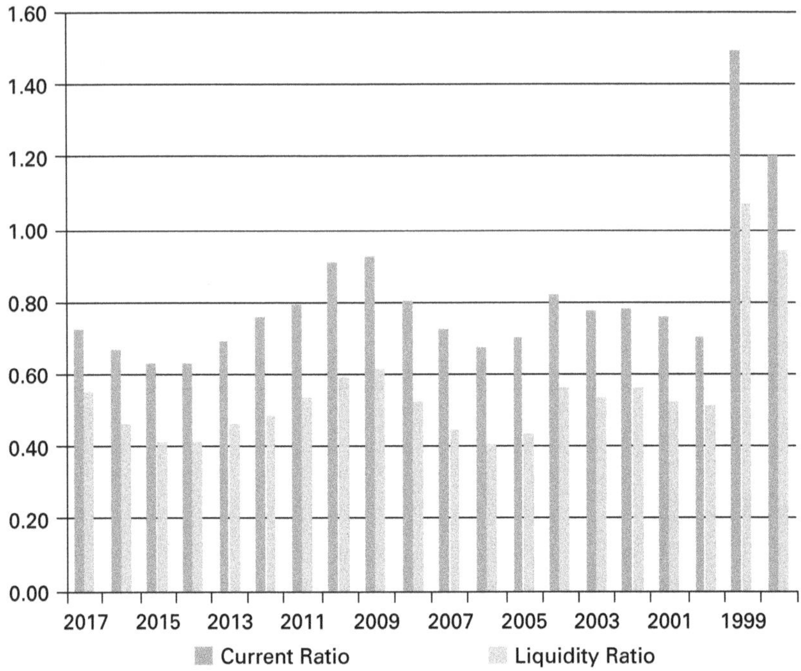

Current Ratio   Liquidity Ratio

Adapted from: *Fame*, published by Bureau van Dijk (2018)

Table 4.13 illustrates the current and acid-test ratios for 5 companies across different industrial sectors.

Table 4.13   Current ratios and acid-test ratios

Company	Financial Year	Current assets	Current liabilities	Current Ratio (X:1)	Inventory	Acid-test Ratio (X:1)	Working capital
BASF Group €m	2017(170)	31,145	14,880	2.093	10,303	1.401	16,265
Deutsche Post DHL Group €m	2017(104)	14,756	13,268	1.112	327	1.088	−1,488
Marks and Spencer Group PLC £m	2017(78)	1,723.3	2,368.0	0.727	758.5	0.407	−644.7
Nestlé Group CHFm	2017 (66 & 67)	32,190	36,054	0.893	9,061	0.642	−3,864
The Procter & Gamble Company $m	2017(38)	26,494	30,210	0.877	4,624	0.724	−3,716

The highest current ratio is 2.093 (BASF Group) and the lowest 0.727 (Marks and Spencer Group PLC PLC) the range of the sample 1.366. These companies also have the highest and lowest asset-test ratio with a range of 0.994. The important point to flag up here is that you must compare like with like with an industrial section as contextual factors relating to the sector will have a significant impact on the calculation of these liquidity ratios.

4.6 Supply chain management and supply chain finance

The importance of working capital and liquidity cannot be overestimated, as was apparent in the 2007–08 financial crisis, which resulted in a significant increase and focus on supply chain finance (SCF). This was highlighted in a press release by UK Prime Minister David Cameron (2012):

> This Government is determined to back all those businesses who aspire to get ahead and take on more people. In the current climate, viable businesses can struggle to get the finance they need to grow – this scheme will not only help them secure finance and support cash flow, but will help secure supply chains for some of our biggest companies and protect thousands of jobs. It can be a win-win, with large companies and small suppliers both benefiting from this innovative scheme.

The Global Supply Chain Finance Forum (2016:8) defines supply chain finance (SCF) as 'the use of financing and risk mitigation practices and techniques to optimise the management of the working capital and liquidity invested in supply chain processes and transactions'. According to Cosse (2011:33), a typical SCF application relates to a 'buyer-driven payables solution, mainly referring to any types of reverse factoring solutions, supported by the appropriate IT technology'.

In this section we will explore further two SCF instruments: reverse factoring and dynamic discounting.

Reverse factoring

Reverse factoring, or approved payables finance, according to the European Banking Association (2014:54), 'allows a supplier to receive a discounted payment of an invoice or account payable due to be paid by a buyer'.

Figure 4.9 illustrates a typical four-corner SCF ecosystem, which includes the four parties involved in the transaction (buyer, seller, buyer and seller banks) and the associated flows that are to be found in the SCM: the physical flow from seller to buyer, the financial flow from buyer to seller and finally the bi-directional information flows between the parties.

Figure 4.9 Four-corner SCF model with associated flows

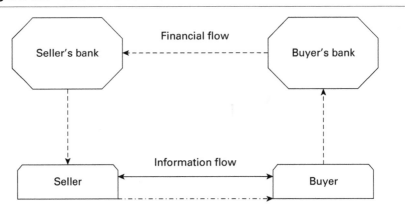

Flow of goods and services

SOURCE Templar et al (2016:151)

Table 4.14 highlights the typical activities relating to the reverse factoring process involving a three-way match.

Table 4.14 Reverse factoring (three-way match) process

Step	Activity
1	Buyer agrees to purchase goods from the supplier and sends a purchase order (PO) to supplier detailing terms and conditions of the transaction.
2	Buyer receives PO and sends goods to buyer's regional distribution centre (RDC) with a goods received note (GRN).
3	Goods are unloaded and checked at the buyer's RDC against PO. If the shipment is correct, the GRN is signed and returned to supplier and a copy is also sent to buyer's accounts payable department (APD).
4	Supplier sends invoice to buyer's APD for payment.
5	Buyer's APD does a three-way match (checks PO with GRN and invoice) and then approves the seller's invoice for payment.
6	Supplier is notified and opts for a reverse factoring solution.
7	Buyer's bank transfers invoice value less early payment discount, which is based on the credit rating of the buyer to the supplier's bank.
8	Supplier is now able to draw down the cash.
9	Buyer pays its bank the full value of the supplier's invoice on the due date for payment.

Dynamic discounting

The European Banking Association (2014:48) defines dynamic discounting as offering 'suppliers the early receipt of accounts payable due from a buyer in return for a variable discount. Typically, the funds are provided by the buyer from its own liquid resources.'

The following fictitious example describes the dynamic discounting approach. Ultra Co Ltd, a supplier to Mega plc, has been onboarded onto the buyer's supply chain finance programme, which is a dynamic discounting solution. Based on Mega plc's standard terms and conditions (T&C), the company will be paid in 90 days once the invoice has been approved for payment. However, if Ultra Co Ltd decides that it wants to take up the offer of an early payment of an invoice after it has been approved, the company can opt to use Mega plc's dynamic discounting programme. They are now able to decide to take an early payment of any of their invoices minus a discount or let the invoice carry on to its due payment date. Table 4.15 illustrates the Mega plc dynamic discounting calculation: if Ultra Co Ltd requires an invoice to be paid immediately, they will receive 95% of its face value; however, if they require the invoice to be paid after 40 days, the invoice will be 97.22% of its original value.

Table 4.15   Mega plc dynamic discounting rates

Payment days	Net invoice value %	Discount %
0	95.00	5.00
10	95.56	4.44
20	96.11	3.89
30	96.67	3.33
40	97.22	2.78
50	97.78	2.22
60	98.33	1.67
70	98.89	1.11
80	99.44	0.56
90	100.00	0.00

Figure 4.10 illustrates Mega plc's dynamic discounting curve: if Ultra Co Ltd decides to take immediate payment, they will receive 95% of their invoice value; however, if they adopt the standard payment T&Cs, they will receive the full value of the invoice in 90 days.

Figure 4.10   Mega plc's dynamic discounting curve

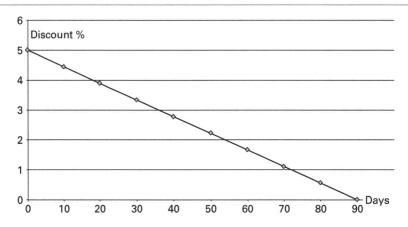

Ultra Co Ltd can use the curve to establish the percent discounted value of an invoice for a given early payment. Currently, Ultra Co Ltd has five invoices which have been approved for payment on Mega plc's SCF platform. Table 4.16 illustrates for Ultra Co Ltd the current value of their discounting invoices on the system at this moment in time. If Ultra Co Ltd now decides to opt for earlier payment of all their invoices in the system, they will receive £112,583.33 and Mega plc will have a saving of £2,416.67 on their accounts payable. The system is dynamic as the discount value of the invoices will change on a daily basis.

Table 4.16   Ultra Co Ltd discounting invoices on the system

Invoice no.	PO no.	Payment due date	Invoice value	Net invoice value
125	47500	10 days' time	£20,000	£19,888.89
154	47578	20 days' time	£25,000	£24,722.22
169	46001	40 days' time	£15,000	£14,666.67
179	46234	50 days' time	£25,000	£24,305.56
201	46645	60 days' time	£30,000	£29,000.00
Total			**£115,000**	**£112,583.33**

The advantages for Ultra Co Ltd are that should they require cash at short notice they are able to require earlier payment, and for Mega plc they are able to generate savings on their accounts payable, which will have a positive impact on their profitability. However, if the buyer (Mega plc) uses their own cash, the cash is unavailable for alternative options, and therefore a potential cost to the buyer.

4.7 Summary

The aim of this chapter was to introduce you to the importance of managing cash flow and working capital. You are now able to explain the importance of cash flow for a business organization. You can construct a cash flow forecast by identifying the relevant cash inflows and outflows for business; you can also calculate the monthly and cumulative cash flows. You can now identify the components of the cash-to-cash cycle calculation (inventory days, accounts receivable, and accounts payable) and calculate the cash-to-cash cycle time. You can recognize the importance and impact that your supply chain decisions can have on the management of working capital. You are able to appreciate the important relationship between supply chain management, supply chain finance and liquidity. You are now able to calculate financial ratios that are relevant to evaluating liquidity and cash flow and can recognize the relationship between liquidity and cash flow.

4.8 References

BASF Group (2017) *Report*, http://report.basf.com/2017/en/ (accessed 15 December 2018)

Brookson, S. (2001) *Understanding Accounts*, Dorling Kindersley, London

Bureau van Dijk (2018) www.bvdinfo.com/en-gb/contact-us/office-locations

Cameron, D (2012) *Prime Minister Announces Supply Chain Finance Scheme*, available at www.gov.uk/government/news/prime-minister-announces-supply-chain-finance-scheme (accessed 23/10/18)

Christopher, M (2011) *Logistics and Supply Chain Management: Creating value-adding networks,* 4th edn, Pearson Education, Harlow

CIMA (1982) *CIMA Official Terminology* (1989 edn), London

CIMA (2005) *CIMA Official Terminology*, CIMA Publishing, Oxford

Cosse, M. (2011) *An Investigation into the Current Supply Chain Finance Practices in Business: A case study approach*, MSc thesis, unpublished, Cranfield University

Deutsche Post DHL Group (2017) *Annual Report*, https://annualreport2017.dpdhl.com/downloads-ext/en/documents/DPDHL_2017_Annual_Report.pdf (accessed 15 December 2018)

European Banking Association (EBA) (2014), *Supply Chain Finance EBA European market guide*, Version 2.0, Paris, France

Global Supply Chain Finance Forum (2016) *Standard Definitions for Techniques of Supply Chain Finance*, available at http://supplychainfinanceforum.org/ICC-Standard-Definitions-for-Techniques-of-Supply-Chain-Finance-Global-SCF-Forum-2016.pdf (accessed 26/06/18)

Marks & Spencer Group Plc (2017) *Annual Report and Financial Statements*, https://corporate.marksandspencer.com/documents/reports-results-and-publications/annual-report-2017.pdf (accessed 15 December 2018)

Marks & Spencer Group Plc (2018) *Annual Report and Financial Statements*, https://corporate.marksandspencer.com/annualreport (accessed 15 December 2018)

Nestlé Group (2017) *Annual Review*, HYPERLINK "http://www.nestle.com/investors/publications#tab-2017" www.nestle.com/investors/publications#tab-2017 (accessed 15 December 2018)

Procter & Gamble Company (2017) *Form 10-K*, www.annualreports.com/HostedData/AnnualReports/PDF/NYSE_PG_2017.pdf (accessed 15 December 2018)

Templar, S, Findlay, C and Hofmann, E (2016) *Financing the End to End Supply Chain: A reference guide to supply chain finance*, 1st edn, Kogan Page, London

4.9 Solutions to the activities

Activity 4.1 solution

Table 4.17 Cash receipts and expenditures for a road haulage company

List as many different cash receipts and expenditures as you can think of that a road haulage company will have.	
Cash receipts	**Cash expenditures**
Selling shares	Wages and salaries
Customer payments	Payments to suppliers
Interest received	Dividends to shareholders
Dividends from investments	Interest to loan providers
Tax rebates	Direct and indirect taxation
Government grants	

Activity 4.2 solution

Ten initiatives that the owners of MakeCo plc could implement to improve their current cash flow situation are illustrated in Table 4.18.

Table 4.18   10 cash flow improvement initiatives for MakeCo plc

1	Start the business with additional share capital.
2	Extend payment terms to suppliers.
3	Rent or lease non-current assets in the short term.
4	Get customers to pay earlier.
5	Introduce a supply chain finance solution to liberate cash tied up in accounts receivable.
6	Reduce the level of purchases as currently there is £160k cash tied up in inventories.
7	Instead of using two 3PL suppliers for inbound and outbound, opt for a single supplier to reduce costs.
8	Pay dividend in the following year January, not in December.
9	Review labour remuneration.
10	Review all factory and SGA costs to look for opportunities to engineer cost out.

Activity 4.3 solution

The information in Table 4.19 has been extracted from the report and accounts of four of your major competitors for the financial year ending 31 December 20XX.

Table 4.19   Cash-to-cash cycle time: four competitors

Company	Alpha	Beta	Delta	Gamma
Inventory days	60	45	30	75
Accounts receivable days	45	75	90	60
Accounts payable days	75	60	45	90
Cash-to-cash cycle days	30	60	75	45

1 The company that has the shortest cash-to-cash cycle time of 30 days is Alpha.

2 Delta's customers take 90 days to pay them, which is the longest time.

3 The company that has the largest number of inventory days is Gamma, with 75 days.

4 Delta pays its suppliers in 45 days, which is the quickest.

5 The company with the lowest inventory days of 30 is Delta.

6 Delta has the longest cash-to-cash cycle time of 75 days.

7 The company which is slowest to pay its suppliers is Gamma with 90 days.

8 Alpha's customers take the shortest time to pay them in 45 days.

Activity 4.4 solution

Table 4.20 illustrates the working capital ratios for three competitors: Red, Yellow and Green.

Green's inventory holding days are 56.15, which is the best out of the three organizations; this means that they turn over their inventory 6.5 times a year. Yellow customers take the shortest time to pay; they pay in 85.17 days. Red takes the longest time to pay its suppliers – on average 152.08 days. The company with the shortest cash-to-cash cycle time is Red; their cash-to-cash cycle time is 30.42 days.

If we were to take the best ratio across the three organizations, the cash-to-cash cycle time will be –10.76 days

$$\text{Cash-to-cash cycle time} = 56.15 \text{ days} + 85.17 \text{ days} - 152.08 \text{ days}$$
$$= -10.76 \text{ days.}$$

Table 4.20   Cash-to-cash cycle ratios

Ratio	Red	Yellow	Green	Best
Inventory holding days	91.25	68.44	56.15	56.15
Accounts receivable days	91.25	85.17	146.00	85.17
Accounts payable days	152.08	85.55	121.67	152.08
Cash-to-cash cycle	30.42	68.06	80.49	–10.76

Workings for yellow

Inventory holding days can be calculated using the following formula:

Inventory holding days = (Average inventory/Cost of sales) * 365
Inventory holding days = (£12,000/£64,000) * 365 = 68.44 days.

Accounts receivable days is derived using the following equation:

Accounts receivable days = (Average accounts receivable/Credit sales)*365
Accounts receivable days = (£28,000/£120,000)*365 = 85.17 days.

Accounts payable days can be calculated using the following formula:

Accounts payable days = (Average accounts payable/Credit purchases)* 365
Accounts payable days = (£15,000/£64,000)* 365 = 85.55 days
Cash-to-cash cycle time = Inventory holding days + Accounts receivable
days – Accounts payable days
Cash-to-cash cycle time = 68.44 days + 85.17 days – 85.55
days = 68.06 days.

4.10 Study questions

Study question 4.1

You have been approached by Pizza Garden Ovens Ltd to assist them in producing a cash flow forecast for their new venture. They wish to start production in January, making pizza ovens for gardens. The company starts business on 1 January 20XX, financed by £120,000 issued share capital. The company rents a factory for £52,000 per annum; the rent is paid quarterly in advance and the first payment will be paid in January. The company purchased plant and machinery for £100,000 and a delivery truck for £25,000 to distribute the finished products; both were paid in January. Production will be 300 ovens a month for the first quarter, increasing to 600 a month in the second quarter. Table 4.21 illustrates the sales figures based on information commissioned by sales and marketing consultants at a cost of £20,000 and paid in January.

Table 4.21 Sales forecast for the six months ending June 20XX

Sales forecast	Jan	Feb	Mar	Apr	May	Jun
Number of ovens	150	320	500	550	580	600

Each oven will sell for £500. All sales are made on 30 days' credit, so sales made in January will be paid in February. Direct wages will be £60,000 a month, but in the second quarter additional overtime will be required, so increasing the monthly wages by 20%. Each oven requires £280 of raw materials and components. The material suppliers will deliver the required parts at the start of each month. They have agreed to allow the company 60 days' credit, so, for example, raw materials delivered in January will be paid for in March. Administration expenses are £6,000 a month and are paid in the month they are incurred. Production expenses are £100 per oven and are paid in the month of production. Depreciation is charged on a straight-line basis. The life span of the plant and machinery is 10 years and of the lorry is 5 years. There will be no inventory at the end of the period, as all ovens made are sold.

You are required to prepare a cash flow forecast for the six months ended 30 June 20XX.

Study question 4.2

Advise Pizza Garden Ovens Ltd what initiatives they could implement to improve their cash flow. Can you identify 10 initiatives and complete Table 4.22?

Table 4.22 Cash flow improvement initiatives for Pizza Garden Ovens Ltd

Cash flow improvement initiatives
1
2
3
4
5
6
7
8
9
10

Study question 4.3

The following information has been extracted from the accounts of four of your competitors for the financial year ending 31 December 20XX. Complete Table 4.23 and then use the information to answer questions 1 to 5.

Table 4.23   Cash-to-cash cycle time for four competitors

Company	Red	Yellow	Green	Blue
Inventory days	30	90	60	
Accounts receivable days	90	60		30
Accounts payable days	60		90	70
Cash-to-cash cycle days		75	90	80

1 Which company has the best cash-to-cash cycle time?

   A Red

   B Green

   C Yellow

   D Blue

2 Which company pays its suppliers the quickest?

   A Yellow

   B Red

   C Blue

   D Green

3 Which company has the worst cash-to-cash cycle time?

   A Red

   B Green

   C Yellow

   D Blue

4 Which company's customers take the shortest time to pay?

   A Red

   B Green

   C Yellow

   D Blue

5 Which company has the highest number of inventory days?

A Red

B Green

C Yellow

D Blue

Study question 4.4

You have been supplied in Table 4.24 with data for three companies from the same industrial sector.

Calculate the following ratios for each company and comment on your findings:

Table 4.24   Cash-to-cash cycle ratios

Company	Alpha	Beta	Gamma
Average inventory £m	16	20	18
Cost of sales £m	52	44	61
Average accounts payable £m	18	20	27
Average accounts receivable £m	32	26	40
Sales (credit) £m	85	92	87
Purchases (credit) £m	48	56	57

1 inventory holding days;

2 accounts receivable days;

3 accounts payable days;

4 cash-to-cash cycle.

4.11 Study question solutions

Study question 4.1 solution

The cash flow forecast is a very important and powerful tool for managing any business, as it illustrates the cash position of the business at various time points, including:

- at the end of the period;
- per month;
- the monthly cumulative cash position.

Figure 4.11 illustrates the cash flow forecast for Pizza Garden Ovens Ltd for the six months ending June 20XX.

Period

Pizza Garden Ovens Ltd has a cash deficit of £57k for the six months ending June 20XX.

Monthly

The current monthly cash flow position illustrates that only two months, April and May, are in surplus. January 20XX has the largest cash deficit of £124k.

Cumulative

Based on the current cash flow forecast, the company will need an overdraft provision from the bank of £145k to cover the cumulative negative cash position at the end of March 20XX.

Figure 4.11 Cash flow forecast for Pizza Garden Ovens Ltd

Pizza Garden Ovens Ltd Cash flow forecast for the six months ending June 20XX							
Period	**Jan**	**Feb**	**Mar**	**Apr**	**May**	**Jun**	**Total**
Sales units	150	320	500	550	580	600	2,700
Production units	300	300	300	600	600	600	2,700
Cash in £k	**Jan**	**Feb**	**Mar**	**Apr**	**May**	**Jun**	**Total**
Share capital	120	–	–	–	–	–	120
Sales	–	75	160	250	275	290	1,050
Total receipts	**120**	**75**	**160**	**250**	**275**	**290**	**1,170**
Cash out £k	**Jan**	**Feb**	**Mar**	**Apr**	**May**	**Jun**	**Total**
Rent	13	–	–	13	–	–	26
Plant and machinery	100	–	–	–	–	–	100
Truck	25	–	–	–	–	–	25
Marketing	20	–	–	–	–	–	20

(*continued*)

Figure 4.11   (Continued)

Pizza Garden Ovens Ltd Cash flow forecast for the six months ending June 20XX							
Period	Jan	Feb	Mar	Apr	May	Jun	Total
Wages	50	50	50	60	60	60	330
Materials & components	–	–	84	84	84	168	420
Administration overheads	6	6	6	6	6	6	36
Production overheads	30	30	30	60	60	60	270
Total expenditure £k	**244**	**86**	**170**	**223**	**210**	**294**	**1,227**
Net cash flow £k	**(124)**	**(11)**	**(10)**	**27**	**65**	**(4)**	**(57)**
Cash brought forward	0	(124)	(135)	(145)	(118)	(53)	
Cash carried forward	(124)	(135)	(145)	(118)	(53)	(57)	

Study question 4.2 solution

Pizza Garden Ovens Ltd could implement the initiatives illustrated in Table 4.25 to improve their cash flow.

Table 4.25   Cash flow improvement initiatives for Pizza Garden Ovens Ltd

Cash flow improvement initiatives
1   Sell additional shares, which would improve their starting cash.
2   Increase the selling price for an oven.
3   Incentivize their customers to pay earlier by giving cash settlement discounts.
4   Adopt a reverse factoring solution.
5   Adopt a dynamic discounting solution.
6   Extend suppliers' payment terms by an additional month.
7   Lease or rent in the short term their non-current assets.
8   Look for alternative low-cost suppliers or negotiate with current suppliers to reduce input costs.
9   Alternative labour remuneration methods to reduce costs.
10   Review all current expenditure to look for savings.

Study question 4.3 solution

To solve these questions, we need to apply the cash-to-cash cycle calculation, which is inventory days plus accounts receivable days minus accounts payable days equals the cash-to-cash cycle time in days. You will also need to remember how to change the subject of the formula. Is that a scream I can hear over the ether as you remember and recount your school algebra classes? Table 4.26 illustrates the cash-to-cash cycle times for the four companies.

Table 4.26 Cash-to-cash cycle time for four competitors

Company	Red	Yellow	Green	Blue
Inventory days	30	90	60	120
Accounts receivable days	90	60	120	30
Accounts payable days	60	75	90	70
Cash-to-cash cycle days	60	75	90	80

1 The company which has the best cash-to-cash cycle time is Red, with 60 days.

   Answer = **A**

2 The company that pays its suppliers the quickest is Red. Their accounts payable days are 60, while Green takes the longest time to pay its customers with an accounts payable of 90 days.

   Answer = **B**

3 The company which has the worst cash-to-cash cycle time is Green, with 90 days.

   Answer = **B**

4 Blue customers take the shortest time to pay, with an accounts receivable time of 30 days, which is 90 days shorter than Green customers, who pay them in 120 days.

   Answer = **D**

5 The company that has the highest number of inventory days is Blue; on average the company has 120 days of inventory, which equates to an inventory turnover rate of three times a year. Red has the least inventory with 30 days, which means that the company turns over its inventory 12.2 times a year.

   Answer = **D**

Study question 4.4 solution

To solve this study question you need to apply the working capital formulas in Table 4.8. The ratios have been calculated and are illustrated in Table 4.27.

Table 4.27   Cash-to-cash cycle ratios

Ratio	Alpha	Beta	Gamma	Best
Inventory holding days	112.31	165.91	107.70	107.70
Accounts receivable days	137.41	103.15	167.82	103.15
Accounts payable days	136.88	130.36	172.89	172.89
Cash-to-cash cycle	112.84	138.70	102.63	37.96

Gamma has the best inventory holding days, which is 107.7 days, which equates to an inventory turnover of 3.39 times a year. Beta's customers take the shortest time to pay; on average they pay in 103.15 days. The organization that takes the longest time to pay its suppliers is Gamma, who pays them in 172.89 days. The company that has the shortest cash-to-cash cycle time is Gamma; their cash-to-cash cycle time is 102.63 days.

Taking the best working capital ratio across all three organizations will produce a cash-to-cash cycle time of 37.96 days.

Cash-to-cash cycle time = 107.70 days + 103.15 days – 172.89 days
= –37.96 days.

An introduction to depreciation 05

The rationale for this chapter is to introduce you to the concept of depreciation and dispel a number of myths related to depreciation. Depreciation is one of the most misunderstood concepts in accounting – just ask the people you know to give you a definition of depreciation and why organizations use it. Here are two examples regarding depreciation from my past experiences – you may have come across both or have your own anecdotes to add to the collection of myths relating to depreciation.

I remember many years ago when I was thinking of buying my first brand-new car and discussing the purchasing decision with family and friends. Often this phrase would come up: 'You don't want to buy new car; as soon as you drive it away from the dealer you've lost a fortune – it's the depreciation.' The second misconception relating to depreciation is: 'It's the amount you save each year to replace a fixed asset.' This suggests that cash is put away on a regular basis, but depreciation is not a cash transaction; however, it is a cost to your business. We will explore this last point in more depth later in this chapter.

Therefore, this chapter will define depreciation, introduce you to three of the most common depreciation methods used in business, explore how depreciation impacts on the financial statement of an organization, and explain why an understanding of the role of depreciation is important for you as a supply chain practitioner and the decisions that you make. Depreciation is a significant cost to any business owning non-current assets such as property, plant and equipment (PPE). Anecdotal statements often refer to 70% of an organization's non-current assets being supply chain related; therefore, supply chain practitioners are responsible for one of the largest operating cost lines in the income statement, which is depreciation.

5.1 Aim and objectives

The aim for this chapter is to introduce you to the concept of depreciation and its application in business with an emphasis on supply chain management. The chapter will use examples taken from practice and a range of activities and study questions will be used to introduce you to the accounting theory, methods and applications relating to depreciation.

At the end of this chapter you will be able to:

- explain the difference between revenue and capital;
- identify different methods of depreciation;
- calculate annual depreciation rates using three methods;
- compare different methods of depreciation;
- explain how depreciation impacts on the income statement and balance sheet of a business.

5.2 Smoke and mirrors

The first thing you need to be aware of is that depreciation is an accounting adjustment. I can now hear you all laughing out loud and shouting, 'It's all smoke and mirrors!' The Chartered Institute of Management Accountants (CIMA) definition of depreciation (2005:66) is: 'Systematic allocation of the depreciable amount of an asset over its useful life.'

There are a few significant words in this definition that need to be explored further, including systematic, allocation and useful life. Systematic is concerned with the approach taken; typing systematic into a thesaurus reveals the following characteristics, including: orderly, regular, organized, efficient and logical, which collectively define the nature of the depreciation transaction. The depreciation calculation is based on a logical rule set: it's verifiable, the transaction is regular and consistent, and the depreciation method chosen by the organization should be the most relevant one related to the type of non-current asset.

For allocation, my trusty thesaurus produces the following words: provision, apportionment, sharing and division – they are all relevant to the role of depreciation. Depreciation is therefore a prescribed mechanism designed to share (apportion) the cost of a non-current asset over its useful life, that is, a number of financial periods. Useful life is an abstract expression, and has a significant impact on the depreciation calculation, as the time period is essential in determining the amount of depreciation to be charged to an accounting period. However, it is also subjective; for example, if I asked you and your friends the question 'How would you calculate the useful life of any asset in your possession (cooker, computer, mobile phone or car)?' and I was to then compare the answers, there would be differences, and hence the useful life will vary because context is important.

I will now put forward the premise that depreciation is more like a supposition: it's an estimate of how much of a non-current asset's value will be consumed by the organization over a period of time. If depreciation is an estimate, you may well ask why depreciation is so important to a business. This is an excellent question, as it's all to do with calculating an organization's profit for an accounting period.

Profit is the difference between the income earned in a period minus expenditure incurred in the same period. Here is an example: while travelling across the USA a couple of years ago I was introduced to the money-making phenomenon of the lemonade stand by a colleague, where people would make and sell lemonade to passers-by during the summer months to earn some cash.

Let's explore this example further. Cash is initially required to buy the ingredients to make the lemonade. Say a mark-up of 100% is applied, giving a healthy profit margin of 50%. Before they can sell the lemonade, they would need to construct a stall or they could borrow from family and friends. They would also need a table, two chairs, a large umbrella, a large ice bucket, two cool boxes, half a dozen glass pitchers, 20 glasses and a tablecloth. However, without those items, they could not have made or distributed the lemonade; in essence, they were their supply chain assets. If these items had to be purchased, the costs would be included in the expenditure; however, all of the items could be used in subsequent years and so the cost of these items should be shared over their useful life against future lemonade sales. Therefore, a proportion of the cost of these items should be included in the associated costs of the lemonade stall and therefore reducing the profits for the enterprise. Thus, in business there are different types of expenditure in our supply chains, which we will explore in the next section.

5.3 Revenue and capital

In business there are two types of expenditure: revenue and capital. Table 5.1 provides you with the CIMA definitions for both types of spend.

Table 5.1   Revenue and capital expenditure

Term	Definition
Revenue expenditure	*Expenditure on the manufacture of goods, the provision of services or on the general conduct of the entity which is charged to the income statement in the period the expenditure is incurred. This will include charges for depreciation and impairment of non-current assets as distinct from the cost of the assets.* **Source: CIMA (2005:77)**
Capital expenditure	*Costs incurred in acquiring, producing or enhancing non-current assets (both tangible and intangible).* **Source: CIMA (2005:61)**

CIMA (2005:74) defines a non-current asset as a 'tangible or intangible asset, acquired for retention by an entity for the purpose of providing a service to the entity and not held for resale in the normal course of trading'.

Typical tangible assets that you can see and touch, for example, in the retail supply chain would include retail premises, distribution centres including material handling and storage equipment such as forklift trucks and racking. In the oil and gas industry, drilling rigs, refineries, pipelines, oil and gas tankers and road tankers for distribution are all examples of non-current assets, while intangible non-current assets include such things as goodwill and patents. Now have a go at Activity 5.1 by completing Table 5.2.

Activity 5.1

List as many different types of revenue and capital expenditure for a road haulier as you can think of.

Table 5.2   Revenue and capital expenditure

Revenue	Capital

In the lemonade stall example, the ingredients used to make the lemonade would be classified as their revenue expenditure and the other items would be classified as their capital expenditure – the non-current assets of their lemonade business. Therefore, depreciation is an accounting technique that is used to estimate a proportion of a non-current asset's value that needs to be matched against the revenue generated by the non-current asset in a particular accounting period, so we can derive profit. The crucial phrase that needs to be explained further is 'needs to be matched'; therefore an important question that now needs to be answered is, what does match mean? To answer this question, you need to be aware of the conventions that underpin accounting. Two important conventions that are relevant to depreciation are the matching and accruals conventions.

The matching convention is defined by Atrill and McLaney (2017:517) as 'the accounting convention that holds that expenses should be matched to the revenue, which they helped generate, in the period in which the revenue is reported'.

CIMA (2005:58) defines the accruals basis of accounting as: 'Effects of transactions and other events are recognized in financial statements when they occur and not when the cash and cash equivalent are received or paid.'

Therefore, the profit calculation from selling lemonade should also include a depreciation charge for the use of the non-current assets in that time period. Here is a question for you to think about: if depreciation is an assumption/estimate, does that not make profit one as well?

5.4 Depreciation methods

In this section we will explore the effect of depreciation on the financial statements of the organization. A fictitious company, Newtown Distribution, will be used to illustrate the impact of three different methods of depreciation. The three different depreciation methods are:

1 straight-line;
2 reducing balance;
3 sum of the digits.

Newtown Distribution currently have a new tractor unit on trial from the dealership and they now plan to purchase it. However, they wish to explore and compare the impact of different depreciation methods on their financial statements using the tractor unit to model the impact of depreciation.

When building any depreciation model, you will need to gather the following information:

- the type of asset;
- the cost of the asset;
- the useful life span of the asset;
- the residual value of the asset at the end of its useful life;
- depreciation method to be used.

The asset is a tractor unit and will be purchased from the dealer for £45,000; it is estimated to have a useful life of six years and has a disposal value of £3,000. The company's current depreciation method is the straight-line method.

Before exploring each method, a couple of points need to be reflected on:

1 The choice of depreciation method should be related to the characteristics of the non-current asset.

2 Depreciation is an accounting adjustment and does not have an impact on the organization's cash flow.

3 The annual depreciation charge is an expense in the income statement.

4 The cumulative depreciation is deducted from the non-current asset's purchase cost to calculate its net book value on the balance sheet.

The net book value (NBV) is the value of the asset after deducting the cumulative depreciation from the asset's purchase price.

Straight-line method

With the straight-line method, the first thing that needs to be calculated is the total value of the depreciation that will be charged to the income statement over the asset's useful life. This will typically be the purchase cost of the asset minus any disposal value and is referred to as the *depreciable amount*.

$$purchase\ cost - disposal\ value = total\ depreciation$$
$$£45,000 - £3,000 = £42,000$$

The annual depreciation charge is calculated by dividing the total depreciation value by the asset's useful life.

total depreciation/asset's useful life = annual depreciation charge
£42,000/6 = £7,000

Every year £7,000 will now be charged as an expense in the company's income statement and the value of the asset on the balance sheet will be decreased by £7,000. The transactions for both financial statements over the asset's life are presented in Table 5.3; note the asset's value at the end of year 6 is its disposal value of £3,000.

When the tractor is sold the company will receive £3,000 in cash, and the tractor will be off the organization's fixed asset register and balance sheet. The fixed asset register is a numbered list of all the non-current assets owned by the business, typically detailing purchase cost, date of purchase and its location; it is an essential document used to calculate depreciation charges.

Table 5.3   Straight-line method of depreciation

| Year | Income statement | Balance sheet | | |
	Annual depreciation £	Historic cost £	Cumulative depreciation £	Net book value £
1	7,000	45,000	7,000	38,000
2	7,000	45,000	14,000	31,000
3	7,000	45,000	21,000	24,000
4	7,000	45,000	28,000	17,000
5	7,000	45,000	35,000	10,000
6	7,000	45,000	42,000	3,000

Reducing balance method

The reducing balance method adopts a different approach from the straight-line method, as this method assumes that the non-current asset's depreciation charge will be higher at the start of its useful life than at its end. Therefore, in those early years a higher amount of depreciation should be charged to the income statement and then a constant percentage is applied to the previous year's net book value.

The following formula is used to derive the reducing balance percentage:

$$Reducing\ balance\ percentage = 1 - \left[n\sqrt{(D\ V/C)} \right]$$

Where:

> n = the life of the non-current asset in years;
> DV = disposal value or residual value or scrap value;
> C = purchase cost of the non-current asset.

We can now derive the reducing balance percentage for the tractor unit.

$$1 - \left[6\sqrt{(£3,000/£45,000)} \right]$$

Step 1: Divide £3,000/£45,0000 = 0.66666;

Step 2: Using a calculator, obtain the 6th root of 0.6666 = 0.6368;

Step 3: 1 – 0.6368 = 0.3632, which is 36.32%.

To calculate the annual depreciation change for year 1, the purchase cost of the vehicle of £45,000 is multiplied by the reducing balance factor 0.3632 to give an annual charge of £16,345 in the income statement. The asset's value on the balance sheet will be reduced by the same amount to give a net book value of £28,655. This figure will be used to derive the annual depreciation charge for year 2 and the asset's net book value on the balance sheet:

$$£28,655 * 0.3632 = £10,408$$

The annual depreciation charges for the remaining years are illustrated in the Table 5.4.

Table 5.4   Reducing balance method of depreciation

Year	Income statement Annual depreciation £	Balance sheet Historic cost £	Cumulative depreciation £	Net book value £
1	16,345	45,000	16,345	28,655
2	10,408	45,000	26,753	18,247
3	6,628	45,000	33,381	11,619
4	4,220	45,000	37,601	7,399
5	2,688	45,000	40,289	4,711
6	1,711	45,000	42,000	3,000

Sum of the digits

The sum of the digits method adopts a similar approach to the reducing balance method, where a greater proportion of depreciation is charged to the income statement in the early years of the asset's life. However, this method does not use a constant percentage, but a predetermined fraction for each year of the asset's life based on the sum of the digits related to the asset's life in years.

In the case of the truck it has a useful life of six years, therefore the sum of the digits will be 6 + 5 + 4 + 3 + 2 + 1 = 21. Table 5.5 illustrates the sum of the digit calculation for years 1 to 10; you may recognize them as triangular numbers.

Table 5.5   Sum of the digits values from 1 to 10 years

Number of years	1	2	3	4	5	6	7	8	9	10
Sum of the digits	1	3	6	10	15	21	28	36	45	55

The depreciation fraction for year 1 for the truck will be 6/21, resulting in £12,000 (£42,000*6/21) depreciation for year 1; the other years' depreciation are as illustrated in Table 5.6.

Table 5.6   Sum of the digits fractions and annual depreciation charges

Year	1	2	3	4	5	6
Sum of the digits fraction	6/21	5/21	4/21	3/21	2/21	1/21
Annual depreciation £	12,000	10,000	8,000	6,000	4,000	2,000

The annual depreciation charges for the tractor unit and its net book value on the balance sheet for the six years are shown in Table 5.7.

Table 5.7   Sum of the digits method of depreciation

Year	Income statement	Balance sheet		
	Annual depreciation £	Historic cost £	Cumulative depreciation £	Net book value £
1	12,000	45,000	12,000	33,000
2	10,000	45,000	22,000	23,000
3	8,000	45,000	30,000	15,000
4	6,000	45,000	36,000	9,000
5	4,000	45,000	40,000	5,000
6	2,000	45,000	42,000	3,000

Comparison of the different depreciation methods

Table 5.8 illustrates the three depreciation methods, and we can see the financial impact for each of the six years. The annual depreciation charge is a constant amount for each year of £7,000 using the straight-line method. The reducing balance method charges the highest amount of £16,345 for year 1 and then in year 6 only £1,711. The sum of the digits method is less extreme than the reducing balance method, but adopts the same premise that more depreciation should be charged early in the asset's life.

Figure 5.1 is derived from the data in Table 5.8 and compares graphically for each method the different annual depreciation charge that will be made in the organization's income statement.

Table 5.8   Income statement annual depreciation charge

Year	Straight-line £	Reducing balance £	Sum of the digits £
1	7,000	16,345	12,000
2	7,000	10,408	10,000
3	7,000	6,628	8,000
4	7,000	4,220	6,000
5	7,000	2,687	4,000
6	7,000	1,711	2,000

Figure 5.1   The three depreciation methods compared

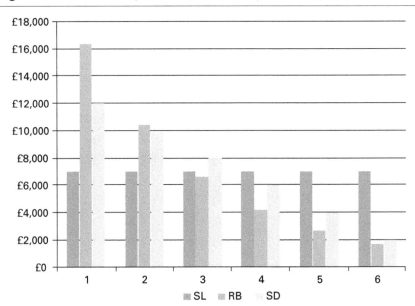

Table 5.9 Balance sheet net book value

Year	Straight-line £	Reducing balance £	Sum of the digits £
1	38,000	28,655	33,000
2	31,000	18,247	23,000
3	24,000	11,619	15,000
4	17,000	7,399	9,000
5	10,000	4,711	5,000
6	3,000	3,000	3,000

As each method will produce different annual depreciation charges, they will also impact differently on the asset's net book value, but all methods will arrive at the same disposal value at the end of the sixth year, as seen in Table 5.9.

Figure 5.2 Net book value by depreciation method

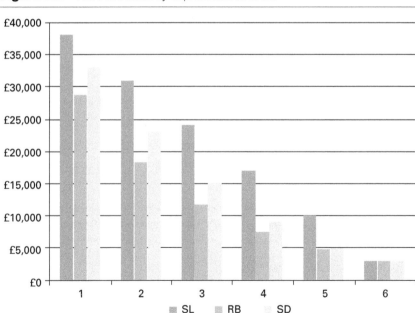

Figure 5.2 compares graphically the net book value for the tractor unit for each of the three depreciation methods for each of the six years.

The information used to calculate the depreciation for the tractor unit is described in the following sentences:

The asset is a tractor unit and will be purchased from the dealer for £45,000 and is estimated to have a useful life of six years and a disposal value of £3,000. The company's current depreciation method is the straight-line method.

Regarding the information required to calculate the annual depreciation for the tractor unit, which is the only fact in the first sentence?

The only fact in the first sentence is the cost of the tractor unit; the useful life and disposal value are assumptions.

Now let's attempt Activity 5.2.

Activity 5.2

A logistics company has purchased a new truck at a cost of £58,000 on 1 January 20X0, and it has a planned life of six years. The disposal value of the system is anticipated to be £4,000 after six years.

a If the company uses the straight-line method of depreciation, what will be the amount of depreciation charged in the income statement for the year ending 31 December 20X3?

b If the company uses the sum of digits method, what fraction will be used to calculate the annual depreciation charge for the year ending 31 December 20X2?

c If the company uses the reducing-balance method, what will be the annual percentage (1 decimal place) used to depreciate the truck?

d What will be the cumulative depreciation amount (to the nearest £) as at 31 December 20X2, if the company uses the sum of digits method of depreciation?

e If the company uses the straight-line method, what will be the net book value of the truck on the company's balance sheet on 31 December 20X4?

For the solution see section 5.10.

5.5 Disposal of an asset

If Newtown Distribution decides to sell the tractor unit at the end of year 3, they will receive £20,000 from the dealership for the vehicle. Table 5.10 indicates the net book value of the tractor at the end of year 3 based on three different methods of depreciation.

Table 5.10 Net book value for the tractor unit at the end of year 3

Year	Straight-line £	Reducing balance £	Sum of the digits £
3	24,000	11,619	15,000

The company would make a profit from the sale of the vehicle if they use the reducing balance method and the sum of the digits; however, if they have adopted the straight-line method, they will make a loss on the disposal as the tractor unit is valued on the balance sheet at £24,000, but they will only receive £20,000, making a loss of £4,000 on disposal. Table 5.11 summarizes the results of the disposal for each of the three depreciation methods; the income and expenditure adjustments will be made in the income statement and the tractor unit will be removed from the motor vehicle account on the balance sheet.

Table 5.11 Financial impact of disposing of the tractor unit

Depreciation method	Outcome
Straight-line	Loss on disposal of £4,000
Reducing balance	Profit on disposal of £8,381
Sum of the digits	Profit on disposal of £5,000

Changing depreciation policy

Say at the end of year 3 the organization decides to change its depreciation method from sum of the digits to straight-line. Using the information in Table 5.12, we can now calculate the impact of changing the company's depreciation policy.

Table 5.12 Tractor unit's net book value year 3

Year	Straight-line £	Reducing balance £	Sum of the digits £
3	24,000	11,619	15,000

The tractor unit's net book value on the balance sheet is £15,000 and the disposal value remains £3,000; therefore, the revised depreciable amount is £12,000. This amount will now be used to calculate the annual depreciation charges for the next three years.

£15,000 – £3,000 = £12,000, £12,000/3 = £4,000 per annum

If the decision was to move from straight-line to reducing balance, a reducing balance percentage will be required.

$$reducing\ balance\ percentage = 1 - \left[3\sqrt{(£3,000/£24,000)} \right] = 0.5$$

The annual depreciation charge for the remaining years would be as follows:

Year 4 = £24,000 * 0.5 = £12,000

Year 5 = £12,000 * 0.5 = £6,000

Year 6 = £6,000 * 0.5 = £3,000

Totalling £21,000, leaving the asset's disposal value of £3,000 on the balance sheet.

Key learning points from the exercise are:

- Accounting is not just a binary world; it is a multifaceted world and the assumptions made by non-accountants can have a big impact on the financial performance of the company.
- Depreciation is an accounting adjustment.
- Depreciation has no impact on cash flow.
- The importance of the asset register and keeping it up to date as it feeds the depreciation calculation.
- The only tangible figure in the depreciation calculation for a non-current asset is the cost of the asset; the others are assumptions, including the life of the asset and its disposal value.
- Need to check out the financial ratio EBITDA.
- The choice of depreciation method can impact on the company's income statement and the value of the total net assets on the balance sheet.

5.6 Depreciation practice in the supply chain

Depreciation policies will vary between organizations based on the depreciation method adopted and the estimated lives allocated to different types of assets, which as discussed earlier will impact on the annual depreciation calculation. To illustrate this, point the depreciation policy and estimated useful lives for different non-current assets have been extracted from the report and accounts of five companies and are illustrated in Table 5.13.

Table 5.13 Depreciation policies and non-current asset useful lives estimates

BASF Group (2017:178)

"Both movable and immovable fixed assets are for the most part depreciated using the straight-line method, with the exception of production licenses and plants in the Oil & Gas segment, which are primarily depreciated based on use in accordance with the unit of production method."

BASF estimates the useful life of its non-current assets based on weight average depreciation periods in years.

"The depreciation methods, useful lives and residual values are reviewed at each balance sheet date. The weighted average depreciation periods were as follows:

Non- current assets	2017	2016
Buildings and structural installations	21	22
Machinery and technical equipment	10	10
Long-distance natural gas pipelines	25	25
Miscellaneous equipment and fixtures	6	7"

Deutsche Post DHL Group (2017:114)

"Depreciation is charged using the straight-line method. The estimated useful lives applied to the major asset classes are presented in the table:

Useful lives	Years*
Buildings	20 to 50
Technical equipment and machinery	10 to 20
Aircraft	15 to 20
IT systems	4 to 5
Technical equipment and vehicle fleet	4 to 18
Other operating an office equipment	8 to 10

*The useful lives indicate represent maximum amounts specified by the Group. The actual useful lives may be shorter due to contractual arrangements or other special factors such as time and location.

Marks and Spencer Group PLC (2018:83)

"Depreciation is provided to write off the cost of tangible noncurrent assets (including investment properties), less estimated residual values on a straight-line basis as follows:

- Freehold land – not depreciated;
- Freehold and leasehold buildings with a remaining lease term over 50 years – depreciated to their residual value over their estimated remaining economic lives;
- Leasehold buildings with a remaining lease term of less than 50 years – depreciated over the shorter of their useful economic lives or the remaining period of the lease; and
- Fixtures, fittings and equipment – 3 to 25 years according to the estimated economic life of the asset."

(continued)

Table 5.13   *(Continued)*

Nestlé Group (2017:90)

"Depreciation is provided on components that have a homogenous useful life by using the straight-line method so as to depreciate the initial cost down to the residual value over the estimated useful lives. The residual values are 30% on head offices and nil for all other asset types
The useful lives are as follows:

	Years
Buildings	*20 to 40*
Machinery and equipment	*10 to 25*
Tools, furniture, information technology and sundry equipment	*3 to 15*
Vehicles	*3 to 15*
Land is not depreciated	

The Procter & Gamble Company (2017:41)

"Depreciation expense is recognized over the assets' estimated useful lives using the straight-line method."

Machinery and equipment includes office furniture and fixtures 15-year life
Computer equipment and capitalized software 3 to 5 year lives
Manufacturing equipment 3 to 20 year lives
Buildings are depreciated over an estimated useful life of 40 years.

Non-current asset register

The non-current asset register is a significant document for an organization, whether it is paper-based or electronic, as it contains the records related to the ownership of a non-current asset. Typically, the information contained in the register will include date of purchase of the asset, its cost, any costs associated with any modifications and enhancements to the asset (computer), asset type, location within the organization (cost centre), its useful life, depreciation method, disposal date and value.

It is important that the asset register is kept up to date as it is essential for audit control and preventing shrinkage, but also the information contained in the register is used to calculate the annual depreciation charge to each cost centre within an organization. If the register is not updated, the amount of depreciation charged to a cost centre would be impacted, causing issues relating to the cost units that flow through the cost centre. We will pick this point up again when looking at full costing.

5.7 Earnings before interest, taxes, depreciation and amortization (EBITDA)

This section will explore the impact of depreciation using data extracted from the BASF Group annual report and accounts for 2017 and focusing on the following financial ratios that are typically used by the organization to measure profitability; they include:

- gross margin (GM) %;

- earnings before interest and taxes (EBIT) %;

- earnings before interest, taxes, depreciation and amortization (EBITDA) %.

Table 5.14 illustrates BASF Group definitions for EBIT and EBITDA.

Table 5.14   EBIT and EBITDA definitions

	BASF Group (2017:250) definitions
EBIT	*'Earnings before interest and taxes (EBIT): EBIT corresponds to income from operations.'*
EBITDA	*'EBITDA corresponds to income from operations before depreciation and amortization (impairments and reversals of impairments).'*
EBITDA margin	*'The margin that we earn on sales from our operating activities before depreciation and amortization. It is calculated as income from operations before depreciation, amortization and valuation allowances as a percentage of sales.'*

When removing depreciation and amortization costs, the EBITDA margin will be higher than the EBIT margin. These are illustrated in Table 5.15.

Table 5.15   BASF Group profitability ratios from 2013 to 2017

Ratio	2017	2016	2015	2014	2013
Gross margin %	31.38	31.39	26.12	24.38	24.53
EBIT margin %	12.86	10.36	8.57	10.44	9.71
EBITDA %	18.87	17.20	13.64	15.09	14.19

When removing depreciation and amortization costs, the EBITDA margin will be higher than the EBIT margin, as illustrated in Figure 5.3.

Figure 5.3   BASF Group profitability ratios from 2013 to 2017

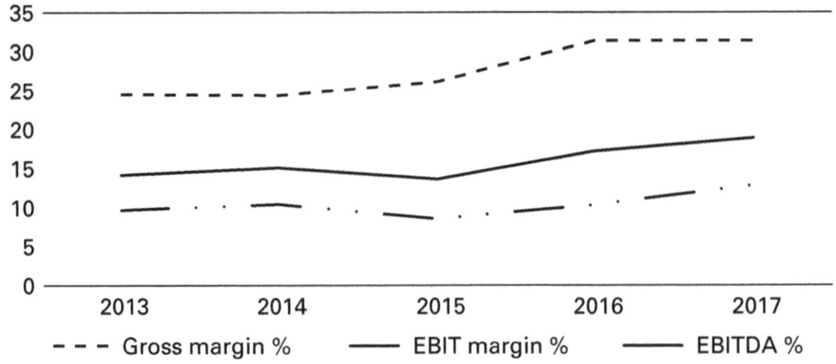

The main advantage of stripping out these costs is that it is now possible to compare profitability across organizations in the same industrial sector if they have adopted different depreciation methods, as described earlier in this chapter. Now have a go at Activity 5.3.

Activity 5.3

Using the data contained in Table 5.16, calculate the following profitability ratios for each company:

- gross margin (GM) %;
- earnings before interest and taxes (EBIT) %;
- earnings before interest, taxes, depreciation and amortization (EBITDA) %.

If you are not sure of the ratio's calculation, see Chapter 2.

Table 5.16   Financial data for companies A, B and C

Company	A	B	C
Sales £m	200	280	350
Cost of goods sold £m	80	126	140
Operating expenses £m	50	80	100
Depreciation included in operating expenses £m	20	30	60

5.8 Summary

The aim of this chapter was to introduce you to the concept of depreciation. You are now able to:

- explain the difference between revenue and capital expenditure;
- describe three different methods of depreciation;
- calculate annual depreciation rates using three methods;
- compare different methods of depreciation;
- explain how depreciation impacts on the income statement and balance sheet of a business.

Key learning points from the chapter include:

- accounting is not just a binary world; it is a multifaceted world and the assumptions made by non-accountants can have a big impact on the financial performance of the company;
- depreciation is an accounting adjustment;
- depreciation has no impact on cash flow;
- the importance of the asset register and keeping it up to date as it feeds the depreciation calculation;
- the only tangible figure in the depreciation calculation for a non-current asset is the cost of the asset; the others are assumptions, including the life of the asset and its disposal value;
- need to check out the financial ratio EBITDA;
- the choice of depreciation method can impact on the company's income statement and the value of the total net assets on the balance sheet.

5.9 References

Atrill, P and McLaney, E (2017) *Accounting and Finance for Non-specialists*, 10th edn, Pearson, London

BASF Group (2017) *Report*, http://report.basf.com/2017/en/ (accessed 15 December 2018)

CIMA (2005) *CIMA Official Terminology*, CIMA Publishing, Oxford

Deutsche Post DHL Group (2017) *Annual Report*, https://annualreport2017.dpdhl.com/downloads-ext/en/documents/DPDHL_2017_Annual_Report.pdf (accessed 15 December 2018)

Marks & Spencer Group Plc (2018) *Annual Report and Financial Statements*, https://corporate.marksandspencer.com/annualreport (accessed 15 December 2018)

Nestlé Group (2017) *Annual Review*, HYPERLINK "http://www.nestle.com/investors/publications#tab-2017" www.nestle.com/investors/publications#tab-2017 (accessed 15 December 2018)

Procter & Gamble Company (2017) *Form 10-K*, www.annualreports.com/HostedData/AnnualReports/PDF/NYSE_PG_2017.pdf (accessed 15 December 2018)

5.10 Solutions to the activities

Activity 5.1 solution

The different types of revenue and capital expenditure for a road haulier are illustrated in Table 5.17.

Table 5.17   Revenue and capital expenditure for a road haulier

Revenue	Capital
Fuel and oil	Articulated tractor units
Wages and salaries	Different type of trailers
Tyres	Forklift trucks
Insurance	Land and buildings
Excise duties	Material handling equipment
Operating licence	Office equipment
Operating overheads	Computer equipment
Spare parts	Communication equipment
Servicing costs	
Consumables	
Road tolls	
Depreciation	
Training	

Activity 5.2 solution

Tables 5.18 to 5.20 illustrate the depreciation calculations for the three methods of depreciation.

a If the company was to use the straight-line method of depreciation, the amount of depreciation charged in the income statement for the year ending 31 December 20X3 will be £9,000.

$$purchase\ cost - disposal\ value = total\ depreciation$$
$$£58,000 - £4,000 = £54,000$$

The annual depreciation charge is calculated by dividing the total depreciation value by the asset's useful life.

$$total\ depreciation/asset's\ useful\ life = annual\ depreciation\ charge$$
$$£54,000/6 = £9,000$$

Table 5.18 Straight-line method

Year	Date	Annual depreciation £	Historic cost £	Cumulative depreciation £	Net book value £
1	20X0	9,000	58,000	9,000	49,000
2	20X1	9,000	58,000	18,000	40,000
3	20X2	9,000	58,000	27,000	31,000
4	20X3	9,000	58,000	36,000	22,000
5	20X4	9,000	58,000	45,000	13,000
6	20X5	9,000	58,000	54,000	4,000

b When the sum of digits method is used the fraction to calculate the annual depreciation charge for the year ending 31 December 20X2 will be 4/21.

$$6 + 5 + 4 + 3 + 2 + 1 = 21$$

Table 5.19 Sum of the digits method

Year	Date	Annual depreciation £	Historic cost £	Cumulative depreciation £	Net book value £	S of D fraction
1	20X0	15,429	58,000	15,429	42,571	6/21
2	20X1	12,857	58,000	28,286	29,714	5/21
3	20X2	10,286	58,000	38,571	19,429	4/21
4	20X3	7,714	58,000	46,286	11,714	3/21
5	20X4	5,143	58,000	51,429	6,571	2/21
6	20X5	2,571	58,000	54,000	4,000	1/21

c When the company uses the reducing balance method, the annual percentage to depreciate the truck will be 35.96%.

$$Reducing\ balance\ percentage = 1 - \left[n\sqrt{(D\ V/C)} \right]$$

Where:

n = the life of the non-current asset in years;
DV = disposal value or residual value or scrap value;
C = purchase cost of the non-current asset.

We can now derive the reducing balance percentage for the truck.

$$1 - \left[6\sqrt{(£4,000/£58,000)} \right]$$

The annual percentage to depreciate the truck will be 35.96%.

Table 5.20 Reducing balance method

Year	Date	Annual depreciation £	Historic price £	Cumulative depreciation £	Net book value £
1	20X0	20,858	58,000	20,858	37,142
2	20X1	13,357	58,000	34,215	23,785
3	20X2	8,554	58,000	42,769	15,231
4	20X3	5,477	58,000	48,246	9,754
5	20X4	3,508	58,000	51,754	6,246
6	20X5	2,246	58,000	54,000	4,000

d The cumulative depreciation on the balance sheet at 31 December 20X2, if the company uses the sum of digits method of depreciation, will be £38,571.

6/21 + 5/21 + 4/21 = 15/21 then multiply 15/21 * £54,000 = £38,571.

e When the company uses the straight-line method the net book value of the truck on the company's balance sheet on 31 December 20X4 will be £13,000.

Multiply the annual depreciation by number of years, then subtract from the historical cost. Therefore £9,000 * 5 = £45,000 derives the cumulative depreciation, subtracting from the historical cost of £58,000, producing an NBV of £13,000.

Activity 5.3 solution

Table 5.21 illustrates the profitability ratios for the three companies.

Companies A and C share the highest gross margin; when operating expenses are included A has the highest EBIT percentage. However, when depreciation costs are taken out of the analysis, company C has the highest profitability when comparing the three companies using EBITDA margin.

Table 5.21   Profitability ratios

Ratio	A	B	C
Gross margin %	60.00%	55.00%	60.00%
EBIT %	35.00%	26.43%	31.43%
EBITDA %	45.00%	37.14%	48.57%

5.11 Study questions

Study question 5.1

You have been supplied with an extract from the asset register in Table 5.22, which details the company's motor vehicles. The company's depreciation policy is straight line and vehicles have a life span of between three and eight years, and a disposal value for each vehicle has been agreed with a local garage.

Table 5.22   Extract from the asset register

MV account	Purchase date	Purchase price	Life span	Residual value
Vehicle A	01.01.20X0	26,000	8	2,000
Vehicle B	01.01.20X1	28,000	8	4,000
Vehicle C	01.01.20X1	23,000	7	2,000
Vehicle D	01.01.20X2	27,000	6	3,000
Vehicle E	01.01.20X3	31,000	7	3,000
Vehicle F	01.01.20X4	27,000	5	2,000
Vehicle G	01.01.20X5	24,000	3	3,000
Vehicle H	01.01.20X6	28,000	4	4,000

You are required to calculate the depreciation charge in the income statement for the year ending 31/12/20X6 and the net book value of the motor vehicles on the balance sheet as at 31/12/20X6.

Study question 5.2

A company purchases a warehouse management computer system for £250,000 on 1 January 2X05; its useful life is estimated to be four years. The scrap value on disposal is assumed to be £10,000. The company uses the reducing balance method.

1 How much depreciation will be charged in the income statement for the year ending 31 December 20X6 and what will its NBV be on the balance sheet?

2 If the company sells the system to another company on 31 December 20X7 for £80,000, what will be the impact on the following:

a income statement;

b balance sheet;

c cash flow?

Study question 5.3

Ultra plc is planning to purchase a non-current asset at a cost of £500,000 on 1 January 20X0; it has a planned life of eight years and a residual value of £60,000 on disposal.

1 If the company uses the straight-line method of depreciation, what will be the amount of depreciation charged in the income statement for the year ending 31 December 20X3 for the non-current asset (to the nearest £)?

2 If the company uses the sum of the digits method of depreciation, what will be the annual depreciation charge for 20X5 (to the nearest £)?

3 If the company uses the reducing balance method of depreciation, what will be the annual depreciation charge for 2X02 (to the nearest £)?

4 If the company uses the straight-line method of depreciation, what is the net book value of the non-current asset on the company's balance sheet on 31 December 20X6?

5 What will be the cumulative depreciation amount (to the nearest £) for the non-current asset as at 31 December 20X3 if the company uses the reducing balance method of depreciation?

6 If the company uses the reducing balance method, what will be the annual percentage (two decimal places) used to depreciate the computer system?

7 If the company uses the sum of the digits method of depreciation, what will be the value of the denominator used to calculate the annual depreciation charge?

8 What will be the cumulative depreciation as at 31 December 20X6 if the company uses the sum of the digits method of depreciation?

Study question 5.4

Your company has purchased a new packing machine for its regional distribution centre at a cost of £1,000,000 on 1 January 20X0, and it has a planned life of 10 years. The scrap value of the system is anticipated to be £60,000 at the end of its useful life.

1 If the company uses the straight-line method of depreciation, what will be the amount of depreciation charged in the income statement for the year ending 31 December 20X7?

A £752,000

B £800,000

C £100,000

D £94,000

2 If the company uses the reducing balance method, what will be the annual percentage (two decimal places) used to depreciate the packing machine?

A 22.45%

B 24.52%

C 25.24%

D 25.42%

3 If the company uses the sum of the digits method of depreciation, what will be the value of the denominator used to calculate the annual depreciation charge for the packing machine?

A 55

B 66

C 45

D 78

4 If the company uses the straight-line method, what is the net book value of the packing machine on the company's balance sheet on 31 December 20X4?

A £376,000

B £624,000

C £470,000

D £530,000

5 What will be the cumulative depreciation as at 31 December 20X2 if the company uses the sum of the digits depreciation method?

A £324,727

B £675,273

C £461,455

D £538,545

5.12 Study question solutions

Study question 5.1 solution

Table 5.23 illustrates the annual depreciation charge in the IS for each vehicle.

Table 5.23   Annual depreciation charge

MV account	Purchase date	Historical cost	Life span	Residual value	Annual depreciation
Vehicle A	01.01.20X0	26,000	8	2,000	3,000
Vehicle B	01.01.20X1	28,000	8	4,000	3,000
Vehicle C	01.01.20X1	23,000	7	2,000	3,000
Vehicle D	01.01.20X2	27,000	6	3,000	4,000
Vehicle E	01.01.20X3	31,000	7	3,000	4,000
Vehicle F	01.01.20X4	27,000	5	2,000	5,000
Vehicle G	01.01.20X5	24,000	3	3,000	7,000
Vehicle H	01.01.20X6	28,000	4	4,000	6,000

Table 5.24 depicts the net book value of each vehicle on the organization's BS.

Table 5.24   Net book value

MV account	Annual depreciation £	Age of vehicle	Cumulative depreciation £	Historical cost £	Net book value £
Vehicle A	3,000	7	21,000	26,000	5,000
Vehicle B	3,000	6	18,000	28,000	10,000
Vehicle C	3,000	6	18,000	23,000	5,000
Vehicle D	4,000	5	20,000	27,000	7,000
Vehicle E	4,000	4	16,000	31,000	15,000
Vehicle F	5,000	3	15,000	27,000	12,000
Vehicle G	7,000	2	14,000	24,000	10,000
Vehicle H	6,000	1	6,000	28,000	22,000
Total	35,000		128,000	214,000	86,000

The depreciation charge for the motor vehicles account in the income statement for the year ending 31/12/20X6 will be £35,000. The net book value
of the motor vehicles on the company's balance sheet as at 31/12/20X6 will
be £86,000.

Study question 5.2 solution

Workings

The company has adopted the reducing-balance method of depreciation.
Before we can solve this question, the annual percentage used to depreciate
the non-current asset needs to be calculated using the following formula:

$$Reducing\ balance\ percentage = 1 - \left[n\sqrt{(D\ V/C)} \right]$$

Where:

n = the life of the non-current asset in years;
DV = disposal value or residual value or scrap value;
C = purchase cost of the non-current asset.

We can now derive the reducing balance percentage for the truck.

$$1 - \left[4\sqrt{(£10,000 / £250,000)} \right]$$

Therefore, the annual percentage to depreciate the non-current asset will be 55.28%.

We can now calculate the annual depreciation for the warehouse management system, as illustrated in Table 5.25.

Table 5.25   Reducing balance method

Year	Date	Annual depreciation £	Historic cost £	Cumulative depreciation £	Net book value £
1	20X5	138,197	250,000	138,197	111,803
2	20X6	61,803	250,000	200,000	50,000
3	20X7	27,639	250,000	227,639	22,361
4	20X8	12,361	250,000	240,000	10,000

1 The amount of depreciation that will be charged in the income statement for the year ending 31 December 20X6 will be £61,803 and the NBV on the balance sheet will be £50,000.

2 If the company were to sell the warehouse management computer system on 31 December 20X7 for £50,000, they would make a profit on the disposal of the asset of £27,639, as it is currently valued on their balance sheet at £22,361.

The income statement for 31 December 20X7 would record a profit of £27,639 on disposal of a non-current asset.

Two things would happen on the balance sheet: first, the computer system account in the non-current assets would be reduced by £22,361. The value of the current assets (cash account) would increase by £50,000 as a consequence of the disposal of the non-current asset. The company would have a cash injection of £50,000 from the proceeds of the disposal of the computer system.

Study question 5.3 solution

Workings

Tables 5.26 to 5.28 illustrate the depreciation calculations for the three depreciation methods.

Table 5.26 Straight-line method

Year	Date	Annual depreciation £	Historic cost £	Cumulative depreciation £	Net book value £
1	20X0	55,000	500,000	55,000	445,000
2	20X1	55,000	500,000	110,000	390,000
3	20X2	55,000	500,000	165,000	335,000
4	20X3	55,000	500,000	220,000	280,000
5	20X4	55,000	500,000	275,000	225,000
6	20X5	55,000	500,000	330,000	170,000
7	20X6	55,000	500,000	385,000	115,000
8	20X7	55,000	500,000	440,000	60,000

Table 5.27 Sum of the digits method

Year	Date	Annual depreciation £	Historic cost £	Cumulative depreciation £	Net book value £	S of D fraction
1	20X0	97,778	500,000	97,778	402,222	8/36
2	20X1	85,556	500,000	183,333	316,667	7/36
3	20X2	73,333	500,000	256,667	243,333	6/36
4	20X3	61,111	500,000	317,778	182,222	5/36
5	20X4	48,889	500,000	366,667	133,333	4/36
6	20X5	36,667	500,000	403,333	96,667	3/36
7	20X6	24,444	500,000	427,778	72,222	2/36
8	20X7	12,222	500,000	440,000	60,000	1/36

Table 5.28 Reducing balance method

Year	Date	Annual depreciation £	Historic cost £	Cumulative depreciation £	Net book value £
1	20X0	116,410	500,000	116,410	383,590
2	20X1	89,307	500,000	205,717	294,283
3	20X2	68,515	500,000	274,232	225,768
4	20X3	52,563	500,000	326,795	173,205

(*continued*)

Table 5.28 (*Continued*)

Year	Date	Annual depreciation £	Historic cost £	Cumulative depreciation £	Net book value £
5	20X4	40,325	500,000	367,120	132,880
6	20X5	30,937	500,000	398,057	101,943
7	20X6	23,734	500,000	421,792	78,208
8	20X7	18,208	500,000	440,000	60,000

1 The amount of depreciation charged in the income statement for the year ending 31 December 20X3 for the non-current asset based on the straight-line method of depreciation will be £55,000.

2 If the company uses the sum of the digits method of depreciation, the annual depreciation charge for 20X5 will be £33,667 (to the nearest £).

3 If the company adopts the reducing-balance method of depreciation, the annual depreciation charge for 20X2 will be £68,515 (to the nearest £).

4 If the straight-line method of depreciation is adopted, the net book value of the non-current asset on the company's balance sheet on 31 December 20X6 will be £115,000.

5 The cumulative depreciation amount for the non-current asset as at 31 December 20X3, if the company uses the reducing-balance method of depreciation, will be £326,795 (to the nearest £).

6 If the company adopted the reducing-balance method, the annual percentage used to depreciate the non-current asset will be 23.28% (two decimal places).

Workings:

$$Reducing\ balance\ percentage = 1 - \left[n\sqrt{(DV/C)} \right]$$

Where:

n = the life of the non-current asset in years;
DV = disposal value or residual value or scrap value;
C = purchase cost of the non-current asset.

We can now derive the reducing balance percentage for the truck:

$$1 - \left[8\sqrt{(£60,000/£500,000)} \right]$$

Therefore, the annual percentage to depreciate the non-current asset will be 23.28%.

7 If the company uses the sum of the digits method of depreciation, the value of the denominator used to calculate the annual depreciation charge will be 36.

Workings:

The life span of the asset is eight years; therefore, the denominator will be the sum of the numbers from 1 to 8, which totals to 36.

8 The cumulative depreciation as at 31 December 20X6, if the company uses the sum of the digits depreciation method, will be £427,778 (to the nearest £).

Study question 5.4 solution

1 If the company uses the straight-line method of depreciation, the amount of depreciation charged in the income statement for the year ending 31 December 20X7 will be £94,000.

First calculate the total depreciation:

$$purchase\ cost - disposal\ value = total\ depreciation$$
$$£1,000,000 - £60,000 = £940,000$$

The annual depreciation charge is calculated by dividing the total depreciation value by the asset's useful life.

$$total\ depreciation/asset's\ useful\ life = annual\ depreciation\ charge$$
$$£940,000/10 = £94,000$$

Answer = **D**

2 If the company uses the reducing-balance method, the annual percentage (two decimal places) used to depreciate the packing machine will be 24.52%.

Workings:

$$Reducing\ balance\ percentage = 1 - \left[n\sqrt{(D\ V/C)} \right]$$

Where:

n = the life of the non-current asset in years;
DV = disposal value or residual value or scrap value;
C = purchase cost of the non-current asset.

We can now derive the reducing-balance percentage for the truck.

$$1 - \left[10\sqrt{(£60,000/£1,000,000)} \right]$$

Therefore, the annual percentage to depreciate the packing machine will be 24.52%.

Answer = **B**

3 If the company uses the sum of the digits method of depreciation, the value of the denominator used to calculate the annual depreciation charge will be the sum of the numbers from 1 to 10, which is 55.

Answer = **A**

4 If the company uses the straight-line method, the net book value of the packing machine on the company's balance sheet on 31 December 20X4 will be £530,000.

To calculate the net book value of the packing machine on the company's balance sheet on 31 December 20X4, we need to calculate the cumulative depreciation for five years and subtract from the historical cost of the asset. We know the annual rate is £94,000; therefore, multiplying this figure by 5 equals £470,000. £1,000,000 minus £470,000 produces a net book value of £530,000.

Answer = **D**

5 The cumulative depreciation as at 31 December 20X2, if the company was to adopt the sum of the digits method, will be £461,455 (to the nearest £).

The value of the denominator is 55 for 10 years; the cumulative depreciation (3 years) will be the sum of the following fractions: 10/55 + 9/55 + 8/55 = 27/55, which is then multiplied by the total depreciable amount of £940,000. Thus, the cumulative depreciation will be £461,455 (to the nearest £).

Answer = **C**

Supply chain management and financial performance

Having spent many years working in and around supply chains, first as a practitioner and then as an academic (researcher and lecturer), I am totally convinced that the decisions that supply chain practitioners take will have a direct impact on the financial performance of their organizations. However, the effect of these decisions extends further than just their immediate internal customers and suppliers; it extends externally to the organizations that they interact with that make up their chain or network, including their external customers and suppliers. However, improving financial performance from an SC perspective is not just about reducing cost; it goes further, according to Ellram and Liu (2002:30): 'The financial impact of purchasing and supply management goes well beyond cost reduction. It extends to such critical performance areas as business growth, profitability, cash flow, and asset utilisation.'

Therefore, SC practitioners need to be aware of the significant strategic impact that their decisions will have on their business, as Christopher (1998:100) points out: 'It is likely that in the future, decisions on logistics strategies will be made based upon a thorough understanding of the impact they have upon the financial performance of the business.'

However, Ellram and Liu (2002:30) stress that practitioners need to go one step further than just recognizing the significant role they play in improving the financial performance of their firm; they need to demonstrate and communicate their contribution: 'Supply chain managers need to be able to quantify that broader impact and then convey that message upward so that top management better understands how purchasing and supply management can contribute to company success.'

Supply chain practitioners can clearly demonstrate their importance to the organization by communicating how their decisions can have a significant impact on the three important financial imperatives facing organizations identified by Christopher (2011:58), which are:

1 The bottom line has become the driving force which, perhaps erroneously, determines the direction of the company.

2 Strong positive cash flow has become as much a desired goal of management as profit.

3 The pressure in most organizations is to improve the productivity of capital – to make the assets sweat.

Hence, it is essential that supply chain practitioners are able to recognize the impact that their decisions have on their organization's profitability, liquidity and asset utilization, as well as the financial ratios and key performance indicators that measure these strategically important financial variables.

6.1 Aim and objectives

The aim of this chapter is to introduce you to the significant impact that your supply chain management decisions have on the financial performance of the organization and enable you to explain the relationship between supply chain management decisions and the financial ratios that are used by organizations as measures of firm performance.

At the end of this chapter you will be able to:

- recognize a set of the financial ratios that are used to measure the impact of your SC decisions on the financial performance of the organization that you work for;
- calculate a typical set of financial ratios;
- explain the relationship between supply chain decisions and their impact on financial ratios;
- recognize the linkages between an organization's financial statements and the different financial ratios used to evaluate financial performance.

6.2 The role of the supply chain

The opening sentences in Braithwaite and Christopher's book (2015:1) emphasize the importance that customers have on the financial success of any business, as well as the significant role that the supply chain has in fulfilling customer demand:

> A company is nothing without customers, and customers are not stupid. They make sophisticated choices in terms of the value they expect to derive from their purchases; this applies to both consumer and business transactions.

Without any customers you have no demand; therefore, you don't have a business and consequently you do not need a supply chain; hence the *raison d'être* for supply chains is to satisfy customer demand. Therefore, the supply chain plays a significant role in contributing to organization sales revenues and can be an enabler in generating top-line growth, reinforcing Ellram and Liu's (2002) argument. Mentzer *et al's* (2001:18) broadly cited definition of supply chain management is:

> The systemic, strategic coordination of the traditional business functions and the tactics across these business functions within a particular company and across businesses within the supply chain for the purposes of improving the long-term performance of the individual companies and the supply chain as a whole.

Hence, the role of supply chain practitioners is to manage the three flows (physical, information and financial) that exist in a typical supply chain operation, as illustrated in Figure 6.1.

Figure 6.1 Supply chain nodes and flows

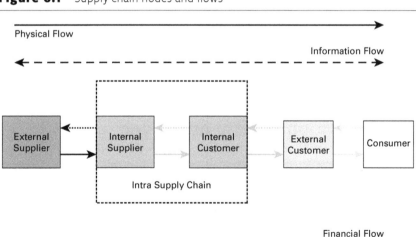

Jay W Forrester's (1958:37) seminal paper recognized the importance of managing the flows that exist in business: 'Management is on the verge of a major breakthrough,' Forrester wrote, 'in understanding how industrial company success depends on the interaction between the flows of information, materials, money, manpower and capital equipment.' However, Forrester makes an important point: these flows are not independent; they interact with each other. 'The way these five flow systems interlock to amplify one another and to cause change and fluctuation will form a basis for anticipating the effects of decisions, policies, organizational forms and investment choices.'

Therefore, supply chain practitioners need to take this into consideration when making decisions regarding one flow: that there can be unforeseen consequences which impact other functions of the business. Hence, decision-makers need to be aware of, and understand, the dynamics of the flows and be prepared to make trade-offs between the other functions whose decisions also impact on the flows.

Ultimately supply chain practitioners will be appraised, and their success evaluated, on their ability to manage the organization's supply operation: economically, efficiently and effectively, providing value for its customers, but also creating value (shareholder) for the owners of the organization, who have invested in the assets that comprise the supply chain infrastructure.

However, a supply chain disruption can have a potential negative impact on the financial performance of the organization. The Procter & Gamble Company (2017:3) highlight the importance of their supply chain operation to the financial performance of their business: 'Disruption in our global supply chain may negatively impact our business results. Our ability to meet our customers' needs and achieve cost targets depends on our ability to maintain key manufacturing and supply arrangements.'

6.3 Return on capital employed

Return on capital employed (ROCE), according to Brookson (2001:43), 'reveals how much profit is being made on the money invested in the business and is a key measure of how well management is doing its job'. ROCE is calculated using information disclosed in both the income statement (IS) and the balance sheet (BS). The ratio takes the earnings before interest and tax (EBIT) from the IS and the value of the organization's capital employed (CE) from the BS. ROCE is calculated by dividing EBIT by CE and then multiplying by 100 to give a percentage. Alternatively, it can be derived by taking EBIT and dividing it by the value of the organization's total assets minus current liabilities, then multiplying by 100 to give a percentage. The two calculation methods are illustrated in Table 6.1.

Table 6.1   Alternative methods of calculating the ROCE percentage

Capital employed	Total assets – current liabilities
(EBIT/CE) * 100	(EBIT/(TA – CL)) *100

The first calculation uses CE from the bottom half of the BS (type 2) as the denominator, while the second method uses the value of the TA – CL from the top half of the BS as its denominator. The figures are actually the same numerically, but they are derived differently. The following user-friendly example will demonstrate this point by revisiting the account equation (Chapter 3). The accounting equation for Ultra plc consists of NCA of £800k, CA of £300k and CL of £100k; the organization is funded by shareholders' equity (EQ) of £750k and non-current liability of £250k, making its total CE £1,000k. The company's NCA + CA – CL = EQ + NCL, which is its BS, as depicted in Table 6.2.

Table 6.2   Ultra plc accounting equation

NCA	+	CA	–	CL	=	EQ	+	NCL
£800k	+	£300k	–	£100k	=	£750k	+	£250k
		£1,000k			=		**£1,000k**	
		Total assets – current liabilities			=		**Capital employed**	

From a supply chain (SC) perspective, the ROCE calculation that adopts TA – CL as the denominator is extremely useful, as the decisions taken by SC practitioners will typically impact on the organization's NCA, CA and CL because SC decisions tend not to impact directly on where an organization raises its finances from (share capital and long-term loans). However, it is important to recognize that SC decisions will have an impact on the retained earnings in the IS, which will either increase or decrease the value of the cumulative retained earnings included as part of the shareholders' funds in the BS.

SC decisions taken by practitioners will have an impact on both the numerator (EBIT) and denominator (TA – CL) of the ROCE ratio. It is essential to deconstruct the ROCE calculation further into its numerator and denominator and then explore these two variables to discover how SC decisions impact on the ratio.

EBIT is calculated using elements from the IS by taking the cost of goods sold plus operating expenses and subtracting them from sales revenue; for example, Ultra plc has sales revenue of £200K, cost of sales of £40k and operating expenses of £60k, therefore its EBIT will be £100k (£200k – £40k – £60k). EBIT is measured as a percentage of sales; in this example the EBIT percentage will be 50% (see Chapter 2). The important point for SC practitioners is to recognize that if you can take decisions that increase sales and also reduce costs, the EBIT percentage will increase and therefore also have a positive impact on the ROCE calculation.

The second element of the ROCE ratio is the denominator (TA – CL), which uses data taken from the BS. For instance, Ultra plc has NCA of £800k, CA of £300k and CL of £100k; therefore its TA – CL would be £1,000K (£800k + £300k – £100k). Therefore, SC decisions that will reduce an organization's NCA and CA and that will increase CL will reduce the denominator and therefore have a positive impact on the ROCE calculation.

Therefore, Ultra plc's ROCE ratio is calculated by dividing the EBIT (£100k) by the sum of the organization's NCA and WC (£1,000k), which produces a ROCE of 10%; this reveals that every £1 of capital employed generates £0.10 in returns before tax.

6.4 EBIT percentage and NCA + WC turnover

The ROCE can also be calculated by multiplying two other ratios together: the EBIT percentage (EBIT/sales*100) and the TA – CL turnover ratio (sales/ TA – CL). The TA – CL turnover is a measure of asset utilization by calculating the value of sales revenue generated by the value of the assets (TA – CL) employed in the business. This ratio uses sales revenue as the numerator and the value of the assets (TA – CL) as the denominator. If we take Ultra plc's sales revenue of £200k and then divide it by the value of £1,000k (TA – CL), we get 0.2; this means that every £1 invested in TA – CL is generating £0.20 in sales revenue.

Ultra plc has an EBIT percentage of 50% (£100k/£200k*100), which equates to £0.50 EBIT for every £1 of sales.

Multiplying the EBIT percentage of 50% by the TA – CL turnover ratio of 0.2 equals a ROCE of 10%. This important relationship between these two ratios is illustrated in Figure 6.2.

Figure 6.2 ROCE calculations

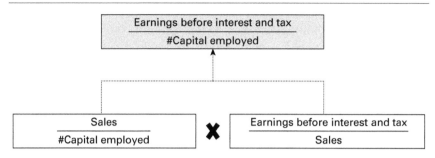

#Non-current assets + working capital = Capital Employed

Therefore, the organization's ROCE will improve if the decisions taken by SC practitioners have the following impacts on the ROCE's numerator and denominator, as illustrated in Table 6.3.

Table 6.3 ROCE and its numerator and denominator

Option	EBIT (numerator)	TA – CL (denominator)
1	Increase	No change
2	No change	Decrease
3	Increase	Decrease
4	Decrease	Decrease
5	Increase	Increase
6	Decrease	Increase
7	Decrease	No change
8	No change	Increase
9	Decrease by the same percentage	Decrease by the same percentage
10	Increase by the same proportion	Increase by the same proportion
11	No change	No change

Options 1 to 3 will increase ROCE; however, options 4 and 5 need further explanation as they relate to the magnitude of the change in the numerator and denominator. For instance, in option 4, if the magnitude of the decrease in the denominator is greater than the size of the reduction in the numerator, the ROCE ratio will increase. Similarly, with option 5, if the magnitude of the increase in the numerator (EBIT) is greater in relation to the increase of the denominator (capital employed), the ROCE will also increase. Options 6 to 8 will reduce the value of the ROCE, while options 9 to 11 will have no impact on the ROCE's percentage. The impact of the 11 options are illustrated in Table 6.4 for Ultra plc using the organization's EBIT and CE values.

Table 6.4   The impact on the ROCE percentage due to changes in its numerator and denominator

Options	Change	ROCE calculation £k	ROCE %
Base case	EBIT	100	10.00%
	CE	1,000	
Option 1	Increase EBIT by 5%	105	10.50%
	No change in CE	1,000	
Option 2	No change in EBIT	100	10.53%
	Decrease CE by 5%	950	
Option 3	Increase EBIT by 5%	105	11.05%
	Decrease CE by 5%	950	
Option 4	Decrease EBIT by 4%	96	10.11%
	Decrease CE by 5%	950	
Option 5	Increase EBIT by 5%	105	10.29%
	Increase CE by 2%	1,020	
Option 6	Decrease EBIT by 5%	95	9.05%
	Increase CE by 5%	1,050	
Option 7	Decrease EBIT by 5%	95	9.50%
	No change in CE	1,000	
Option 8	No change in EBIT	100	9.80%
	Increase CE by 2%	1,020	
Option 9	Decrease EBIT by 5%	95	10.00%
	Decrease CE by 5%	950	
Option 10	Increase EBIT by 5%	105	10.00%
	Increase CE by 5%	1,050	
Option 11	No change	100	10.00%
	No change	1,000	

Therefore, it is essential that SC practitioners have an understanding of the impact that an SC decision will have on the elements that make up the numerator (sales and costs) and the denominator (NCA, CA and CL) of the ROCE calculation, and then they will be able to quantify the effect of their decision on the ratio.

Table 6.5 illustrates the relationship between the two ratios, EBIT percentage and TA – CL turnover; when they are multiplied together, they produce the ROCE %. The table also illustrates that the same ROCE percentage can be derived by using different values of the two ratios EBIT percentage and TA – CL turnover. For example, an organization that has an EBIT percentage of 4% and TA – CL turnover of 6 will have an ROCE percentage of 24%, but another organization can have an EBIT percentage of 24% and TA – CL turnover of 1 and can achieve the same ROCE %.

Table 6.5 Constant ROCE percentage given different values of EBIT percentage and TA – CL turnover

(EBIT/sales) *100 = EBIT%	1	2	3	4	6	8	12	24
Sales/(TA – CL) = TA – CL turnover	24	12	8	6	4	3	2	1
ROCE %	24	24	24	24	24	24	24	24

Figure 6.3 illustrates the constant ROCE percentage curve for different combinations of the EBIT percentage and TA – CL turnover ratio.

Figure 6.3 ROCE percentage curve for combinations of the EBIT percentage and TA – CL turnover ratio

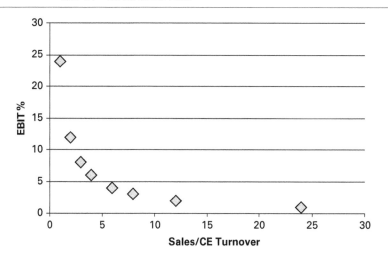

It is important to recognize that organizations that operate in different industrial sectors will have diverse EBIT percentages and TA – CL turnover ratios, but they can achieve the same ROCE %. In Figure 6.4 two ratios are deconstructed further into their components; you may have come across this approach before in the form of the Du Pont model. As mentioned earlier, the ROCE percentage uses elements from both the BS and the IS in its calculation.

Figure 6.4 illustrates the relationship between the EBIT percentage and TA – CL turnover ratio.

Figure 6.4   ROCE and its relationship with EBIT percentage and TA – CL turnover ratio

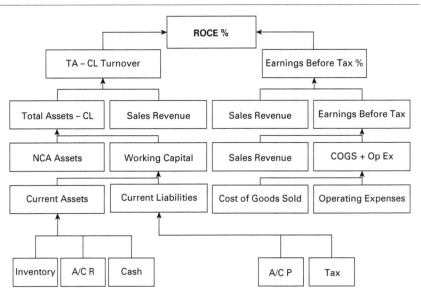

6.5 Case study: Qwerty Ltd

This case study explores the impact of SC decisions on a fictitious organization's ROCE %. Qwerty Ltd imports computer keyboard components and assembles them into unique wireless keyboards in various colour combinations to meet their customers' specifications.

The company currently has an EBIT percentage of 15.4%, a TA – CL turnover ratio of 2.778 and an ROCE percentage of 42.78%. Figure 6.5 illustrates the organization's current BS as at 31 March 20XX. The company's IS

Figure 6.5   Qwerty Ltd balance sheet

Qwerty Ltd – balance sheet as at 31 March 20XX	
Non-current assets	**£k**
Property, plant and equipment	114
	114
Current assets	
Inventories	140
Accounts receivable	220
Cash	0
	360
Total assets	**474**
Equity	
£1 ordinary shares	200
Retained profit	100
	300
Non-current liabilities	
Long-term loan	60
Current liabilities	
Accounts payable	60
Taxation	54
	114
Total equity and liabilities	**474**

Figure 6.6   Qwerty Ltd income statement

Qwerty Ltd – income statement for the year ending 31 March 20XX	**£k**
Revenue	**1,000**
Cost of goods sold	660
Gross profit	**640**
Operating expenses	186
Earnings before tax	**154**
Taxation	54
Earnings after tax	**100**
Dividend	0
Retained earnings	**100**

for the year ending 31 March 20XX is depicted in Figure 6.6 and the ROCE calculation is outlined in Figure 6.7.

Figure 6.7 Qwerty Ltd ROCE percentage calculation

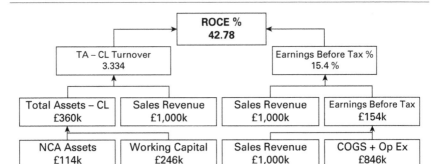

The company's board has a number of SC initiatives they want to implement; however, they are unsure of the potential impact on the organization's ROCE %. Using the current financial statements as the base case, they want to discover the impact of each SC initiative on the existing ROCE %. The four SC initiatives are:

1 a 10% reduction in the cost of goods sold;

2 to reduce the organization's accounts receivable by £60k;

3 a £60k reduction in inventories plus related savings in the inventory holding costs;

4 a supply chain outsourcing opportunity that will reduce non-current assets by £60k.

SC initiative 1: 10% reduction in the cost of goods sold calculation

Qwerty Ltd owners recognize that the organization will be faced with significant competition from its rivals in the near future, which will put pressure on the organization's gross margin; their customers are already discussing potential price reductions for next year. The owners have asked the procurement team to look into the potential of a 10% reduction on the company's cost of goods sold (COGS) calculation and to discover the impact on the ROCE %. Figure 6.8 illustrates the change in ROCE %.

Figure 6.8   The impact of a 10% reduction in Qwerty Ltd's cost of goods sold on ROCE percentage

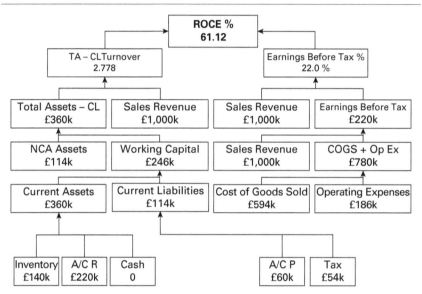

This initiative has reduced the COGS from £660k to £594k, a saving of £66k, as this change will have a direct impact on the company's EBIT, increasing it from £154k to £220k; therefore, the EBIT percentage will increase from 15.4% to 22.0%, with a resulting increase in the ROCE percentage to 61.12% (EBIT% * TA – CL turnover ratio = 22.0% * 2.778). The percentage uplift in the ROCE percentage is 42.87%.

SC initiative 2: to reduce the organization's accounts receivable by £60k

Qwerty Ltd's CEO has targeted the marketing and supply chain teams to reduce the cost of serving their customers and has asked them to reduce the cash tied up in the accounts receivable. The cash generated from this activity will be used to pay off the organization's long-term loan, which matures this year, and improve the business's gearing percentage. The impact on the company's ROCE percentage of a £60k reduction in their accounts receivable and the paying off of its long-term loan is illustrated in Figure 6.9.

Figure 6.9 The impact of a £60k reduction in Qwerty Ltd's accounts receivable on the ROCE percentage

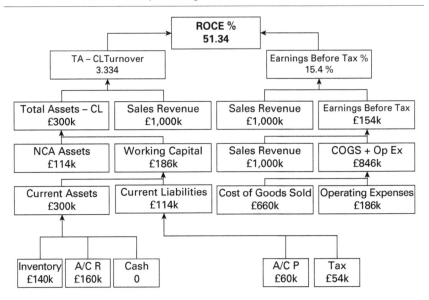

The company's accounts receivable have decreased from £220k to £160k; the injection in cash has been used to pay off the existing long-term loan of £60k. The £60k reduction in accounts receivable has reduced the organization's CA from £360k to £300k, which in turn has reduced Qwerty Ltd's WC (CA – CL) to £186k, resulting in the TA – CL reducing to £300k. The TA – CL turnover ratio has increased from 2.778 to 3.334 (sales revenue/ TA – CL = £1,000k/£300k), an increase of just over 20%; this has increased the company's ROCE percentage to 51.34%. This change has only impacted on the items in their BS.

SC initiative 3: a £60k reduction in inventories plus related inventory holding cost savings

A recent benchmarking exercise by the organization's CFO has revealed that the company's inventories were significantly higher than its competitors and that the company was also having to write off obsolescent components, which was having a negative impact on the company's earnings. The CFO is seeking a one-off reduction of £60k in the company's inventory levels; the cash liberated would be used to redeem the organization's long-term loan. The impact of the inventory reduction on the ROCE percentage is depicted in Figure 6.10.

Figure 6.10   A £60k inventory reduction and related inventory holding costs on the ROCE percentage

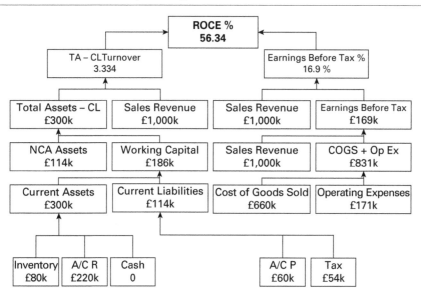

The £60k reduction in the level of the organization's inventories will have an impact on the company's BS, IS and its cash flow. The effect on the BS will be the same as the reduction in accounts receivable, with the TA – CL turnover ratio increasing to 3.334; however, with the inventory reduction there will also be a reduction in the costs of holding inventory. Typically the cost of holding inventory is on average 25% of its cost for a year. An inventory reduction of £60k will generate £15k savings in operating expenses in the income statement, therefore increasing the company's EBIT to £169k. The combined impact of the inventory reduction and the holding cost savings has increased the company's ROCE percentage to 56.34%.

SC initiative 4: an SC outsourcing opportunity that will reduce non-current assets by £60k

Qwerty Ltd's SC director has been approached by a third-party logistics operator with a proposal to outsource their current distribution operation, which would involve a reduction of £60k in NCA on the BS. There will also be operational savings including costs such as wages, fuel, depreciation, and so on, but there will be a management fee from the outsourcing company. The impact on Qwerty Ltd's ROCE is illustrated in Figure 6.11.

Figure 6.11 An SC outsourcing opportunity that will reduce non-current assets by £60k

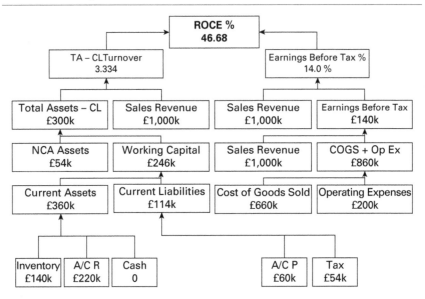

The company's NCA assets have been reduced by £60k to £54k, which has reduced the TA – CL to £300k, increasing the TA – CL turnover ratio to 3.334. However, the impact of the outsourcing decision has increased the company's operating costs by £14k to £200k, which has reduced the EBIT to £140k and the EBIT percentage to 14%. The outsourcing opportunity has had a positive impact on the ROCE %, increasing it to 46.68%; the reduction in NCA has outweighed the decrease in earnings, and the cash injection from the sale of the assets can be used to repay the company's long-term loan.

6.6 Supply chain management and ROCE

This section will identify and explore typical SC initiatives adopted by organizations that will have an impact on the ROCE's numerator and denominator. Examples taken from business will be incorporated to illustrate the relationship between SC decisions and financial performance.

Sales

An improvement in EBIT can also be achieved by increasing sales revenue, which typically focuses on price and quantity initiatives.

Price

- increasing price;
- developing value-adding services that can be charged, such as same-day deliveries;
- reducing the time to market for new product introductions;
- developing customer loyalty programme;
- improving product mix;
- enhancing customer service levels and charging appropriately;
- ensuring that you are charging for the activities a customer is consuming.

Quantity

- promotions;
- reduce customer churn;
- volume discounts to increase order size.

Cost reduction

There are numerous supply chain initiatives that practitioners can implement that will have a positive impact on reducing expenditure in their organization's income statement, including:

Revenue expenditure

Upstream supply chain initiatives

- Review your organization's incoterms.
- Consider moving to just in time (JIT) deliveries.
- Evaluate the adoption of vendor-managed inventories (VMIs).
- Review and rationalize supplier base.
- Consider changing suppliers.
- Reduce the cost of holding inventory.
- Review SC productivity and performance measures.
- Consider an inbound logistics outsourcing opportunity.
- Collaborate with suppliers to reduce your cost of goods sold.

- Reduce inbound packaging costs.
- Reduce obsolescence and inventory write-off.
- Reduce shrinkage and damages.

Conversion, manufacturing and production initiatives:

- Reduce waste and non-value activities in your processes.
- Reduce utilities costs by changing supplier or renegotiating with existing supplier.
- Increase productivity.
- Consider using toll manufacturers in the SC.
- Reduce indirect costs.

Downstream supply chain initiatives:

- Consider an outbound logistics outsourcing opportunity.
- Introduce driver skills training courses to reduce fuel, maintenance and tyre costs.
- Reconfigure network to optimize costs.
- Improve vehicle utilization by reducing empty running and increase back hauling.
- Collaborate with customers to increase vehicle utilization and increase drop sizes.
- Reduce customer returns and refusals.

Customer relationship management initiatives

- Reduce the cost of capturing a customer's order by moving away from manual process to electronic.
- Reduce the cost of serving different customers.
- Improve customer billing and invoice accuracy.

Post sales and returns management initiatives:

- Collaborate with other organizations to reduce the cost of reverse logistics.
- Pool and share spare parts with competitors to reduce cost of holding inventory.

Central support initiatives:

- Collaborate with other external organizations using shared services for central functions including payroll, HRM, training and development.
- Outsource non-core activities.

People management and remuneration initiatives:

- Review employee remuneration.
- Review employee ways of working to balance peaks and troughs across the organization.

Data management, communication and information technology initiatives:

- Consider cloud-based IT services when replacing ageing systems.
- Introduce RFID to track and trace inbound and outbound deliveries.
- Adopt shared service platforms.
- Data-share between SC collaborators.
- Consider block chain technology.
- Consider introducing analytics across the organization.

Supplier relationship management initiatives:

- Adopt target costing and total cost of ownership approaches to procurement decisions.
- Introduce supplier relationship management programmes with strategic suppliers.
- Adopt smart contracts.
- Introduce supply chain finance programmes to build financially sustainable SC networks.
- Audit your supplier base to avoid reputational damage to your brand.

Total assets – current liabilities

It is important to identify SC initiatives that impact on an organization's TA – CL on its BS.

Non-current asset initiatives:

- Remove redundant assets that remain on the BS.
- Change asset ownership and consider renting instead of owning.
- Consider outsourcing supply chain activities such as transport and distribution which will remove non-current assets off your BS.
- Migrate IT to cloud-based solutions, reducing non-current assets.

Current asset initiatives:

- Reduce inventories by adopting JIT or VMI.

- Reduce accounts receivable by introducing supply chain finance instruments.

Current liability initiatives:

- Review standard terms and conditions with suppliers to extend payment day.

- Introduce supply chain finance instruments to build financially sustainable supply chains.

The following examples are taken from practice and illustrate SC initiatives that are having a positive impact on the financial performance of organizations: the income statement and the balance sheet. FMCG organization The Procter & Gamble Company in 2017 (viii) highlighted areas where they were looking to reduce expenditure:

> We have plans to save up to $10 billion from fiscal year 2017 through fiscal year 2021. This is on top of the $10 billion saved from fiscal year 2012 through fiscal year 2016. There are four elements of our planned productivity savings: cost of goods sold, marketing spending, trade spending and overhead spending.

The second example focuses on the organization's BS (2017:46):

> Lower inventory generated $71 million of cash mainly due to supply chain optimizations, partially offset by increases to support business growth and increased commodity costs. Inventory days on hand decreased approximately 1 day primarily due to supply chain optimizations.

Conversely, the following quotation was taken from Marks & Spencer Group plc's (2018:2) annual report and illustrates the significant impact and contribution that the supply chain has on the financial performance of an organization:

> Our supply chains in both Clothing & Home and in Food require significant re-engineering. In fast-moving fashion this means we are slower than most of our major competitors to market and carry high levels of stock. Although online sales are growing, our online capability is behind the best of our competitors, and our fulfilment centre at Castle Donington has struggled to cope with peak demand. Our technology support is improving as we migrate off legacy systems and an old mainframe. In both main retail businesses, our customer base has narrowed and we have lost share of younger family-age customers.

Table 6.6 Marks & Spencer Group plc profitability ratios 2009–2018

Profitability ratios	2018	2017	2016	2015	2014	2013	2012	2011	2010	2009
Return on shareholders' funds (%)	2.26	5.59	14.19	18.75	21.44	22.52	23.58	29.20	32.40	33.92
Return on capital employed (%)	1.41	3.38	8.85	10.67	10.84	11.01	12.71	15.77	13.35	14.44
Gross margin (%)	37.83	38.48	39.11	38.65	37.54	37.86	37.80	38.24	37.94	37.21
EBIT margin (%)	1.46	2.38	5.53	6.80	6.74	7.54	7.51	8.59	8.93	9.61
EBITDA margin (%)	9.39	8.61	12.38	11.87	11.29	12.03	12.83	13.39	13.42	14.12

SOURCE Fame, published by Bureau van Dijk (2018)

Table 6.6 illustrates a set of profitability ratios for Marks & Spencer Group plc between 2009 and 2018. Over the 10-year period their return on capital employed has decreased from 14.44% in 2009 to 1.41% in 2018; likewise, their EBIT has also declined, which you would expect, as EBIT is included in the ROCE calculation. Interestingly, the gross margin percentage has been fairly consistent over the same period.

When these ratios are plotted on a graph, as illustrated in Figure 6.12, the trends of each of the five profitability ratios can be clearly seen over the 10 years.

Figure 6.12   Marks & Spencer Group plc profitability ratios 2009–2018

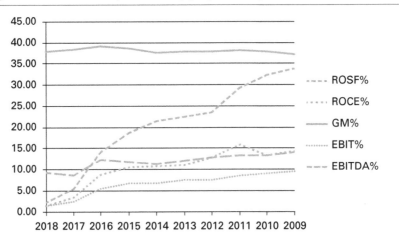

SOURCE Fame, published by Bureau van Dijk (2018)

The following quotation was taken from Marks & Spencer Group plc's 2018 (50) annual report; the heading of the section was 'Supply chain fit for purpose' and directly makes the link between the supply chain and business performance: 'In order to be a faster and more commercial business we must improve our supply chain, which is slow, inefficient and expensive.'

6.7 Supply chain management financial ratios

In this supply chain management (SCM) and financial ratios' case study, supply chain practitioners will be introduced to a set of financial ratios that they impact on or need to know. Typical financial ratios are grouped into different classifications, as illustrated in Table 6.7; you have already been introduced to some of these ratios in earlier chapters (Chapters 2 and 3).

Table 6.7 Financial ratio categories and their function

Category	Function
Profitability	Profitability ratios focus on measuring profit at prescribed points in the income statement, for example gross margin. They illustrate how an organization's top-line revenue has been eroded by different costs, eventually ending up at the organization's bottom line, its retained earnings. Other profitability ratios measure earnings as a percentage of the capital employed in the business (see ROCE and ROSF).
Liquidity	Liquidity ratios measure the proportion of an organization's short-term current assets with their short-term current liabilities (current ratio and acid-test ratio), providing an indication of whether they have sufficient assets to cover their liabilities if they fall due.
Working capital	These ratios focus on the variables that constitute working capital, including inventories, accounts receivable and accounts payable.
	They measure your average inventory held in days, the average time taken by your customers to pay you and the average time you take to pay your suppliers, and the time taken to recoup your cash back using the cash-to-cash cycle to calculate your liquidity gap.
Asset utilization	These ratios focus on the ability of different asset categories to generate sales revenue. They are calculated by dividing sales revenue by any asset category, for instance total asset turnover.
Productivity	These ratios measure different aspects of productivity, including sales per employee and different cost categories as a percentage of sales value.
Financial structure	Focuses on how the company is funded, in particular the relationship between the shareholder's funds and long-term debt, typically referred to as gearing.

Investment ratios have been excluded as typically SC practitioners tend not to be involved with this category of ratios.

Certain ratios can be calculated from a single financial statement, including EBIT percentage (IS) and the current ratio (BS); however, the majority of the ratios are derived from data in both the IS and BS, for example ROCE percentage and inventory days. Figure 6.13 illustrates the source of the financial statements used to calculate the various ratios.

Figure 6.13   Financial ratios and financial statements

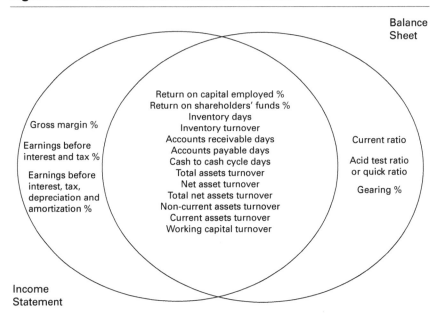

Balance Sheet

Return on capital employed %
Return on shareholders' funds %
Inventory days
Inventory turnover
Accounts receivable days
Accounts payable days
Cash to cash cycle days
Total assets turnover
Net asset turnover
Total net assets turnover
Non-current assets turnover
Current assets turnover
Working capital turnover

Gross margin %

Earnings before interest and tax %

Earnings before interest, tax, depreciation and amortization %

Current ratio

Acid test ratio or quick ratio

Gearing %

Income Statement

Table 6.8 illustrates a set of financial ratios by category, including the method of calculation, which are extremely useful for SC practitioners to explain the impact of their SC decisions on the financial performance of the organization and can be used to communicate the effect to the organization's top team.

Table 6.8   Financial ratios and calculation by category

Abbreviation	Profitability ratios
GM%	Gross margin % *(Gross profit/sales) *100*
EBIT%	Earnings before interest and tax % *(Earnings before interest and tax/sales) *100*
EAT%	Earnings after tax % *(Earnings after tax/sales) *100*
ROCE%	Return on capital employed % *(Earnings before interest and tax/average capital employed) *100*
ROTA%	Return on total assets % *(Earnings before interest and tax/total assets) *100*

(continued)

Table 6.8 (Continued)

ROE%	Return on equity % *(Earnings after interest and tax/Equity) *100*
EBITDA%	Earnings before interest, tax, depreciation and amortization % *(Earnings before interest, tax, depreciation and amortization/sales) *100*
Abbreviation	**Liquidity ratios**
CR	Current ratio *Current assets: Current liabilities*
AT	Acid-test ratio or quick ratio (Current assets – inventories): Current liabilities
Abbreviation	**Working capital ratios**
WC	Working capital *Current assets – Current liabilities*
INVD	Inventory days *(((Opening inventory + Closing inventory)/2)/cost of goods sold) *365*
ARD	Accounts receivable days *(((Opening receivables + Closing receivables)/2)/credit sales) *365*
APD	Accounts payable days *(((Opening payables + Closing payables)/2)/credit purchases) *365*
C2C	Cash-to-cash cycle days *Inventory days + Accounts receivable days – Accounts payable days*
Asset utilization	**Ratio**
INVT	Inventory turnover (per annum) *365/inventory days*
FAT	Fixed asset turnover *Sales/fixed assets*
TAT	Total asset turnover *Sales/total assets*
NCA + WCT	Non-current assets + working capital turnover *Sales/(non-current assets + working capital)*
NAT	Net assets turnover *Sales/(non-current assets + working capital – non-current liabilities)*

(continued)

Table 6.8   (*Continued*)

Abbreviation	Productivity ratios
COGS%	Cost of goods sold as a percentage of sales *(Cost of goods sold/sales) *100*
OPEX%	Operating expenses as a percentage of sales *(Operating expenses/sales) *100*
SPE	Sales per employee *Sales/number of employees*
EBITPE	Earnings before interest and tax per employee *Earnings before interest and tax /number of employees*

Abbreviation	Financial structure ratios
GR	Gearing ratio *(Non-current liabilities/capital employed) *100*
IC	Interest cover (times) *Earnings before interest and tax/interest paid*

Activity 6.1

The following information has been extracted from the report and accounts of FMCG Ltd for the period ending 31 March 20XX and is illustrated in Table 6.9.

Table 6.9   Financial data extracted from FMCG Ltd for the period ending 31 March 20XX

Account	£m
Accounts receivable	95
Cash	10
Cost of goods sold	30
Current liabilities	60
Intangible fixed assets	25
Inventories*	15
Non-current liabilities	40
Operating expenses	60
Reserves	80
Sales	150
Tangible fixed assets	75

*Use £15m to calculate inventory ratios.

Calculate the following:

1 the value of the shareholders' funds;

2 the value of the capital employed;

3 the earnings before interest and tax percentage;

4 the return on total assets – current liabilities percentage;

5 the value of the company's current assets;

6 the value of the company's working capital;

7 operating expenses as a percentage of sales;

8 non-current asset turnover ratio;

9 the value of total assets;

10 total asset turnover ratio;

11 the value of total net assets;

12 total net asset turnover ratio;

13 the value of total assets – current liabilities;

14 the total assets – current liabilities turnover ratio;

15 inventory days;

16 inventory turnover;

17 the current ratio;

18 the acid-test or quick ratio;

19 the gross profit margin;

20 the gearing percentage.

6.8 EBIT after asset charge (EAC)

An enhancement to the EBIT ratio is EBIT after asset charge (EAC); this ratio takes the EBIT generated by the organization in the financial year and then subtracts an asset charge. The asset charge effectively is the benefit that the organization could have received if it decided to invest its capital in an alternative investment opportunity instead of their organization. The asset charge is based on the weighted average cost of capital they could have earned from an alternative investment opportunity. If the EAC is positive after the asset charge, the organization has added value; if negative, value has been eroded.

An organization that is currently using EAC is Deutsche Post DHL (Deutsche Post World Net Annual Report 2007:8); their reasoning for adopting this financial ratio is as follows:

> We are introducing EBIT after asset charge as a new primary performance metric to focus all divisions on sustained value growth. From 1 January 2008, management incentives will also be tied to this metric. In this way, we aim to improve cash generation.

EAC will be applied across all their business divisions (Deutsche Post DHL Annual Report 2013:50) and will be used to compare divisional performance: 'Making the asset charge a part of business decisions encourages all divisions to use resources efficiently and ensures that the operating business is geared towards increasing value sustainably while generating cash flow.'

Table 6.10 illustrates the EAC for Deutsche Post DHL Group between 2015 and 2017 (Deutsche Post DHL Group Annual Report 2016:52 and 2017:55).

Table 6.10   Deutsche Post DHL Group EAC ratio 2015 to 2017

Financial year	2015	2016	2017
Earnings before interest and tax €m	2,411	3,491	3,741
minus asset charge €m	1,534	1,528	1,566
EBIT after asset charge (EAC) €m	877	1,963	2,175
Weighted average cost of capital (WACC) %	8.5	8.5	8.5

6.9 Summary

The aim of this chapter was to introduce you to the significant impact that your supply chain decisions will have on the financial performance of the organization and enable you to explain the relationship between the decisions you are planning to take and the financial ratios that are used by organizations to measure firm performance.

At the end of this chapter you are able to:

- recognize a set of the financial ratios which are used to measure different aspects of an organization's financial performance;
- identify the impact of your SC decisions on the financial performance of an organization.

- calculate a typical set of financial ratios that measure profitability, liquidity, asset utilization, working capital, productivity and financial structure;
- explain the relationship between supply chain decisions and an organization's return on capital employed;
- recognize the important linkages between an organization's financial statements and the different financial ratios used to evaluate financial performance.

6.10 References

Braithwaite, A and Christopher, M (2015) *Business Operations Models: Becoming a disruptive competitor,* 1st edn, Kogan Page, London

Brookson, S (2001) *Understanding Accounts,* Dorling Kindersley, London

Bureau van Dijk (2018) available at www.bvdinfo.com/en-gb/contact-us/office-locations (accessed 18th November 2018)

Christopher, M (1998) *Logistics and Supply Chain Management: Strategies for reducing cost and improving service networks,* 2nd edn, Pearson Education, Harlow

Christopher, M (2011) *Logistics and Supply Chain Management: Creating value-adding networks,* 4th edn, Pearson Education, Harlow

Deutsche Post DHL Group (2007) *Annual Report,* www.dpdhl.com/content/dam/dpdhl/en/media-center/investors/documents/annual-reports/dpwn_annual_report_2007_en.pdf (accessed 15 December 2018)

Deutsche Post DHL Group (2013) *Annual Report,* http://geschaeftsbericht2013.dpdhl.com/dpdhl_gb2013/static/export/docs/DPDHL_Annual_Report_2013.pdf (accessed 15 December 2018)

Deutsche Post DHL Group (2016) *Annual Report,* www.dpdhl.com/content/dam/dpdhl/en/investors/agm/2017/DPDHL_2016_Annual_Report.pdf (accessed 15 December 2018)

Deutsche Post DHL Group (2017) *Annual Report,* https://annualreport2017.dpdhl.com/downloads-ext/en/documents/DPDHL_2017_Annual_Report.pdf (accessed 15 December 2018)

Ellram, LM and Liu, B (2002) The financial impact of supply chain management, *Supply Chain Management Review,* 6 (6), pp 30–37

Forrester, JW (1958) Industrial dynamics: a major breakthrough for decision makers, *Harvard Business Review,* (July–August), pp 37–66

Marks & Spencer Group Plc (2018) *Annual Report and Financial Statements,* https://corporate.marksandspencer.com/annualreport (accessed 15 December 2018)

Mentzer, JT, Dewit, W, Keebler, JS, Min, S, Nix, NW, Smith, CD and Zacharia, ZG (2001) Defining supply chain management, *Journal of Business Logistics*, **22** (2), pp 1–25

Procter & Gamble Company (2017) *Form 10-K*, www.annualreports.com/ HostedData/AnnualReports/PDF/NYSE_PG_2017.pdf (accessed 15 December 2018)

6.11 Solutions to the activities

Activity 6.1 solution

Accounting equation = balance sheet = NCA + CA – CL = SC + R + NCL

Where:

NCA	non-current assets	Tangible = plant, property and equipment Intangible = goodwill
CA	current assets	Inventory, accounts receivables and cash
CL	current liabilities	Accounts payable, dividend payable and tax
SC	share capital	Ordinary share capital
R	reserves	Earnings
NCL	non-current liabilities	Long-term loans

To solve the questions, we need to balance the accounting equation in Table 6.11; however, there is one figure missing. We need to find the value of FMCG Ltd's share capital. Remember, the balance sheet shows where the company has raised its finance from and where it has gone into the business.

As non-current assets – working capital is equal to capital employed, the missing figure, which represents FMCG Ltd's share capital, will be £40m.

Table 6.11 Accounting equation

		To			=			From		
		Net assets			=			Capital employed		
NCA	+	CA	–	CL	=	SC	+	R	+	NCL
100	+	120	–	60	=	?	+	80	+	40
		160			=	?	+		120	

1 The value of the shareholders' funds is the total of the shareholders' capital and reserves; therefore the value will be £40m plus £80m, which is £120m.

2 The value of the capital employed is £160m.

3 The earnings before interest and tax (EBIT) percentage is calculated by dividing earnings before interest and tax by sales and multiplying by 100 to give a percentage. EBIT is £60m (sales – cost of goods sold – operating expenses) (EBIT/sales) * 100 = (£60m/£150m) * 100 = 40%.

4 The return on total assets less current liabilities percentage is the same as the return on capital employed (ROCE) percentage. ROCE is calculated by dividing EBIT by capital employed (CE) and multiplying by 100 to give a percentage. EBIT = £60m and CE = £160m, therefore ROCE percentage = (£60m/£160m) * 100 = 37.5%.

5 The value of FMCG Ltd's current assets is £120m (inventories + accounts receivable + cash).

6 Working capital (WC) is derived by subtracting current liabilities (CL) from current assets (CA), so for FMCG Ltd it's WC = CA – CL = £120m – £60m = £60m.

7 FMCG Ltd operating expenses (OPEX) as a percentage of sales is 40% [(OPEX/Sales) * 100].

8 The non-current asset turnover ratio for FMCG Ltd is 1.5; therefore £1 invested in non-current assets is producing £1.50 in sales revenue.

9 The value of the company's total assets (NCA + CA) is £220m.

10 The total asset turnover (TAT) ratio for the company is derived by dividing sales by the value of the company's total assets, which equates to 0.68 (£150m/£220m). Therefore, every £1 invested in total assets produces sales of £0.68.

11 The value FMCG Ltd's total assets – current liabilities (NCA + CA – CL) is £160m.

12 FMCG Ltd's total assets – current liabilities turnover (TA – CL) ratio is calculated by dividing sales by the company's total assets – current liabilities. This equates to 0.68 (£150m/£160m), so every £1 invested in total assets – current liabilities by the company generates £0.94 in sales revenue.

13 The value of total net assets (TNA) is £120m (NCA + CA – CL – NCL).

14 FMCG Ltd's net asset turnover ratio is 1.25 (£150m/£120m).

15 Inventory days (ID) is calculated by dividing the value of the company's inventory by the cost of goods sold value and multiplied by 365, the number of days in a year. The inventory days ratio for (£15m/£30m) * 365 = 182.5 days.

16 Inventory turnover (IT) is calculated by dividing the number of days in the year by the company's inventory days' ratio. FCMG Ltd's inventory turnover ratio is 2 (365/182.5), which means the business turns over its inventory twice a year.

17 The current ratio (CR) is the ratio between the company's current assets and current liabilities. The company's current ratio is 2:1 (£120m:£60m).

18 FMCG Ltd's acid-test (AT) or quick ratio (QR) is 1.75:1 (£105m:£60m). This ratio excludes inventories from the value of the company's current assets when compared with current liabilities.

19 The company's gross profit margin is 80%. The ratio is calculated by deducting the cost of goods sold from sales to derive gross profit, then gross profit is divided by sales and multiplied by 100 to generate the margin: (£120m/£150m) * 100.

20 The gearing percentage measures the amount of an organization's capital employed which is funded by non-current liabilities. The ratio is non-current liabilities divided by capital employed multiplied by 100 to give a percentage. FMCG Ltd's gearing percentage is 25%: (£40m/£160m) * 100.

6.12 Study questions

Study question 6.1

Using the information contained in Figures 6.14 and 6.15, calculate the financial ratios in Table 6. 12 for JIT plc for the financial year ending 31 March 20XX.

Figure 6.14 JIT plc – balance sheet as at 31 March 20XX

JIT plc – balance sheet as at 31 March 20XX	
Non-current assets	**£m**
Land and buildings	45
Fixtures and fittings	25
Plant and machinery	15
Motor vehicles	5
	90
Current assets	
Inventories	26
Accounts receivable	22
Cash	2
	50
Total assets	**140**
Equity	
£1 ordinary shares	30
Retained profit	40
	70
Non-current liabilities	
Long-term loan	30
Current liabilities	
Accounts payable	34
Taxation	6
	40
Total equity and liabilities	**140**

Figure 6.15 JIT plc – income statement as at 31 March 20XX

JIT plc – income statement for the year ending 31 March 20XX	£m
Revenue	**120**
Cost of sales	54
Gross profit	**66**
Operating expenses	30

(continued)

Figure 6.15 *(Continued)*

JIT plc – income statement for the year ending 31 March 20XX	£m
Operating profit	**36**
Interest paid	3
Earnings before tax	**33**
Taxation	9
Earnings after tax	**24**
Dividend	6
Retained earnings	**18**

Notes to Figures 6.14 and 6.15

1 JIT plc cost of goods sold calculation

	£m	£m
Revenue		120
Less cost of goods sold		
Opening inventory	28	
plus, purchases	52	
minus closing inventory	26	
equals cost of goods sold		54
Gross profit		**66**

2 JIT plc depreciation charge for year ending 31 March 20XX was £6m.

3 The company employs 1,000 people.

4 Opening balances:

- accounts receivable were £25m;
- accounts payable were £28m;
- capital employed was £80m.

Calculate the following financial ratios in Table 6.12 for JIT plc for the financial year ending 31 March 20XX.

Table 6.12 Financial ratios

Abbreviation	Profitability ratios
GM%	Gross margin %
EBIT%	Earnings before interest and tax %
EAT%	Earnings after tax %
ROCE%	Return on capital employed %
ROTA%	Return on total assets %
ROSF%	Return on shareholders' funds %
EBITDA%	Earnings before interest, tax, depreciation and amortization %
Abbreviation	**Liquidity ratios**
CR	Current ratio
AT	Acid-test ratio or quick ratio
Abbreviation	**Working capital ratios**
INVD	Inventory days
ARD	Accounts receivable days
APD	Accounts payable days
C2C	Cash-to-cash cycle days
Asset utilization	**Ratio**
INVT	Inventory turnover (per annum)
FAT	Fixed asset turnover
TAT	Total asset turnover
NCA+WCT	Non-current assets + working capital turnover
NAT	Net assets turnover
Abbreviation	**Productivity ratios**
COGS%	Cost of goods sold as a percentage of sales
OPEX%	Operating expenses as a percentage of sales
SPE	Sales per employee
EBITPE	Earnings before interest and tax per employee
Abbreviation	**Financial structure ratios**
GR	Gearing ratio
IC	Interest cover (times)

Study question 6.2

Identify five supply chain initiatives that an organization can implement that will improve its return on capital employed. For each initiative identified, describe how it will impact on the components of the return on capital employed calculation.

Study question 6.3

The information in Table 6.13 has been derived from the accounts of Ultra plc for the financial year ending 31 March 20XX.

Table 6.13   Financial data extract from Ultra plc's report and accounts March 20XX.

Account items	£m
Accounts receivable (average)	10
Cash	2
Current liabilities	8
Intangible fixed assets	5
Inventories	4
Long-term loan	10
Operating expenses	24
Reserves	7
Sales (credit sales)	30
Share capital	15
Tangible fixed assets	19

1 What is the company's current ratio?

  a 1.0:1.0

  b 1.5:1.0

  c 2.0:1.0

  d 2.5:1.0

2 What is the value of the company's capital employed?

  a £19 million

  b £24 million

  c £32 million

  d £40 million

3 What is the company's total asset turnover ratio (two decimal places)?

a 1.58

b 1.24

c 0.94

d 0.75

4 What is the average settlement period for accounts receivable (to the nearest day)?

a 31 days

b 60 days

c 90 days

d 122 days

5 What is the return on capital employed (ROCE) percentage for the company?

a 12.50%

b 15.00%

c 18.75%

d 25.00%

Study question 6.4

The information in Table 6.14 has been taken from the accounts of Mega plc for the financial year ending 31 December 20XX.

Use the data in the table to answer the following questions:

Table 6.14 Financial data extract from Mega plc's report and accounts December 20XX

Account items	£m
Accounts receivable	67
Cash	10
Accounts payable	45
Dividend payable	10
Inventories	33
Share capital	80

(continued)

Table 6.14   *(Continued)*

Account items	£m
Operating expenses	64
Reserves	25
Sales	160
Cost of goods sold	40
Non-current assets	85

1 What is the earnings before interest and tax (EBIT) percentage?

   a 25%

   b 30%

   c 35%

   d 40%

2 What are Mega plc's return on total assets – current assets and gross profit margin percentages?

   a 40% and 35%

   b 35% and 75%

   c 30% and 35%

   d 40% and 75%

3 What is the value of the non-current liabilities?

   a £25 million

   b £30 million

   c £35 million

   d £40 million

4 What is the value of the company's total assets?

   a £110 million

   b £85 million

   c £140 million

   d £195 million

5 What is the company's acid-test (quick) ratio?

a 2.0:1.0

b 1.4:1.0

c 1.0:1.0

d 0.4:1.0

6.13 Study question solutions

Study question 6.1 solution

Table 6.15 Financial ratios for JIT plc for the financial year ending 31 March 20XX

Abbreviation	Profitability ratios	Ratio
GM%	Gross margin % *(£66m/£120m) *100*	55.00%
EBIT%	Earnings before interest and tax % *(£36m/£120m) *100*	30.00%
EAT%	Earnings after tax % *(£24m/£120m) *100*	20.00%
ROCE%	Return on capital employed % *(£36m/£90m) *100*	40.00%
ROTA%	Return on total assets % *(£36m/£140m) *100*	25.71%
ROSF%	Return on equity % *(£24m/£70m) *100*	34.29%
EBITDA%	Earnings before interest, tax, depreciation and amortization % *(£42m/£120m) *100)*	35.00%
Abbreviation	**Liquidity ratios**	**Ratio**
CR	Current ratio *£50m:£40m*	1.25:1.00
AT	Acid-test ratio or quick ratio *(£50m – £26m):£40m*	0.6:1.00

(continued)

Table 6.15   *(Continued)*

Abbreviation	Working capital ratios	Ratio
INVD	Inventory days *(£27m/£54m) *365*	182.5 days
ARD	Accounts receivable days *(£23.5m/£120m) *365*	71.48 days
APD	Accounts payable days *(£31m/£52) *365*	217.60 days
C2C	Cash-to-cash cycle days *182.50 + 71.48 – 217.60*	36.38 days
Abbreviation	**Asset utilization ratios**	**Ratio**
INVT	Inventory turnover (per annum) *365/182.5 days*	2 times
FAT	Fixed asset turnover *£120m/£90m*	1.33 times
TAT	Total asset turnover *£120m/£140m*	0.86 times
NCA + WCT	Non-current assets + working capital turnover *£120m/£100m*	1.20 times
NAT	Net assets turnover *£120m/£70m*	1.71 times
Abbreviation	**Productivity ratios**	**Ratio**
COGS%	Cost of goods sold as a percentage of sales *£54m/£120m*	45%
OPEX%	Operating expenses as a percentage of sales *£30m/£120m*	25%
SPE	Sales per employee *£120m/1,000*	£120,000
EBITPE	Earnings before interest and tax per employee *£36m/1,000*	£36,000
Abbreviation	**Financial structure ratios**	**Ratio**
GR	Gearing ratio *£30m/£100m*	30.00%
IC	Interest cover (times) *£36m/£3m*	12 times

Study question 6.2 solution

Five supply chain initiatives that an organization can implement that will improve its return on capital employed are illustrated in Table 6.16.

Table 6.16   Supply chain initiatives and their impact on ROCE.

Initiatives	EBIT	TA - CL
Inventory reduction	Reduce the costs associated with holding inventory in the IS and therefore improve EBIT and ROCE.	Reduce CA on the BS and also TA – CL, which will have a positive impact on ROCE.
Extending accounts payable	No effect on EBIT	Increase CL on the BS and reduce TA – CL, which will have a positive impact on ROCE.
Outsourcing outbound logistics	Reduce the costs associated with owning the outbound logistics but will now incur a management fee from the third-party logistics operator; if the savings are greater than the fee, will be an improvement in EBIT and ROCE.	Reduce NCA on the BS and also TA – CL, which will have a positive impact on ROCE.
Reducing the cost to serve customers	Reduce the costs associated with serving customers will improve EBIT and ROCE.	No effect on TA – CL, only if NCA are reduced.
Reducing factory waste	Reducing the costs associated factory waste the costs will improve EBIT and ROCE.	No direct impact on TA – CL.

Study question 6.3 solution

Table 6.17   Ultra plc's accounting equation.

NCA	+	CA	–	CL	=	SC	+	R	+	NCL
24	+	16	–	8	=	15	+	7	+	10
Total assets – current liabilities = 32					=	Capital employed = 32				

Table 6.18 Ultra plc's EBIT calculation.

S	–	OpEx	=	EBIT
30	–	24	=	6

Table 6.19 Ultra plc current assets and current liabilities.

Current assets	£m	Current liabilities	£m
Inventories	4		
Accounts receivable	10		
Cash	2		
Total	**16**	Total	8

1 The company's current ratio is the ratio between its current assets and current liabilities.

Answer = C

2 The value of the company's capital employed is the sum of the shareholder funds plus its non-current liabilities. The company's capital employed is £32m, comprising shareholder funds (share capital and reserves) of £22m and non-current liabilities of £10m.

Answer = C

3 The company's total asset turnover ratio is derived by dividing sales by its total assets (non-current assets + current assets). The company's sales are £30m and its total assets are £40m, therefore its total asset turnover ratio is 0.75. Every £1 of total assets generates £0.75 in sales value.

Answer = D

4 The average settlement period for accounts receivable is calculated by dividing the average accounts receivable by the sales made on credit and then multiplied by 365 days. As we have limited information, we need to make a couple of assumptions. The first is that all sales are made on credit and as we have only a single figure for accounts receivable, we will take this figure as the average. Therefore, average accounts receivable = (£10m/£30m) * 365 = 122 days.

Answer = D

5 Return on capital employed (ROCE) percentage is calculated by dividing earnings before interest and tax (EBIT) from the income statement by the capital employed (CE) on the company's balance sheet, then multiplying by 100 to give a percentage. The ROCE for the organization will be (£6m/£32m) * 100 = 18.75%.

Answer = C

Study question 6.4 solution

Table 6.20   Mega plc's accounting equation.

NCA	+	CA	−	CL	=	SC	+	R	+	NCL
85	+	110	−	55	=	80	+	25	+	35
Total assets − current liabilities = 140					=	Capital employed = 140				

Table 6.21   Mega plc's EBIT calculation.

S	−	COGS	−	GP	−	OPEX	=	EBIT
160	−	40	−	120	−	64	=	56

Table 6.22   Mega plc current assets and current liabilities.

Current assets	£m	Current liabilities	£m
Inventories	33	Accounts payable	45
Accounts receivable	67	Dividend payable	10
Cash	10		
Total	110	Total	55

1 Mega plc's earnings before interest and tax (EBIT) percentage is calculated by dividing its EBIT (£56m) by sales (£160m) and then multiplying by 100 to give 35%.

Answer = C

2 The return on total assets − current liabilities (TA -CL) percentage is the same figure as the ROCE %. The company's TA − CL percentage is calculated by dividing EBIT (£56m)/TA − CL (£140m) multiplied by 100 = 40%.

The gross profit (GP) is derived from Mega plc's income statement, taking its gross profit (sales − COGS), which is £120m. GP (£120m) is then divided by sales (£160m) and multiplied by 100, which equals 75%.

The company's TA − CL percentage is 40% and its GP percentage is 75%.

Answer = D

3 The company's non-current liabilities (NCL) are the missing figure as they were not in the figures extracted from Mega's accounts. To find the value of the NCL, we change the subject of the accounting equation as NCL will be the balancing item.

NCL = TA − CL − share capital − reserves = £140m − £80m − £25m = £35m.

Answer = C

4 Mega plc's total assets are the sum of its non-current assets (£85m) plus current assets (£110m), which is £195m. The company's total asset turnover ratio is 0.82 (£160m/£195m).

Answer = D

5 The company's acid-test or quick ratio is the ratio between its current assets minus the value of its inventories compared with its current liabilities. The acid-test is a more rigorous liquidity ratio than the current ratio, as the value of current assets is reduced by deducting the company's inventory.

Mega plc's current assets (£110m) minus the value of its inventories (£33m) are £77m and its current liabilities are £55m; the ratio is £77m:£55m, which is 1.4:1.0.

Answer = B

Marginal costing 07

The concepts of marginal costing have been around in business since ancient times and are still being applied today to underpin costing and forecasting models used by numerous organizations that operate in a diverse range of industrial sectors, such as airlines, hotels, road freight and theatres – this list is not exhaustive.

This chapter introduces the concepts that underpin marginal costing, its applications in business, and its strengths and weaknesses as an approach to costing products and facilitating management decisions. Finally, its role as an enabler in improving relationships between internal functions, including accounting, sales, marketing and the supply chain community, is examined.

Now consider that you are formulating a business case for introducing a new product or service into the marketplace. It is essential that you are able to provide answers to the following questions, which you will typically be asked, either by your board of directors or potential investors:

- How much does the product cost to make?
- How many units do we need to sell to break even?
- What is the product's contribution per unit?
- What are the fixed costs of making the product?
- What is the product's margin of safety?
- How much profit will the product make if we sell X units?

First of all, don't panic! There may be a number of terms you are not familiar with, such as marginal cost, contribution, margin of safety and break even; this chapter will introduce and define them for you. Also, numerous examples and activities have been designed to help you grasp marginal costing.

7.1 Aim and objectives

The aim of this chapter is to recognize the value of applying a marginal costing approach to supply chain decisions.

At the end of this chapter you will be able to:

- identify the different types of cost that exist within a typical supply chain;
- recognize how changes in output impact on different cost types;
- define marginal cost;
- calculate a product's contribution per unit;
- calculate a product's break-even point, by formula and graphically;
- apply marginal costing to solve capacity problems with a single constraint;
- identify the strengths and weaknesses of applying marginal costing.

7.2 Different types of cost

This section introduces you to two main types of cost used in a marginal costing: fixed and variable. However, in the vocabulary of the business they often have many aliases. For instance, in road freight they are referred to as standing and running costs. We come across these different costs in our everyday life: for example, you have telephone line rental and usage costs on your telephone account; when you pick up a taxi at an airport or railway station to take you home, your taxi fare will contain fixed and variable cost elements. Let us now explore these cost types a little further.

Fixed cost

Fixed costs typically do not vary up or down with changes in output over a specific period of time. CIMA (2005:13) defines a fixed cost as: 'Cost incurred for an accounting period that within certain output or turnover limits, tends to be unaffected by fluctuations in the levels of activity (output or turnover).'

Road freight companies refer to these costs as standing costs, and Rushton *et al* (2006:421) define standing costs as:

> These costs will not vary over a fairly long period of time (say a year) and they are not affected by the activity of the vehicle, ie distance the vehicle runs over this period.

Table 7.1 illustrates the nature of fixed costs from two perspectives: as output increases, fixed costs remain constant; however, as output increases, the proportion of costs per unit decreases. The latter can lead to conflict between departments if manufacturing increases volume to get unit cost reductions, which then results in additional inventory being produced; there

Table 7.1 Fixed costs

Output units (000s)	0	10	20	30	40	50	60	70	80	90	100
Fixed cost £ (000s)	100	100	100	100	100	100	100	100	100	100	100
Fixed cost £ per unit	0	10.00	5.00	3.33	2.50	2.00	1.67	1.43	1.25	1.11	1.00

is now a trade-off between lower production costs and inventory holding costs that needs to be calculated, as the savings in production costs can be cancelled out by additional warehousing costs.

If you plot the coordinates relating to output and fixed cost on a graph, it will be a horizontal straight line that intercepts the vertical axis (y-axis) at some point above the origin and remains constant as output increases. In Figure 7.1 the fixed cost curve intercepts the y-axis at £100,000.

Figure 7.1 Fixed cost curve

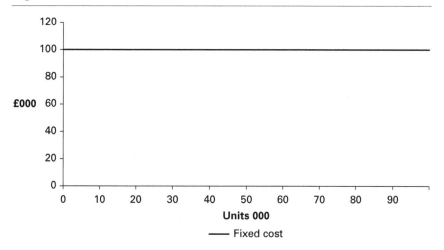

Fixed cost

If the fixed cost per unit (Table 7.1) was to be plotted on a graph, the curve would slope diagonally downwards from left to right; as output increases, the unit cost decreases.

Stepped fixed cost

A stepped fixed cost is where at certain levels of output there is need to incur additional fixed costs. For example, a road haulage company has secured a new contract, increasing demand for its services, so the business needs to purchase an additional truck. Or customer demand increases for an online retailer, so another distribution centre is needed to hold inventory to meet increasing customer demand and maintain customer service levels, resulting in a stepped fixed cost increase. As the cost's name implies, the curve is stepped in nature, beginning above the origin on the y-axis, and is constant for a given level of output until, at a specific point on the x-axis, the curve increases vertically as additional fixed costs are incurred and then the curve remains constant again until the next point in time when it shifts vertically when fixed costs increase once more, as illustrated in Figure 7.2.

Figure 7.2   Stepped fixed cost curve

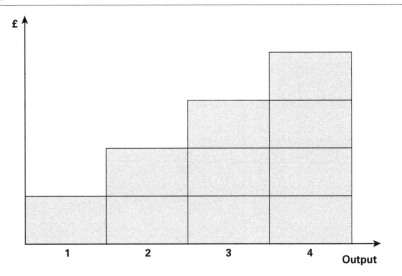

Everyday examples of step costs include car parking charges or traveling on the London Underground. Let's take a journey on the London Tube.

Our journey on the Metropolitan line starts from Aldgate station in central London and terminates at Amersham in Buckinghamshire. Our journey takes us 1 hour and 8 minutes; we stop at 22 stations and travel across 9 fare zones. A typical zonal pricing policy for different journeys starting at station 1 is illustrated in Table 7.2.

Variable cost

CIMA (2005:13) defines a variable cost as a 'cost that varies with a measure of activity'. A variable cost increases in direct proportion to changes in output; for instance, the greater the distance travelled, the more fuel is consumed by a truck. Road freight operators refer to these costs as running costs. In manufacturing, raw material costs are typical variable costs; just

Table 7.2   Zonal pricing on a tube journey

Starting station	Terminating station	Starting zone	Terminating zone	£
1	2	A	A	5.00
1	4	A	B	5.00
1	7	A	D	6.00
1	10	A	E	6.00
1	12	A	F	7.00
1	15	A	G	7.00
1	18	A	H	9.00
1	20	A	I	9.00

take a look at any product's bill of materials (BOM), which breaks down a product into its constitute components, for example your mobile phone or ingredients of your favourite chocolate bar. Table 7.3 illustrates a BOM for making a unit of product ZX12.

Table 7.3   ZX12 bill of materials

Component	Price	Quantity
AB67	£2.50	10
AZ67	£3.60	5
BK12	£0.90	20

If the company makes a batch of 100 units, the total raw material cost will be £6,100 as the sub-components increase in proportion with the number of ZX12 produced, as illustrated in Table 7.4.

Table 7.4   Variable cost ZX12

Component	Price per unit	Quantity	ZX12 cost per unit	ZX12 – 100 units
AB67	£2.50	10	25.00	2,500
AZ67	£3.60	5	18.00	1,800
BK12	£0.90	20	18.00	1,800
ZX12		**1**	**61.00**	**6,100**

Graphically, a variable cost curve begins at the origin, has a positive gradient and increases at a constant rate, as depicted in Figure 7.3.

Figure 7.3 Variable cost curve for ZX12

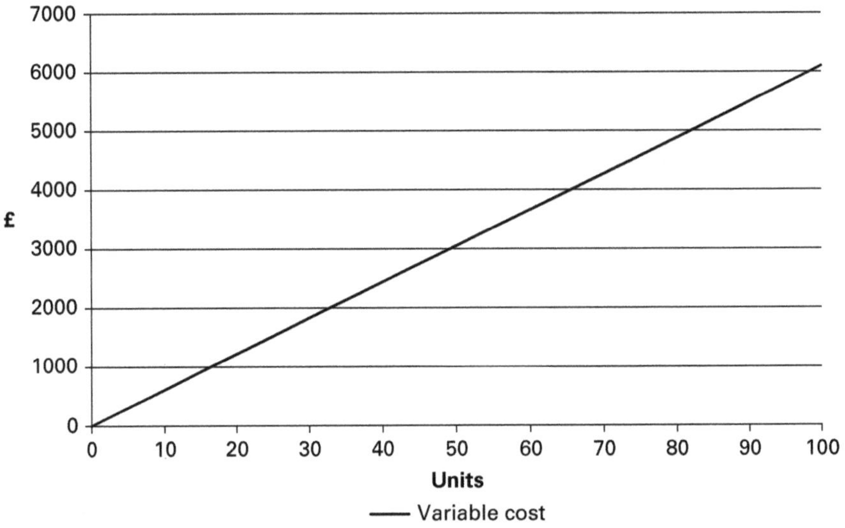

The variable cost per unit, if plotted, would be a horizontal straight line as the cost per unit is constant as output increases.

Now have a go at the following activity.

Activity 7.1

Try to identify as many standing (fixed) and running (variable) costs for a road haulage company as you can in Table 7.5.

Compare your list with mine at the end of this chapter.

Table 7.5 Standing and running costs

List as many different standing and running costs for a road haulage company as you can.	
Standing costs	**Running costs**

Marginal cost

CIMA (2005:13) defines a marginal cost as 'the part of the cost of one unit of product or service, which would be avoided if that unit were not produced, or which would increase if one extra unit were produced'. In marginal costing, the marginal cost is the same as the variable cost.

Total cost

A total cost contains elements of fixed and variable costs; for example, a taxi fare will contain fixed costs which can include a charge for luggage, a time charge for out of hours and road tolls. These costs don't typically increase as the distance travelled increases. However, your taxi fare contains a variable cost, which is based on a complex formula relating to time and distance travelled. Another example is a utility account, which has a standing cost and also a variable charge based on consumption.

7.3 Break-even analysis

Finding a product's break-even point is important to any business, because at this unique point the product does not make a profit, but neither does it make a loss. It is the tipping point where a product's sales revenues are equal to the total costs of making the product; this single point is the product's break-even point.

The break-even point can be derived graphically and also by formula. In this section both methods are introduced.

The graphical method

Table 7.6 Product XX6

Forecast	Sales units	Sales revenue £	Total cost £	Profit/ loss £
High	75,000	1,500,000	1,300,000	200,000
Low	25,000	500,000	700,000	−200,000

You are given forecast data for a new product XX6 in Table 7.6. We do not know the product's variable cost per unit, fixed costs, or its selling price per unit, but we have been given by the marketing team two forecasts which can be used to solve this problem. Both the sales revenue and total cost curves are straight lines and data in Table 7.6 can be used to derive coordinates for each curve.

Sales revenue coordinates are (25,000:500,000) and (75,000:1,500,000).

Total cost coordinates are (25,000:700,000) and (75,000:1,300,000).

You can now plot these coordinates on a graph, as illustrated in Figure 7.4, and, connecting each pair by a straight line, you have a revenue curve and a total cost curve. If you extend the total cost line to intercept the vertical axis, you will derive the product's fixed costs; the gradient on the line represents the variable cost per unit. If you extend the sales revenue line downwards and to the left, it will pass through the origin of the graph; at this point sales revenue and the number of units sold will be zero and the gradient of the line is the selling price per unit.

The break-even point occurs when the sales revenue curve intersects the total cost curve. To the left of the break-even point, the sales revenue line is below the total cost curve and the product is losing money; to the right of the break-even point, where the sales revenue curve is above the total cost curve, the product is making a profit, as illustrated in Figure 7.4.

Figure 7.4   Product XX6 break-even chart

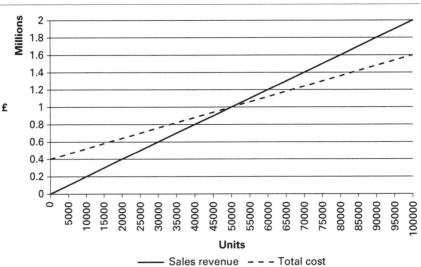

Drawing a vertical line downwards from the break-even point to the x-axis indicates the level of sales units required to break even; a horizontal line from the break-even point to the y-axis gives you the value of sales needed to break even. The vertical distance between the sales revenue curve and the total cost curve represents the profit for a given level of output on the x-axis to the right on the break-even point; conversely, the distance between the two lines represents the amount of loss made to the left of the break-even point.

Product XX6's break-even point will be when 50,000 units are sold, which will generate sales revenue of £1,000,000 for the business.

Alternatively, we can draw a profit/loss chart (see Figure 7.5), which can find the break-even point with just a single line by plotting the profit coordinates for the two forecasts from Table 7.6. Your x-axis is units produced and your y-axis represents profit/loss. The profit coordinates are (25,000: –200,000) and (75,000:200,000); now connect these two sets of coordinates with a straight line and then extend the line diagonally downwards to the left. The line will intercept the x-axis, which is the break-even point, and then continue your line until it intercepts the y-axis, which derives your fixed costs.

Figure 7.5   Profit/loss chart

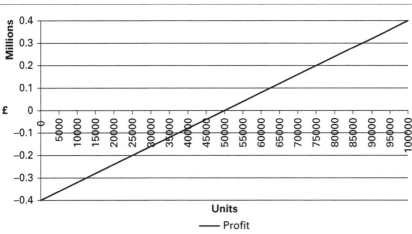

The break-even point for product XX6 can be now be derived at the point where the profit line intercepts the x-axis, which will be 50,000 units. When the curve intercepts the y-axis, the fixed costs for making XX6 are revealed, which are £400,000. The gradient of the profit line equates to the contribution of £8 per unit up to the break-even point to cover fixed costs; after the break-even point, contribution becomes profit of £8 per unit.

By formula

The break-even point can also be derived by formula using a seven-stage approach, as explained in the marginal costing approach in Table 7.7.

Table 7.7   Marginal costing seven-stage approach

Stage	Activity	Method
1	Calculate the variable cost of making the product.	Variable cost per unit = change in total cost divided by the change in quantity = Δ Cost/Δ Quantity.
2	Calculate the product's selling price per unit.	Selling price per unit = change in revenue divided by the change in quantity = Δ Revenue/Δ Quantity.
3	Derive the fixed costs of making the product.	Total cost = fixed cost + (variable cost per unit * quantity). Therefore, by changing the subject of the formula we get fixed cost = total cost – (variable cost per unit * quantity).
4	Calculate the contribution per unit.	Contribution per unit = selling price per unit – variable cost per unit.
5	Determine the break-even point.	The break-even point in units is calculated by dividing fixed costs by contribution per unit. To find the break-even point in sales revenue, the number of units is then multiplied by selling price per unit.
6	Calculate the forecast profit.	The forecast profit is calculated by multiplying contribution per unit by the forecast quantity sold to arrive at total contribution, and then subtracting fixed costs to derive the forecast profit.
7	Determine the product's margin of safety.	The margin of safety can be calculated in units by taking the forecast sales in units and subtracting the number of units at the break-even point. The margin of safety in sales revenue is calculated by multiplying the number of units by its selling price.

Using the data for product XX6 in Table 7.6 and the marginal cost approach stages 1 to 5, we can calculate the break-even point (Table 7.7). The first stage is to calculate the differences between the two forecasts, as illustrated in Table 7.8.

Table 7.8   Product XX6 differences between high and low forecasts

Forecast	Sales units	Sales revenue	Total cost
High	75,000	1,500,000	1,300,000
Low	25,000	500,000	700,000
Difference	50,000	1,000,000	600,000

The remaining stages are illustrated in Table 7.9.

Table 7.9 Marginal costing seven-stage approach for product XX6

Stage 1	Variable cost per unit = £600,000/50,000 = £12 per unit
Stage 2	Selling price per unit = £1,000,000/50,000 = £20 per unit
Stage 3	Total cost – (variable cost per unit * quantity) = fixed costs £1,300,000 – (£12*75,000) = £400,000
Stage 4	Selling price per unit – variable cost per unit = contribution per unit £20 – £12 = £8
Stage 5	Break-even point in units = fixed costs/contribution per unit £400,000/£8 = 50,000 units and in sales revenue equates to £1,000,000
Stage 6	If the company actually sells 65,000 units, we can now calculate the profit. £8 * 65,000 = £520,000 – £400,000 = £120,000
Stage 7	Margin of safety = 65,000 – 50,000 = 15,000 units and sale revenue of £300,000.

Now have a go at Activity 7.2. The solution can be found in section 7.9.

Activity 7.2

Ultra-Manufacturing Ltd has produced the following information regarding the future production of their new product QT45 in Table 7.10.

Table 7.10 Product QT45 forecast

Forecast	Low	Medium	High
Sales units	300,000	600,000	900,000
Sales revenue	£3,600,000	£7,200,000	£10,800,000
Total costs	£5,000,000	£6,200,000	£7,400,000

1 For each of the three forecasts, calculate the expected profit.

2 What is the variable cost of making a unit of QT45?

3 What are the total fixed costs?

4 Calculate the break-even point in terms of units sold and sales revenue.

5   How much profit will the company make if they achieve sales of 725,000 units?

6   The company is considering a change to its manufacturing process which will increase its variable costs by £2 per unit and result in a saving of £2,000,000 of fixed costs. What will be the impact on the company's profit at 725,000 units, its break-even point and margin of safety?

7.4 Limiting factor analysis

Contribution analysis can be used to solve problems when a business is faced with an unplanned constraint, such as:

- machine breakdown:
- shortage in materials;
- reduction in labour hours due to illness or a dispute.

Marginal costing can identify the optimum production mix that needs to be produced to maximize profitability given the constraint. Contribution per limiting factor is used to decide which products should be made and the order in which they are produced. The limiting factor ratio is calculated by dividing the contribution £ per unit by the limiting factor £ per unit. The product ratios are ranked and the product with the highest ratio is produced first, then the second highest and so on, until the entire limiting factor is consumed. Table 7.11 illustrates the limiting ratio calculation and the ranking process; in this example the limiting factor is a shortage of raw materials that are required to produce all three products.

Table 7.11   Limiting factor ratios

Product	Alpha	Beta	Gamma
Contribution £ per unit	10.00	12.00	8.00
Raw material £ per unit	4.00	6.00	2.00
Limiting factor ratio	2.50	2.00	4.00
Ranking	2	3	1

Gamma has the highest limiting factor ratio and would be manufactured first, as every £1 spent on raw materials returns £4 in contribution, followed by Alpha, then Beta.

Activity 7.3 explores contribution analysis and the limiting factor ratio further by following a logical process:

1 Calculate variable cost per unit.

2 Calculate contribution per unit.

3 Calculate limiting factor ratio.

4 Rank the products according to the highest limiting factor ratio.

5 Calculate the quantity of production for each product until the limiting factor is consumed.

Now have a go at Activity 7.3. The solution can be found in section 7.9.

Activity 7.3

Opal Productions Ltd has prepared its budget for the next financial year for their product portfolio, as illustrated in Table 7.12.

Table 7.12　Production budget

Product	QW3	XC9	RX8	GA2
Sales units	3,000	3,000	3,000	3,000
Price per unit	200	220	250	155
Direct labour cost £ per unit	38	36	34	57
Direct materials cost £ per unit	40	50	60	25
Direct expenses £ per unit	2	4	6	3

Total fixed costs are £1,000,000 and raw material costs are £5 per kg.

1 Calculate the Opal Productions Ltd profit for the year ending 31 December 20XX.

2 The company has been sent an urgent email from their raw material supplier that because of a machine breakdown they are only able to supply 80% of the company's needs for the year. Calculate the forecast production mix that will maximize profitability given the constraint.

7.5 Inventory valuation

As you have seen in Activities 7.2 and 7.3, marginal costing does not charge fixed costs to individual products, as they are kept separate. When using marginal costing, inventory is valued at marginal cost only, not full cost. This is an important issue, as inventory, according to financial accounting, is 'valued at the lower of cost or net realizable value'; however, not all of the costs of making the product are included in the marginal cost valuation as fixed costs are excluded. Therefore, if inventory is carried forward to the next accounting period, only the marginal cost of making the inventory moves into the next accounting period. The fixed costs remain in the previous accounting period and this does not meet the matching concept, as sales revenue is now not matched with the costs associated with making the product in the same accounting period.

A company manufactures 1,000 units of product XYZ each month. The product's selling price is £15 per unit and has a cost of £5 per unit; the fixed costs for the period are £5,000 per month. In March the company sells 800 units and 1,200 units in April. Table 7.13 illustrates the income statements for both months.

Table 7.13   Marginal costing and inventory valuation

March sales		800 * £15 = £12,000
Less cost of goods sold		
Opening inventory	0	
Plus production	1,000 * £5 = £5,000	
Minus closing inventory	200 * £5 = £1,000	800 * £5 = £4,000
Contribution		£8,000
Fixed costs		£5,000
Profit for the period		£3,000
April sales		1,200 * £15 = £18,000
Less cost of goods sold		
Opening inventory	200 * £5 = £1,000	
Plus production	1,000 * £5 = £5,000	
Minus closing inventory	0	1,200 * £5 = £6,000
Contribution		£12,000
Fixed costs		£5,000
Profit for the period		£7,000

In Table 7.13, the profit for March is reduced because the whole of the fixed costs of making the 1,000 units is charged against sales of 800 units. But in April the profits are increased, as 1,200 units are sold and the opening inventory valuation from the previous month does not contain the full costs of making the products, just the marginal costs.

7.6 Practical applications of marginal costing in supply chains

The principles of marginal costing in conjunction with revenue management are used in a variety of supply chain situations across different industrial sectors for managing products and services, including:

- introducing new products;
- allocating a limited resource;
- off-peak transport pricing;
- pricing tickets and load factors on flights;
- road freight pricing for backhaul;
- hotel room pricing at weekends;
- meal deals at restaurants;
- ticket pricing for theatre, conferences and charity fundraising events.

Marginal costing, however, has its weaknesses, as in business we don't live in a straight-line world. A product's selling price is not always constant, as buyers ask for quantity discounts, and variable costs per unit are not always constant, as raw material prices vary due to supply and demand factors; for example, oil prices and labour rates can also change by government policy. Fixed costs are not always constant during a period and they can be stepped as output increases, which has implications for break-even analysis.

A key strength of marginal costing is its important role as enabler of improving relationships between internal functions within an organization, including accounting, sales, marketing and the supply chain community, especially if the business is introducing a new product or launching a new service. Marginal costing can be used to collect costing data, confirm assumptions, communicate information between functions and coordinate inter-departmental activities, such as the impact of different scenarios on the product's break-even point.

7.7 Summary

In this chapter you are now aware of the different types of cost that are typically found in a supply chain operation: fixed and variable. You have seen how changes in output impact on these different cost types. You now recognize that in accounting, marginal cost is the same as the variable cost. You are also able to calculate a product's contribution per unit. You can now derive the break-even point for a product or service by formula and graphically. You can apply marginal costing to solve capacity problems with a single constraint and can identify the strengths and weaknesses of applying marginal costing in practice.

7.8 References

CIMA (2005) *CIMA Official Terminology*, CIMA Publishing, Oxford
Rushton, A, Croucher, P and Baker, P (2006) *The Handbook of Logistics and Distribution Management*, 3rd edn, Kogan Page, London

7.9 Solutions to the activities

Activity 7.1 solution

Standing and running costs, which are associated with road haulage operations, are illustrated as follows:

Standing costs	Running costs
• insurance;	• fuel;
• driver costs;	• tyres;
• depreciation;	• lubricants;
• licences;	• maintenance.
• maintenance.	

Activity 7.2 solution

1 For each of the three forecasts, subtract total costs from sales revenue to derive the expected profit or loss as illustrated in Table 7.14.

Table 7.14   QT45 profit/loss by forecast sales

QT45 forecast	Low	Medium	High
Sales revenue £	3,600,000	7,200,000	10,800,000
Minus total costs £	5,000,000	6,200,000	7,400,000
Equals profit or loss £	−1,400,000	1,000,000	3,400,000

2 The variable cost per unit can be calculated by dividing the change in total cost by the change in output between a higher and lower scenario (see Table 7.15), such as:

- high–low;
- high–medium;
- medium–low.

Table 7.15   QT45 variable cost per unit and selling price per unit

Forecast	Sales units	Total costs £	Sales revenue £
High	900,000	7,400,000	10,800,000
Low	300,000	5,000,000	3,600,000
Difference	600,000	2,400,000	7,200,000
QT45 £ per unit		4	12

In this example the difference between the high and low forecasts has been used. The variable cost of a unit of QT45 is £4 per unit and its selling price is £12.

3 The fixed costs can now be calculated by rearranging the following formula:

total costs = fixed costs + (variable cost per unit * output) into
fixed costs = total costs − (variable cost per unit *output),
            so for 300,000 units
fixed costs = £5,000,000 − (£4 * 300,000) = £3,800,000,
            just check for 600,000 units
fixed costs = £7,400,000 − (£4 * 900,000) = £3,800.000.

4 The break-even point in units can be calculated by dividing the fixed costs by contribution per unit. The contribution per unit is £12 − £4 = £8; therefore every unit will contribute £8 to cover the business's fixed costs.

The break-even points can now be calculated by dividing £3,800,000 by £8, which equals 475,000 units, and when multiplied by £12 equates to £5,700,000 in sales revenue.

5 If the company sales are 725,000, the expected profitability will be as follows:

profit = (contribution per unit * sales units) – fixed costs
(£8 * 725,000) – £3,800,000 = £2,000,000 profit.

6 The change to the current manufacturing process will increase variable costs by £6 per unit, but reduce fixed costs by £2,000,000, as shown in Table 7.16.

Table 7.16   QT45 scenarios

	Current	Proposed
Sales units	725,000	725,000
Sales revenue £	8,700,000	8,700,000
Variable costs £	2,900,000	4,350,000
Contribution £	5,800,000	4,350,000
Fixed costs £	3,800,000	1,800,000
Profit £	2,000,000	2,550,000
Contribution per unit £	8	6
Break-even point units	475,000	300,000
Break-even point sales revenue £	5,700,000	3,600,000
Margin of safety units	250,000	425,000
Margin of safety sales revenue £	3,000,000	5,100,000

The proposed change will improve the profitability of the business by £550,000, as the increase in variable costs is offset by a great reduction in the company's fixed costs. The break-even point and margin of safety have also improved by the proposed change to the manufacturing process.

Activity 7.3 solution

1 If Opal Productions Ltd achieves its budget, the business will make a profit before tax of £410,000. Table 7.17 shows the breakdown per product.

Table 7.17   Opal Productions Ltd budgeted profit

Product	QW3	XC9	RX8	GA2	Total
Sales revenue £	600,000	660,000	750,000	465,000	2,475,000
Variable cost £	240,000	270,000	300,000	255,000	1,065,000
Contribution £	360,000	390,000	450,000	210,000	1,410,000
Fixed costs £					1,000,000
Profit £					410,000

2 The forecast production mix that will maximize profitability given the raw material constraint is illustrated in Table 7.18.

Table 7.18   Opal Productions Ltd limiting factor ratio calculations

Product	QW3	XC9	RX8	GA2
Sales units	3,000	3,000	3,000	3,000
Price per unit	200	220	250	155
Direct labour cost £ per unit	38	36	34	57
Direct materials cost £ per unit	40	50	60	25
Direct expenses £ per unit	2	4	6	3
Total variable cost £ per unit	80	90	100	85
Contribution £ per unit	120	130	150	70
Limiting factor ratio	3.00	2.60	2.50	2.80
Ranking	1	3	4	2

The forecast production mix that will maximize profitability given the raw material constraint is illustrated in Table 7.19.

Table 7.19   Opal Productions Ltd forecast production mix

Product	QW3	XC9	RX8	GA2	Total
Kg per unit	8	10	12	5	
Total kg required	24,000	30,000	36,000	15,000	105,000
Total kg available	24,000	30,000	15,000	15,000	84,000
Production units	3,000	3,000	1,250	3,000	

Given the raw material constraint, the company's profit before tax will now be £147,500, as illustrated in Table 7.20, a reduction of £262,500, which equates to the contribution of 1,750 units of RX8 (1,750 * £150), which could not be produced.

Table 7.20   Opal Productions Ltd revised profit forecast based on raw material constraint

Product	QW3	XC9	RX8	GA2	Total
Sales revenue £	600,000	660,000	312,500	465,000	2,037,500
Variable cost £	240,000	270,000	125,000	255,000	890,000
Contribution £	360,000	390,000	187,500	210,000	1,147,500
Fixed costs £					1,000,000
Profit £					**147,500**

7.10 Study questions

Study question 7.1

You are planning to introduce a new product; the forecast has been supplied to you in Table 7.21 from the marketing team.

Table 7.21   Product forecast

Demand	Units	Total cost	Total revenue
Low	25,000	£600,000	£500,000
High	60,000	£1,020,000	£1,200,000

1 What is the variable cost of making the new product?

   A £20

   B £10

   C £12

   D £8

2 What are the fixed costs of making the product?

   A £600,000

   B £500,000

   C £400,000

   D £300,000

3 How many units need to be sold to break even?

   A 75,000

   B 62,500

C 37,500

D 25,000

4 How much profit will be made if the company sells 45,000 units?

A £120,000

B £90,000

C £60,000

D £30,000

5 If the company sells 42,500 units, what is their margin of safety in sales value?

A £100,000

B £80,000

C £60,000

D £40,000

Study question 7.2

Revenue and costing information has been provided by Ultra plc in Table 7.22 for their four products.

Table 7.22   Product data

Product	Red	Green	Yellow	Blue
Sales units	5,000	5,000	5,000	5,000
Price per unit	£333	£367	£417	£267
Direct labour cost per unit	£63	£60	£57	£95
Direct materials cost per unit	£67	£83	£100	£42
Direct expenses per unit	£3	£7	£10	£5

1 Which product produces the highest contribution per unit?

A Red

B Green

C Yellow

D Blue

2 Which product produces the lowest contribution per unit?

A Red

B Green

C Yellow

D Blue

3 If direct materials are the limiting factor, which product has the lowest limiting factor ratio per unit?

A Red

B Green

C Yellow

D Blue

4 If direct labour is the limiting factor, which product has the highest limiting factor ratio per unit?

A Red

B Green

C Yellow

D Blue

5 If direct expenses are the limiting factor, which product has the highest limiting factor ratio per unit?

A Red

B Green

C Yellow

D Blue

Study question 7.3

You have been supplied with the information in Table 7.23 regarding a new product OE 52 from marketing and production.

Table 7.23 Product OE 52 data

Forecast	Units sold	Total cost	Sales revenue
Low	6,000	860,000	600,000
Medium	12,000	1,220,000	1,200,000
High	18,000	1,580,000	1,800,000

Draw a profit/loss chart to calculate the following:

1 the break-even point in terms of units sold;

2 the fixed costs;

3 the margin of safety in terms of units sold and sales revenue if 20,000 units are sold;

4 the expected profit the company could make if they achieve sales of 20,000 units.

Study question 7.4

Qwerty plc has supplied you with a forecast in Table 7.24 for the next month's sales for the five products they manufacture at their factory.

The cost of a kg of variable material is £0.25 and the fixed costs for the month are £48,000.

Table 7.24 Product data

September 20XX	ZA1	BC4	CH6	DK3	EE7
Forecast monthly sales (units)	4,000	3,000	1,000	5,000	2,000
Selling price £ per unit	10	12	18	20	24
Variable material cost £ per unit	2	6	4	8	10
Other variable costs £ per unit	3	4	6	4	6

1 Calculate the forecast profit for the month if the company achieves the sales forecast for its five products.

2 To make the monthly forecast, the company requires 360,000kg of materials. Unfortunately, the major supplier of raw materials has had a production problem and can only supply Qwerty plc with 288,000kg. You are required to calculate the production mix that will maximize profitability for the month.

7.11 Study question solutions

Study question 7.1 solution

1 The variable cost per unit can be calculated by dividing the change in total cost by the change in output between a higher and lower scenario, as illustrated in Table 7.25.

variable cost per unit = £420,000/35,000 = £12 per unit

Answer = C

Table 7.25 Variable cost per unit

Forecast	Sales units	Total costs £	Total revenue £
High	60,000	1,020,000	1,200,000
Low	25,000	600,000	500,000
Difference	35,000	420,000	700,000

2 The fixed costs can now be calculated by rearranging the following formula:

total costs = fixed costs + (variable cost per unit * output) into
fixed costs = total costs – (variable cost per unit *output) so for
        60,000 units
fixed costs = £1,020,000 – (£12 * 60,000) = £300,000, just check for
        25,000 units
fixed costs = £600,000 – (£12 * 25,000) = £300,000.

Answer = **D**

3 The break-even point in units can be calculated by dividing the fixed costs by contribution per unit. The contribution per unit is calculated by taking the selling price per unit of £20 and deducting the variable cost of £12 to give a contribution of £8 per unit. Therefore, every unit will contribute £8 to cover the business's fixed costs. The break-even points can now be calculated by dividing £300,000 by £8, which equals 37,500 units, and when multiplied by £20 equates to £750,000 in sales revenue.
   The company would need to sell 37,500 units to break even.
Answer = **C**

4 If the company sales are 45,000 units, they expect profitability will be as follows:

profit = (contribution per unit * sales units) – fixed costs
(£8 * 45,000) – £300,000 = £60,000 profit.

Answer = **C**

5 The margin of safety can be calculated in units by taking the forecast sales in units, which is 42,500, and then subtracting the number of units at the break-even point, 37,500, which equates to 5,000 units. The margin of safety in sales revenue is calculated by multiplying the margin of safety in units by its selling price per unit, which will be £20 by 5,000 units equals £100,000.
   Therefore, if the company sells 42,500 units, its margin of safety in sales value will be £100,000.
Answer = **A**

Study question 7.2 solution

The first thing to do is to calculate the contribution per unit for each product, as illustrated in Table 7.26.

Table 7.26   Contribution per unit by product

Product	Red	Green	Yellow	Blue
Sales units	5,000	5,000	5,000	5,000
Price per unit	£333	£367	£417	£267
Direct labour cost per unit	£63	£60	£57	£95
Direct materials cost per unit	£67	£83	£100	£42
Direct expenses per unit	£3	£7	£10	£5
Total variable cost per unit	£133	£150	£167	£142
Contribution per unit	£200	£217	£250	£125

Remember, the limiting factor ratio is calculated by dividing the contribution £ per unit by the limiting factor £ per unit. Therefore, if direct labour is the limiting factor, the ratio for Red will be £200/£63 = 3.175. The limiting factor ratios for each variable cost are depicted in the Table 7.27.

Table 7.27   Limiting factor ratios for each variable cost

Limiting factor ratio	Red	Green	Yellow	Blue
Direct labour	3.175	3.617	4.386	1.316
Direct materials	2.985	2.614	2.500	2.976
Direct expenses	66.667	31.000	25.000	25.000

1 The product that produces the highest contribution per unit is Yellow.
   Answer = **C**

2 The lowest contribution per unit is generated by Blue.
   Answer = **D**

3 If direct materials are the limiting factor, the product that has the lowest limiting factor ratio per unit is Yellow.
   Answer = **C**

4 When direct labour is the limiting factor, Yellow has the highest limiting factor ratio per unit.
   Answer = **C**

5 If direct expenses are the limiting factor, the product that has the highest limiting factor ratio per unit is Red.
   Answer = **A**

Study question 7.3 solution

Figure 7.6 illustrates a profit/loss chart for new product OE 52.

Figure 7.6   Profit/loss chart for OE 52

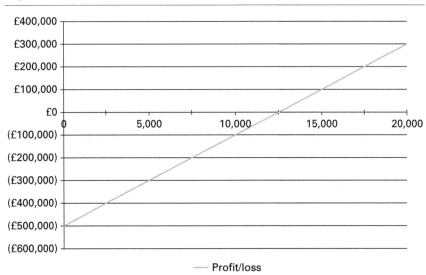

—— Profit/loss

1 The break-even point in terms of units sold for the new product OE 52 can be obtained from the profit/loss chart, where the line intercepts the x-axis, which is 12,500 units.

2 The fixed costs for the production of the new product OE 52 can be derived when the line intercepts the y-axis.

3 The margin of safety is the difference between the forecast sales, which is 20,000 units, and the break-even point of 12,500; therefore the margin of safety is 7,500 units. This equates to £750,000 in sales revenue.

4 The expected profit if the company sells 20,000 units can be determined from the graph by finding 20,000 units on the x-axis. Now draw a vertical line until it intercepts the profit curve; at this point now draw a horizontal line until it intercepts the y-axis, which reveals the company will achieve a profit of £300,000 if it sells 20,000 units.

Study question 7.4 solution

Table 7.28 illustrates the total contribution by product for the month of September 20XX.

Table 7.28 Contribution by product for September 20XX

September 20XX	ZA1	BC4	CH6	DK3	EE7
Forecast monthly sales (units)	4,000	3,000	1,000	5,000	2,000
Selling price £ per unit	10	12	18	20	24
Variable material cost £ per unit	2	6	4	8	10
Other variable costs £ per unit	3	4	6	4	6
Total variable costs £ per unit	5	10	10	12	16
Contribution £ per unit	5	2	8	8	8
Total contribution £ per product	**20,000**	**6,000**	**8,000**	**40,000**	**16,000**

The company's forecast total contribution for September will be £90,000 (£20,000 + £6,000 + £8,000 +£40,000 + £16,000); subtracting fixed costs for the month of £48,000 will generate a profit of £42,000.

However, to make the monthly forecast the company requires 360,000kg of materials; unfortunately, the major supplier of raw materials has had a production problem and can only supply Qwerty plc with 288,000kg. To calculate the production mix that will maximize profitability for the month, the limiting factor ratio for each product needs to be calculated, as shown in the Table 7.29.

Table 7.29 Limiting factor ratio by product

Product	ZA1	BC4	CH6	DK3	EE7
Contribution £ per unit	5	2	8	8	8
Material cost £ per unit	2	6	4	8	10
Limiting factor ratio	2.50	0.33	2.00	1.00	0.80
Order of production	**1**	**5**	**2**	**3**	**4**

The limiting factor ratios for each product have been calculated so as to maximize the total contribution given the material constraint. The order of production will be ZA1, CH6, DK3, EE7 and finally BC4 if there is sufficient raw materials available.

The company's forecast total contribution for September after taking into consideration the raw material constraint will now be £84,000; subtracting fixed costs for the month of £48,000 will generate a profit of £36,000. The revised contribution for September is given in Table 7.30.

Table 7.30 Revised production given the materials constraint

September 20XX	ZA1	BC4	CH6	DK3	EE7	Total
Forecast monthly sales (units)	4,000	3,000	1,000	5,000	2,000	
Required materials	32,000	72,000	16,000	160,000	80,000	360,000
Material consumed	32,000	0	16,000	160,000	80,000	288,000
Production	4,000	0	1,000	5,000	2,000	
Contribution £ per unit	5	2	8	8	8	
Total contribution £ per product	**20,000**	**0**	**8,000**	**40,000**	**16,000**	**84,000**

The profit decreases by £6,000 as they are unable to produce any of BC4; this is the optimum solution given the constraint. However, if the company is contracted to produce the product, the order of production will need to be revised, but this would produce a lower profit.

Absorption costing and variance analysis

The origins of absorption costing are as old as time itself. You have just received a text from your garage telling you that your car is ready to be collected after its annual service. You arrive at the garage's art deco revival designed reception area to pay for the service. You are presented with the invoice, your eyes scan down the right-hand column and then arrive at the final total in bold. You sigh, hand over your credit card, type in its pin number, fold the invoice in two and pick up your keys. As you walk over to your car, you look at the invoice once again and you wonder to yourself, why is the labour rate £50 per hour? You quickly do the mental maths: £50 multiplied by 40 hours is £2,000 a week, then by 52 equates to £104,000. You consider whether to change your career. Welcome to the world of absorption (full) costing and overhead recovery. We all encounter full costing every single day, whether it's the coffee you buy at the railway station, the call you make on your mobile phone, the cinema ticket for the latest movie or the loaf of bread you purchase from the bakery.

The next time you unwrap that chocolate bar or struggle with the cork when opening a bottle of Italian red wine, which you have just purchased for £1 and £10 respectfully, recognize that the price paid for these two items enables the retailer, the manufacturers, the growers and the farmers to make a profit. An understanding of full costing is essential for anyone working in supply chains. For example, Table 8.1 illustrates five items from our weekly shopping receipt; the question is, how many organizations were involved in fulfilling my shopping order? Also, how much profit was made by these organizations at every stage of each item's supply chain?

This chapter introduces the thinking behind absorption costing and variance analysis, exploring its application within the context of the supply chain. The chapter highlights the importance of capturing the relevant costs associated with producing a product or delivering a service. The fragilities

Table 8.1 Five items from Templar's shopping basket

Item	Price
Persil Bio 840ml	£3.00
Heinz tomato ketchup	£2.00
Uncle Ben's rice	£1.00
Cod fishcakes	£0.93
Kitchen scissors	£2.50

of the costing method are discussed. An opportunity to discuss alternative cost approaches that are able to address these deficiencies is provided in the subsequent chapter.

8.1 Aim and objectives

The aim of this chapter is to introduce you to the application of absorption costing and variance analysis.

At the end of this chapter you will be able to:

- identify the different types of costs that make up a product or service using absorption costing;
- explain the use of cost units and cost centres within an organization's supply chain;
- appreciate the difference between the three methods used to distribute indirect costs to products and services;
- recognize how indirect costs are charged to products and services;
- appreciate the difference between mark-up and margin;
- explain why absorption costing is important in placing a value on inventory;
- calculate price and usage variances for direct and indirect costs;
- recognize the benefits and limitations of absorption costing.

8.2 The need for full costing

In the previous chapter you were introduced to marginal costing. A significant weakness of this costing approach is that fixed costs are not distributed to the cost of a product or service; they are kept separate. The cost of a product only includes its marginal costs and at the end of the financial year, if there are any unsold products, the closing inventory is valued at marginal cost. The problem is that the closing inventory of the previous year becomes the opening inventory of the subsequent year. With marginal costing, only the marginal cost of the product moves forward to next year; the fixed costs associated with making the inventory stay in the previous. There are two important issues associated with this policy: it does not meet the matching concept, therefore will have an impact on the profitability of both financial years; and the inventory valuation protocol, which has implications for the balance sheet. Table 8.2 illustrates the income statement (IS) for the two financial years using marginal costing to value inventory. In year 1 the company makes a profit of £350, which is margin of 15.6%, and in year 2 the profit is £650 with a margin of 23.6%. In Table 8.2 the fixed costs of £1,000 are the same for both years and these costs are expensed against the sales for each year. Only the marginal production cost of the inventory, which is £100 (50 units at £2) moves forward to the next accounting period to become the opening inventory; hence this does not meet the matching concept for both years as the relevant costs are not matched against the appropriate revenue for each year.

Table 8.2 Marginal costing

	Year 1					**Year 2**			
Sales	**Units**	**£**	**£**	**£**	**Sales**	**Units**	**£**	**£**	**£**
	450	5		2,250		550	5		2,750
Opening inventory	0	2	0		Opening inventory	50	2	100	
Plus production	500	2	1000		Plus production	500	2	1000	
Less closing inventory	50	2	100		Less closing inventory	0	2	0	
Equals cost of goods				900	Equals cost of goods				1,100
Fixed costs				1,000	Fixed costs				1,000
Profit				350	Profit				650

Table 8.3 Full costing

Sales	Year 1 Units £	£	£	£	Sales	Year 2 Units £	£	£	£
	450	5		2,250		550	5		2,750
Opening inventory	0	4	0		Opening inventory	50	4	200	
Plus production	500	4	2000		Plus production	500	4	2,000	
Less closing inventory	50	4	200		Less closing inventory	0	4	0	
Equals cost of goods				1,800	Equals cost of goods				2,200
Profit				450	Profit				550

Table 8.3 illustrates the income statement (IS) for the two financial years using full costing to value inventory; the fixed costs are now absorbed into the product cost using the number of units produced (£1,000 divided by 500 units produced = £2 per unit), making the full cost of a unit £4. In year 1 the company makes a profit of £450, which is a margin of 20%, and in year 2 the profit is £550 with a margin of 20%.

When applying the full costing method, the relevant income streams are now matched with the appropriate costs incurred to produce the units sold in each accounting period. The closing inventory valuation in year 1 now contains a proportion of the fixed costs used in their production and these costs travel forward to the next financial year and then are matched with the revenue generated in year 2 when they are sold.

The profit for the two years is the same, £1,000, for both costing methods, but the range between the annual profits is smaller: using full costing it is £100, compared with £300 using marginal costing. This has implications for financial ratios, tax and inventory valuation on the balance sheet.

In this simple example indirect costs are absorbed to cost units using the absorption basis of the number of units produced to derive the full cost per unit. Hang on a minute, I hear you cry; what's all this terminology you've just mentioned, such as indirect costs, absorption basis and full cost per unit? In the next section we will explore and explain the terminology relating to full costing, or absorption costing, as it is also known.

8.3 Margin vs. mark-up

The selling price of the Italian bottle of red wine includes all the direct costs, indirect costs and also a mark-up to provide a profit margin for the winery. Typically, a profit margin is calculated by dividing the profit by the selling price of the product. In the following example a product, WT45, sells for £20 and it costs £12 to produce; therefore it makes a profit of £8. Its profit margin percentage is derived by £8 divided by £20 and then multiplied by 100 to give 40% profit margin. Its mark-up percentage on cost is 66.67%; to achieve a 20% profit margin, £8 is added to derive the product's selling price. CIMA (2005:49) terminology defines mark-up as 'addition to the cost of goods or services which results in a selling price'. While a mark-down, according to CIMA (2005:49), is the 'reduction in the selling price of damaged or slow-selling goods'.

A mark-down is calculated by multiplying the original selling price by 1 – the mark-down percentage expressed as a decimal. For example, a retailer currently sells an item for £500 and decides to mark it down by 15%; the new selling price will be £425 (£500 * 0.85).

Table 8.4 illustrates the profit margin and mark-up percentages for a product which costs £100.

Table 8.4   Profit margin and mark-up percentages

Product cost £	Selling price £	Profit £	Profit margin	Mark-up %
100	105.26	5.26	5%	5.26%
100	111.11	11.11	10%	11.11%
100	117.65	17.65	15%	17.65%
100	125.00	25.00	20%	25.00%
100	133.33	33.33	25%	33.33%
100	142.86	42.86	30%	42.86%
100	153.85	53.85	35%	53.85%
100	166.67	66.67	40%	66.67%
100	181.82	81.82	45%	81.82%
100	200.00	100.00	50%	100.00%
100	222.22	122.22	55%	122.22%
100	250.00	150.00	60%	150.00%

(continued)

Table 8.4   (Continued)

Product cost £	Selling price £	Profit £	Profit margin	Mark-up %
100	285.71	185.71	65%	185.71%
100	333.33	233.33	70%	233.33%
100	400.00	300.00	75%	300.00%
100	500.00	400.00	80%	400.00%
100	666.67	566.67	85%	566.67%
100	1000.00	900.00	90%	900.00%
100	2000.00	1900.00	95%	1900.00%
100	10000.00	9900.00	99%	9900.00%

If the company requires a profit margin of 60% on a product with a total cost of £100, it would have to mark up the product by 150% of its cost to derive a selling price of £250. If the product sells for £250 and its cost is £100 to make, it will produce a profit of £150, which is a margin of 60% (£150/£250 * 100). A useful formula can be used to derive the selling price for a target margin and given cost.

The formula is:

$$SP = C/(1-M)$$

Where:

SP = selling price;

C = total cost;

M = is the required profit margin expressed as a decimal.

To derive the selling price for a product that costs £240 to make and requires a profit margin of 25%:

$$SP = £240/(1-0.25) = £240/0.75 = £320$$

The mark-up on cost is £80, which is 33.33% of cost. If you have the selling price and profit margin percentage, to find the product's cost SP*(1–M), in this example it will be £320*(1–0.25) =£320*0.75 = £240.

8.4 Absorption costing

In marginal costing you were introduced to two cost types: marginal costs (variable costs) and fixed costs. In full costing you will also be introduced to two more types of costs: direct costs and indirect costs (overheads). Every product produced or service delivered will contain both these cost elements in their total cost (full cost) plus a margin to derive its selling price. Figure 8.1 illustrates the selling price for product WR56.

Figure 8.1 Selling price for product WR56

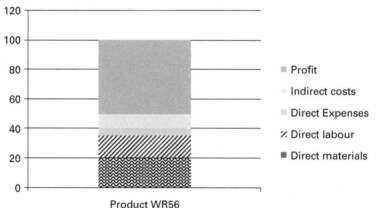

Product WR56

Legend:
- Profit
- Indirect costs
- Direct Expenses
- Direct labour
- Direct materials

The selling price is £100, its profit is £50, and its total cost is the sum of its direct materials (£20), direct labour (£15), direct expenses (£5) and indirect costs (£10), which is £50.

Direct and indirect costs

CIMA (2005:12) defines a direct cost as 'expenditure that can be attributed to a specific cost unit, for example material that forms part of the product'. Typical direct costs can be sub-divided into direct materials, direct labour and direct expenses. When these costs are aggregated together, they form a product's prime cost.

The direct material costs can be obtained from the product's bill of materials (BOM), which is defined by CIMA (2005:4) as the 'detailed specification, for each product, of the subassemblies, components and materials required, distinguishing items purchased externally from those manufactured in-house'.

Table 8.5 illustrates the BOM required to make a unit of TZ96. The BOM states the standard quantity of materials required by each sub-component, including their standard price per kg.

Table 8.5 Bill of materials for TZ96

Raw material component	Price £ per kg	Quantity kg	Cost £
KB6	30.00	8	240.00
GW5	15.00	12	180.00
DQ6	10.00	5	50.00
Total			**470.00**

The direct material cost is £470. Now if the company were to manufacture 250 units, Table 8.6 illustrates total direct materials required and the total cost.

Table 8.6 Total material cost for 250 units of TZ96

Raw material component	Price £ per kg	Quantity kg	Total cost £
KB6	30.00	2,000	60,000
GW5	15.00	3,000	45,000
DQ6	10.00	1,250	12,500
Total			**117,500**

Direct labour costs are typically derived based on the hours used to manufacture the product and are captured using time sheets or other time recording methods. The time and the grade of the labour are captured as the grade of labour used will impact on the cost of the product and will be factored into the standard cost of the direct labour used. An example of direct expenses is a royalty payment, which is paid to the owner of the copyright.

Indirect costs (CIMA, 2005:14) are defined as 'expenditure on labour, materials or services that cannot be economically identified with a specific saleable cost unit'. Typically, indirect costs are referred to as overheads and will include the supporting service functions within a business, such as finance and accounting, administration, human resource management, sales and marketing, information technology, and so on. The sum of the direct and indirect costs is referred to as the total cost.

8.5 Cost units and cost centres

In the previous sections of this chapter, the term cost unit has been used but not defined. A cost unit (CIMA, 2005:15) is a 'unit of product or service in relation to which costs are ascertained'. In a university a cost unit could be a student taking a specific degree programme; in a regional distribution centre the cost unit could be the handling unit (pallet, case or an item); in consulting it would be the chargeable unit (day or hour); typically in the oil industry, cost per barrel is the cost unit; in manufacturing it can be the cost per tonne produced. Every industrial sector has their own cost unit.

Closely connected to cost unit is cost centre. A cost centre is defined by CIMA (2005:7) as the 'production or service location, function, activity or item of equipment for which costs are accumulated'. Table 8.7 illustrates numerous examples of cost centres that you may find in a supply chain operation. The list is not exhaustive; you can think of additional examples. The important point to recognize is that they can be classified into primary and support cost centres.

Table 8.7 Supply chain cost centres

Goods in	Security	Payroll
Storage	Production maintenance	Training
Picking	Information technology	Research
Co-packing	Site services	Administration
Goods out	Human resource management	Procurement
Transport	Sales	Customer services
Distribution	Marketing	Maintenance
Manufacturing	Financial accounting	Utilities
Health and safety	Management accounting	Industrial engineering
Quality control	Treasury	Returns management

8.6 Allocation, apportion and absorption

Indirect costs, those costs which cannot be traced to specific cost units, have to be processed using three management accounting processes: allocation, apportion and absorption. The mathematics is fairly straightforward. It is the process that can be complex. It is at this point I will confide that there is no such thing as a true cost – I will demonstrate this to you in this section.

I will summarize the overall process briefly, then explore each of the three processes individually in more depth.

Once the prime cost has been established for the product, the indirect costs can be added to calculate the full cost/total cost. It is important to identify all the cost centres involved in the manufacturing of the product. This can be done by following each stage of the product's production process, from the receipt of the raw materials to the dispatch to the customers. However, the product will not flow through numerous service cost centres, such as sales and marketing, human resource management, accounting and finance, and information technology; these are just some of the supporting functions typically found in an organization. These service cost centres provide support and services to the production centres and therefore their costs need to be distributed to the production centres. The processes of distributing these indirect costs to cost units is outlined in the following six steps:

1 All indirect costs that can be allocated to a single cost centre are distributed first.

2 All indirect costs are now apportioned to all the cost centres (production and service) using appropriate apportionment basis.

3 Service centre costs are then secondary apportioned to the relevant production cost centres they support; however, some service centres will also serve other service centres. For example, payroll will pay HR employees and HR will provide services to payroll, such as training and development. This is often complex and requires reciprocal apportionments, as will be explored and explained later in this section.

4 Once all the service centre costs have been apportioned to production cost centres, the cost centre costs are absorbed to cost units using an appropriate overhead recovery or absorption rate.

5 The total cost of the product can now be calculated as it flows through each production cost centre, where costs are accumulated to products.

6 The final stage is to calculate the selling price of the product by adding a mark-up.

Allocation

CIMA (2005:4) terminology defines allocate as: 'to assign a whole item of cost, or of revenue, to a single cost unit, centre, account or time period'. Here is an example of an allocation: if you are using heavy goods vehicles to distribute your products, the indirect costs for applying (£257), issue (£401) and continuation fee after five years (£401) are applicable to the transport cost centre and therefore are allocation (UK Government, 2018):

> You need a licence to carry goods in a lorry, van or other vehicle with either:

- *a gross plated weight (the maximum weight that the vehicle can have at any one time) of over 3,500 kilograms (kg)*
- *an unladen weight of more than 1,525 kg (where there is no plated weight).*

Apportion

The second process is apportionment. CIMA terminology (2005:4) defines apportion as: 'to spread revenues or costs over two or more cost units, centres, accounts, or time periods'. Typing apportion into my computer's thesaurus produces the following results: allocate, allot, assign, distribute, dispense, share out, dish out, divide up and dole out.

Apportionment is the process of sharing out an indirect cost across more than one cost centre. For example, a regional distribution manager is responsible for three distribution centres; how should the manager's costs be shared across the three cost centres? This is not an easy question to answer: should we use time spent at each location to apportion costs, or should I charge them a third of the cost? Whichever apportionment basis we use will impact on the costs of the cost centre.

The following example will explore the apportionment calculations in more depth.

Apportion example

A manufacturing company has decided to apportion their central overhead costs of £120 million to their four factories, which are currently operated by the organization as cost centres, therefore making them profit centres. The company has supplied you with the information illustrated in Table 8.8 concerning their four factories, including production percentages, percentage of employees per factory, sales revenue and factory costs.

Using the data in Table 8.8, solve the following five questions:

1 How much profit will Factory **A** make if the percentage of people is used to apportion central overhead costs?

Table 8.8   Factory data

Data	Factory A	Factory B	Factory C	Factory D
Production (%)	35	30	15	20
People (%)	10	35	25	30
Sales (£ million)	350	300	100	250
Factory costs (£ million)	280	210	35	175

2 How much profit will Factory **A** make if production percentage is used to apportion central overhead costs?

3 How much profit will Factory **D** make if sales revenue is used to apportion central overhead costs?

4 How much profit will Factory **B** make if factory costs are used to apportion central overhead costs?

5 How much profit will Factory **A** make if central overhead costs are apportioned equally to each factory?

Now look at the solution to the five questions.

Apportion example solution

When solving an apportion problem, there are a number of logical steps that need to be followed in a strict order:

1 Decide on the basis for the apportionment. The first question asks you to adopt the production percentage as the basis for apportioning central overhead costs to each factory, then to calculate the profit for Factory A.

2 For each apportionment basis, sum up the individual costs, percentages, sales, and so on, to find the total, as illustrated in Table 8.9.

3 Then convert each one into a percentage of the total, as shown in Table 8.10.

4 Now multiply the percentage for each factory by the amount needed to be apportioned across each factory. Remember, apportion is just an alternative word for sharing. In the case of Factory A, it generates 35% of production for the organization; therefore the factory will be apportioned with 35% of the central overhead costs of £120 million, which equates to £42 million.

Table 8.9   Basis of apportionment

Data	A	B	C	D	Total
Production (%)	35	30	15	20	100
People (%)	10	35	25	30	100
Sales (£ million)	350	300	100	250	1,000
Factory costs (£ million)	280	210	35	175	700

Table 8.10   Basis of apportionment

Data	A	B	C	D	Total
Production	35%	30%	15%	20%	100%
People	10%	35%	25%	30%	100%
Sales	35%	30%	10%	25%	100%
Factory costs	40%	30%	5%	25%	100%

5 First calculate the contribution for each of the four factories by deducting factory costs from sales revenue, as shown in Table 8.11.

Table 8.11   Factory contribution

	A	B	C	D	Total
Sales (£ million)	350	300	100	250	1,000
Factory costs (£ million)	280	210	35	175	700
Contribution (£ million)	70	90	65	75	300

6 To calculate the factory's profit, deduct its apportioned share of central overhead costs from its contribution, as illustrated in Table 8.12. When the production percentage is used as the basis for apportioning central overhead costs, Factory A will make a profit of £28 million, as illustrated in the following Table 8.12.

Table 8.12   Factory profitability using the production percentage

Production (%)	A	B	C	D	Total
Contribution (£ million)	70	90	65	75	300
Central overheads (£ million)	42	36	18	24	120
Profit (£ million)	28	54	47	51	180

For each apportionment basis, the profit for each factory is illustrated in Tables 8.13 to 8.16.

Table 8.13   Factory profitability using the percentage of people

People (%)	A	B	C	D	Total
Contribution (£ million)	70	90	65	75	300
Central overheads (£ million)	12	42	30	36	120
Profit (£ million)	58	48	35	39	180

Table 8.14   Factory profitability using the percentage of sales revenue

Sales (%)	A	B	C	D	Total
Contribution (£ million)	70	90	65	75	300
Central overheads (£ million)	42	36	12	30	120
Profit (£ million)	28	54	53	45	180

Table 8.15   Factory profitability using the percentage of factory costs

Factory Costs (%)	A	B	C	D	Total
Contribution (£ million)	70	90	65	75	300
Central overheads (£ million)	48	36	6	30	120
Profit (£ million)	22	54	59	45	180

Table 8.16 Factory profitability based on apportioning equally central overheads

Apportioned equally	A	B	C	D	Total
Contribution (£ million)	70	90	65	75	300
Central overheads (£ million)	30	30	30	30	120
Profit (£ million)	40	60	35	45	180

Table 8.17 summarizes the profit for each factory according to the apportionment basis used by the organization.

Table 8.17 Factory profit by different apportionment basis used by the organization

Profit (£ million)	Production (%)	People (%)	Sales (%)	Factory costs (%)	Apportioned equally	Range
Factory A	28	58	28	22	40	36
Factory B	54	48	54	54	60	12
Factory C	47	35	53	59	35	24
Factory D	51	39	45	45	45	12
Total profit	180	180	180	180	180	

Using the relevant and appropriate apportionment basis is key. However, choosing an inappropriate basis to apportion the central overheads to cost centres can lead to:

- conflict between the cost centres;
- conflict between the centre and the individual cost centres;
- product pricing and profitability;
- cross-subsidization;
- financial performances issues;
- motivation and goal congruence.

Now have a go yourself; try the following activity.

Activity 8.1

A manufacturing company has decided to apportion their central overhead costs of £120 million to their four factories. The company has supplied you with the information in Table 8.18 concerning their four factories.

Table 8.18 Factory data

Data	Factory A	Factory B	Factory C	Factory D
Production (%)	35	30	15	20
People (%)	10	35	25	30
Sales (£ million)	350	300	100	250
Factory costs (£ million)	280	210	35	175

Use the data to answer questions 1 to 5.

1 How much profit will Factory **A** make if the percentage of people is used to apportion central overhead costs?

2 How much profit will Factory **C** make if production percentage is used to apportion central overhead costs?

3 How much profit will Factory **D** make if sales revenue is used to apportion central overhead costs?

4 How much profit will Factory **B** make if factory costs are used to apportion central overhead costs?

5 How much profit will Factory **A** make if central overhead costs are apportioned equally to each factory?

The apportion example and activity focus on apportioning central overheads to factories; however, apportioning happens within a factory as well. The logic, methodology and mathematical rationale are the same; choice of apportionment basis will be determined by the type of cost. Table 8.19 provides you with examples, illustrating the relationship between a cost type, its apportionment basis and potential data sources to assist you with the apportionment calculation.

Table 8.19 Apportionment basis

Cost	Apportionment basis	Data source
Heating and lighting Rent Cleaning	Square metres	Architect drawings Floor plans
Depreciation Insurance	Net book value of assets	Asset register

(continued)

Table 8.19   *(Continued)*

Cost	Apportionment basis	Data source
Machine maintenance	Number of breakdowns	Fault log
Procurement	Purchase requisitions	Purchase order records
Canteen HR costs	Number of people	HR records

Earlier in this section you were introduced to the complex issue of service centres within an organization that supply each other with services. The following example illustrates the reciprocal apportionment method. The organization has three production cost centres and two service cost centres. The service centres support the three production centres but also support each other. Table 8.20 illustrates the indirect costs apportioned to the five cost centres and the percentage of time that each service centre supports its internal customers; for example, the procurement service spends 35% of its time supporting the forming cost centre, but also spends 15% supporting the IT service centre. Likewise, IT spends 10% of its time supporting procurement.

Table 8.20   Indirect costs and service centre apportionment basis

Cost centre	£	Procurement time %	IT support time %
Forming	2,400	35	40
Finishing	1,200	30	35
Packing	1,000	20	15
Procurement	800	0	10
IT support	600	15	0
Total	6,000	100	100

It really doesn't matter which service centre you start with; just carry out the apportionment process using the basis in Table 8.20. In Table 8.21 the apportionment began with the procurement service centre; once all those costs have been apportioned to the other cost centres, do the next service centre. You will notice in the shaded row of the table that £120 of procurement costs have been apportioned to IT support. Now £720 of IT support costs are apportioned across its internal customers. The process is repeated to all the service centres until costs have been apportioned to the three production centres.

The next stage is to absorb the total production cost centre costs to the cost units that flow through each centre using a relevant absorption basis.

Table 8.21 Reciprocal apportionment

Cost centre	Forming	Finishing	Packing	Procurement	IT support	Total
Total cost	2,400.00	1,200.00	1,000.00	800.00	600.00	6,000.00
Procurement apportionment	280.00	240.00	160.00	(800.00)	120.00	–
Total cost	2,680.00	1,440.00	1,160.00	–	720.00	6,000.00
IT support apportionment	288.00	252.00	108.00	72.00	(720.00)	–
Total cost	2,968.00	1,692.00	1,268.00	72.00	–	6,000.00
Procurement apportionment	25.20	21.60	14.40	(72.00)	10.80	–
Total cost	2,993.20	1,713.60	1,282.40	–	10.80	6,000.00
IT support apportionment	4.32	3.78	1.62	1.08	(10.80)	–
Total cost	2,997.52	1,717.38	1,284.02	1.08	–	6,000.00
Procurement apportionment	0.38	0.32	0.22	(1.08)	0.16	–
Total cost	2,997.90	1,717.70	1,284.24	–	(0.16)	6,000.00
Final total	**2,997.98**	**1,717.75**	**1,284.27**	**–**	**–**	**6,000.00**

Absorption

CIMA (2005:20) defines absorption as 'a means of attributing overheads to a product or service, based on a pre-determined overhead absorption rate'. There are six different overhead absorption rates that can be used in absorbing cost centres to cost units:

- direct labour hour rate £
- direct labour wage %
- machine hour rate £
- direct materials %
- £ per unit produced
- prime cost %

The following example will be used to assist you through the absorption methodology.

Absorption example

A company has been asked to make a special batch of products for a customer. The direct costs and factory resources for batch QX4 are detailed in Table 8.22, together with the organization's annual factory budget. The company's shareholders require a profit margin of 30% on batch QX4. Use the data in the Table 8.22 to calculate the following:

Table 8.22 Annual factory production budget and details for batch QX4

Annual factory production budget		Batch QX4
Direct labour hours	250,000	450
Direct labour wages £	2,500,000	4,000
Machine hours	50,000	95
Direct materials consumed £	10,000,000	20,000
Number of units produced	12,500	30
Overheads for the period £	5,000,000	

1 Calculate the selling price for batch QX4 if direct labour hours are used to absorb overheads to production.

2 Calculate the profit for batch QX4 (two decimal places) if the direct material percentage is used to absorb overheads to production.

3 Calculate the profit for batch QX4 if the prime cost percentage is used to absorb overheads to production.

4 Calculate the total cost for batch QX4 if units produced are used to absorb overheads to production.

5 Calculate the selling price for batch QX4 if direct machine hours are used to absorb overheads to production.

6 Calculate the total cost for batch QX4 if the direct wage percentage is used to absorb overheads to production.

Now look at the solution to the six calculations.

Absorption example solution

A six-stage approach can be used to solve the questions in this activity.

1 **Calculate the prime cost for the batch.** Add together all of the batch's direct costs to calculate prime cost. Direct labour cost plus direct material costs = £4,000 + £20,000 = £24,000.

2 **Calculate overhead recovery rate.** To derive the overhead recovery rate, first take the annual factory overheads for the period and then divide by the chosen recovery basis. For example, annual factory overheads for the period are £5,000,000; let's use the number of units produced as the basis for charging overheads to products. Now divide £5,000,000 by 12,500, which equals £400 per unit. Therefore, every unit produced by the factory would have £400 added to its prime cost.

All the overhead recovery rates are calculated in Table 8.23.

Table 8.23 Overhead recovery rates

Overhead recovery basis	Calculation	Rate
Direct labour hour rate £	£5,000,000/250,000	£20
Direct labour wage %	(£5,000,000/£2,500,000) *100	200%
Machine hour rate £	£5,000,000/50,000	£100
Direct materials %	(£5,000,000/£10,000,000) *100	50%
£ per unit produced	£5,000,000/12,500	£400
Prime cost %	£5,000,000/£12,500,000	40%

3 **Calculate the amount of overhead to be recovered to the batch.** When using units produced, multiply the number of units in the batch by the overhead recovery rate per unit. In the case of batch QX4, it is 30 units multiplied by £400, which is £12,000.

4 **Add prime cost to overhead absorbed to give total cost.** The total cost of the batch when using an overhead recovery rate based on units produced is prime cost: £24,000 + £12,000 overheads, which is £36,000.

5 **Calculate selling price based on desired profit margin percentage.** Selling price is calculated by dividing total cost by 1 minus the margin percentage expressed as a decimal. In the case of batch QX4, the company expects to earn a margin of 30%; therefore the formula for the batch's selling price is £36,000/0.7 = £51,428.57.

6 **Selling price minus total cost to derive margin.** The margin is the difference between the batch's selling price and its total cost, which is £51,428.57 − £36,000 = £15,428.57. To check, divide margin by selling price, then multiply by 100 to generate margin percentage:

$$(£15,428.57/£51,428.57) * 100 = 30\% \text{ margin}$$

The overhead recovered, total cost, margin and selling price for each of the six bases are illustrated in Table 8.24.

Table 8.24 Selling prices for batch QX4 (£)

Overhead recovery basis	Prime cost	Overhead	Total	Margin	Selling price
Direct labour hours	24,000	9,000	33,000	14,143	47,143
Direct labour wage %	24,000	8,000	32,000	13,714	45,714
Machine hours	24,000	9,500	33,500	14,357	47,857
Direct materials %	24,000	10,000	34,000	14,571	48,571
Number of units produced	24,000	12,000	36,000	15,429	51,429
Prime cost %	24,000	9,600	33,600	14,400	48,000

1 If direct labour hours are used to absorb overheads, the selling price for batch QX4 will be £47,143.

2 If the direct material percentage is used to absorb overheads to batch QX4, it will make a profit of £14,571.

3 If the prime cost percentage is used to absorb overheads, batch QX4 will make a profit of £14,400.

4 The total cost for making batch QX4 if units produced are used to absorb overheads is £36,000.

5 If direct machine hours are used to absorb overheads, the selling price for batch QX4 will be £47,857.

6 The total cost for making batch QX4, if the direct wage percentage is used to absorb overheads, will be £45,714.

Now you have a go at the next activity.

Activity 8.2

Mega plc has asked for your help to calculate different budgeted overhead absorption rates. They have supplied you with the information in Table 8.25.

Table 8.25   Annual factory production budget

Annual factory production budget	
Direct labour hours	200,000
Direct labour wages	£2,000,000
Machine hours	40,000
Direct materials consumed	£8,000,000
Number of units produced	10,000
Fixed overheads for the period	£2,000,000

Use the data to answer questions 1 to 6.

1 What is the overhead recovery rate if the prime cost percentage is used?

2 What is the overhead recovery rate if labour hours are applied?

3 What is the overhead recovery rate if the direct material percentage is applied?

4 What is the overhead recovery rate if units produced is adopted?

5 What is the overhead recovery rate if machine hours are applied?

6 What is the overhead recovery rate if the direct wage percentage is applied?

The next section is a case study that takes you through the absorption process.

8.7 Absorption costing case study

You have been asked to calculate a budgeted overhead absorption rate for the fabrication and finishing departments within the factory. Both are production cost centres and they share a common purchasing department (service centre).

You have been supplied with the budget information in Tables 8.26 to 8.28.

Table 8.26   Budgeted indirect costs

Budgeted indirect costs	£
Heating and lighting	50,000
Supervisors' wages	250,000
Cleaning contract	60,000
Rent and rates	100,000
Plant and machinery maintenance contract	40,000
Plant and machinery insurance	30,000
Plant and machinery depreciation	220,000
Total	750,000

Table 8.27   Cost centre data

Cost centre data	Fabrication	Finishing	Purchasing	Total
Floor area m²	500	300	200	1,000
Purchasing requisitions	80	120	0	200
Number of supervisors	2	2	1	5
Plant and machinery value £	600,000	150,000	50,000	800,000
Number of breakdowns	80	15	5	100
Machine hours	5,000			
Labour hours		7,500		

Table 8.28   Prime cost and processing times

Product	Red	Blue	Yellow
Budgeted prime cost per unit (£)	100	150	200
Fabrication (hours) per unit	1.5	2.0	1.5
Finishing (hours) per unit	2.5	0.5	1.5

You are required to:

1 Apportion the indirect costs to the production cost centres and the purchasing service centre.

2 Use a suitable basis to apportion the total cost of the purchasing between the fabrication and finishing cost centres.

3 Calculate a suitable overhead recovery rate for fabrication and finishing cost centres.

4 Using the overhead absorption rates calculated in part 3 of the question, now calculate the total cost for the products Red, Blue and Yellow.

5 Calculate the selling price for each product. The company expects to earn a 30% profit margin.

Absorption costing case study solution

1 The first step is to apportion all the unallocated indirect costs in Table 8.26 into the three cost centres (two production and one service) using the appropriate apportionment basis. The data in the cost centre table (8.27) can be used.

2 The purchasing service centre costs are then secondary apportioned to the two production cost centres they support.

3 Once all the purchasing centre costs have been apportioned to production cost centres, the cost centre costs are then absorbed to cost units using an appropriate overhead recovery or absorption rate. In this example machine hours are used for the fabrication cost centre and labour hours for the finishing cost centre (Table 8.29).

4 The total cost of the product can now be calculated as it flows through each of the two production cost centres, where costs are accumulated to products.

Table 8.29 Apportionment and absorption basis

Budgeted indirect costs	£	Apportionment basis	Fab £	Fin £	Purchasing £	Total £
Heating and lighting	50,000	Floor area m²	25,000	15,000	10,000	50,000
Supervisors' wages	250,000	Number of supervisors	100,000	100,000	50,000	250,000
Cleaning contract	60,000	Floor area m²	30,000	18,000	12,000	60,000
Rent and rates	100,000	Floor area m²	50,000	30,000	20,000	100,000
Plant and machinery maintenance contract	40,000	Number of breakdowns	32,000	6,000	2,000	40,000
Plant and machinery insurance	30,000	Plant and machinery value	22,500	5,625	1,875	30,000
Plant and machinery depreciation	220,000	Plant and machinery value	165,000	41,250	13,750	220,000
Total	**750,000**		**424,500**	**215,875**	**109,625**	**750,000**
Purchasing		Number of stores requisitions	43,850	65,775		
		Total	**468,350**	**281,650**		**750,000**
		Absorption rates	**93.67**	**37.55**		

5 The final stage is to calculate the selling price of the product by adding a mark-up that will generate a 30% profit margin.

The total cost for Red is calculated in Table 8.30; a summary of the calculation process is described below.

Table 8.30   Product total costs and selling price for the three products

Product	Red £	Blue £	Yellow £
Prime cost	100.00	150.00	200.00
Fabrication indirect costs	140.51	187.34	140.51
Finishing indirect costs	93.88	18.78	56.33
Total cost	334.39	356.12	396.84
Mark-up	143.31	152.62	170.07
Selling price	477.70	508.74	566.91
Sales margin %	30.00%	30.00%	30.00%

The prime cost of £100 is added to the overheads from the fabrication cost centre using the overhead recovery rate based on machine hours, which is £93.67 per hour. A unit of Red will spend 1.5 hours in the fabrication cost centre and therefore will absorb £140.51 of indirect costs, making its cumulative cost now £240.51. The cost unit then moves on to the finishing cost centre, where it spends 2.5 hours; the overhead recovery rate for this cost centre is based on labour hours and is £37.55 per hour, resulting in £93.88, making its total cost £334.39. The company expects to earn a margin of 30%; using the formula $SP = C/(1-M)$, it is possible to derive Red's selling price of £477.70. The same process is then repeated for Blue and Yellow.

8.8 Standard costing and variance analysis

In this section it is worth exploring the relationship between absorption and standard costing. CIMA (2005:15) defines a standard cost as 'the planned unit cost of the products, components or services produced in a period'. Establishing a full cost for a product using planned prime costs, allocating apportioning and absorbing indirect costs by applying a predetermined basis and then incorporating an expected profit margin to establish a selling price for a product in effect is achieving a standard cost using absorption costing. Standard costs can be derived using other costing methods, including marginal costing and activity-based costing. It is important to define the term standard. A standard (CIMA, 2005:27) is defined as 'a benchmark measurement, of resource usage, set in defined conditions'.

Therefore, the product costs calculated are established according to the defined conditions at the time, factoring in resource usage and planned costs to formulate a benchmark cost, which can then be compared with the actual cost and the difference analysed. In accounting, the difference is referred to as a variance, which according to the CIMA (2005:29) is 'the difference between a planned, budgeted or standard cost and the actual cost incurred'.

Cost variances can be positive (underspend) or negative (overspend); a positive variance in the language of accounting is described as favourable (F) and negative variance as adverse (A). Investigating and explaining why a variance has arisen are referred to as variance analysis, which CIMA (2005:29) defines as 'the evaluation of performance by means of variances whose timely reporting should maximise the opportunity for managerial action'.

Variances and variance analysis are subjects that deserve their own chapter, but in this section we are going to explore only six variances – there are many more. These six variances, typically used in manufacturing related to direct material and labour, will introduce you to the logic, methodology and calculations. Table 8.31 illustrates the calculations for the variances.

Table 8.31   The direct labour and material formulas

Variance	Calculation
Direct labour rate	(standard rate – actual rate) * actual hours
Direct labour efficiency	(standard hours - actual hours) * standard rate
Direct labour variance	direct labour variance + direct labour rate
Direct material price	(standard price – actual price) * actual quantity
Direct material usage	(standard quantity – actual quantity) * standard price
Direct material variance	direct material price + direct material usage

Typically a total variance comprises two sub-variances that have an emphasis on price and quantity; for example, the direct material is the sum of the direct material price variance and the direct material usage variance.

Variance analysis example

The distribution manager at Swift Service plc has asked you to help the team with reconciling last month's distribution accounts. They on average use 8,000 litres of petrol per month at a cost of £1.30 per litre. Their drivers on average work 1,600 hours a month at a cost of £25 per hour. The actual figures for last month were as follows:

- 9,000 litres at a cost of £10,080;
- 1,760 hours at a cost of £49,280.

Using the data supplied by Swift Service plc, we will now calculate the following variances for the month:

1 the total variance;

2 the direct material variance;

3 the direct labour variance;

4 the direct material price variance;

5 the direct material usage variance;

6 the direct labour rate variance;

7 the direct labour efficiency variance.

The first step is to calculate the budget for the month. The direct material budget is derived by multiplying the standard price per litre of petrol, £1.30, by the standard quantity, 8,000 litres, budgeted for the month, which equates to £10,400. The direct labour budget is derived using the same approach: the standard hourly rate of £25 is multiplied by the budgeted monthly standard hours, which are 1,600, to give a cost of £40,000. Table 8.32 illustrates the budget, actual spend and variances for materials, labour and total.

Table 8.32   Swift Service plc total variances for the month

	Budget	**Actual**	**Variance**	**Percentage**
Petrol £	10,400	10,080	320F	3.08
Labour £	40,000	49,280	9,280A	23.20
Total £	50,400	59,360	8,960A	17.78

Just subtract the actual spend fom the budget to produce the variance.

The total variance for the month is £8,960A, which is derived from the material variance of £320F and the labour variance of £9,280A.

It can be seen from Table 8.32 that both direct materials and labour costs are overspent as they both have adverse variances for the month. Therefore, Swift Service plc's total variance for the month is £8,960A.

The calculations for direct material and labour sub-variances for Swift Service plc are illustrated in Table 8.33.

Table 8.33 Swift Service plc direct material and labour sub-variances

Variance	Calculation
Direct labour rate	(standard rate – actual rate) * actual hours (£25 per hour – £28 per hour) * 1,760 hours = £5,280A
Direct labour efficiency	(standard hours – actual hours) * standard rate (1,600 hours – 1,760 hours) * £25 per hour = £4,000A
Direct material price	(standard price – actual price) * actual quantity (£1.30 per litre – £1.12 per litre) * 9,000 litres = £1,620F
Direct material usage	(standard quantity – actual quantity) * standard price (8,000 litres – 9,000 litres) * £1.30 per litre = £1,300A

The sum of all the monthly sub-variances will add up to the total variance for the month, as illustrated in Figure 8.2.

Figure 8.2 Swift Service plc monthly variances

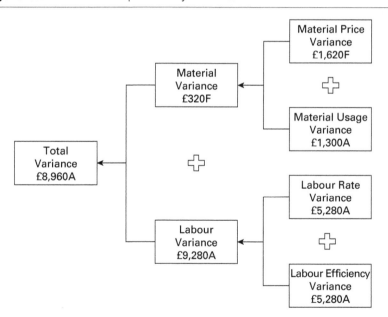

The next stage is to investigate and explain the potential root causes of the variances, as illustrated in Table 8.34.

Table 8.34 Potential root causes of the variances

Variance	Potential root causes of the variances
Direct labour rate £5,280A	The actual labour rate is £3 more than the standard rate; this could be explained: • new rates negotiated by the drivers; • inflation; • overtime; • different grade of labour was used.
Direct labour efficiency £4,000A	The actual hours were 160 hours more than the standard hours; this could be explained: • diversion due to roadworks; • delays due to congestion; • inexperience of the drivers; • reduced speed limits on the road network; • weather conditions; • unloading and loading times at delivery locations; • increased waiting times at delivery locations.
Direct material price £1,620F	The actual material price is £0.18 per litre less than the standard rate of £1.30; this could be explained by: • a reduction in global price of oil; • quantity discount negotiated by procurement; • new supplier.
Direct material usage £1,300A	The actual quantity of petrol was 1,000 litres more than the standard quantity; this could be explained: • diversion due to roadworks; • delays due to congestion; • inexperience of the drivers and their driving style; • reduced speed limits on the road network; • weather conditions; • the age and maintenance of the vehicle.

Now have a go at the following activity.

Activity 8.3

To make one unit of AF53, the materials illustrated in Table 8.35, the product's bill of materials, are required.

Table 8.35 AF53 bill of materials

Raw material component	Price per kg	Kg per unit
MK92	£8	4
ST46	£12	8
MA07	£6	11

The actual figures for this month's production of 150 units of AF53 were as follows:

- MK92 620kg at a cost of £4,650;
- ST46 1,220kg at a cost of £14,884;
- MA07 1,700kg at a cost of £9,350.

Use the data to answer questions 1 to 7.

1 What is the total material variance for the monthly production of AF53?

2 What is the material price variance for the raw material component MK92 when 150 units of AF53 are produced?

3 What is the material usage variance for the raw material component ST46 when 150 units of AF53 are produced?

4 What is the total material variance for the raw material MA07 component when 150 units of AF53 are produced?

5 What is the material price variance for the raw material MA07 component when 150 units of AF53 are produced?

6 What is the total material variance for the raw material MK92 component when 150 units of AF53 are produced?

7 What is the material price variance for the raw material ST46 component when 150 units of AF53 are produced?

8.9 Supply chain implications

The application of absorption and standard costing can have a significant impact on the decisions taken by supply chain practitioners.

Make or buy decision

The make or buy decision in a supply chain will occur when an organization is looking to reduce the cost of a product, component or service, often associated with a target cost exercise. The option to buy externally will be a cost comparison decision between the internal cost and the bought-in cost of the component. Before making the decision it is worth examining the cost assumptions regarding how indirect costs are absorbed, as different overhead recovery rates can result in different costs for the item.

Economic order quantity model

The economic order quantity (EOQ) model establishes the optimal reorder size that will (CIMA, 2005:48) 'minimize the sum of stock ordering costs and stock holding costs'.

$$\sqrt{\frac{2CoD}{ch}}$$

Where:
  D is demand for a time period;
  Co is the cost of placing one order;
  ch is the cost of holding one item for that time period.
The model incorporates the two cost elements Co and ch, which are in effect standard costs, and will contain direct and indirect costs. If the assumptions underpinning the apportionment and absorption basis are incorrect, this will have profound implications for the EOQ calculation.

Transfer pricing

A transfer price is the price of a good that is sold between an internal buyer and seller, typically between a manufacturing division and a marketing division, who then sells the product on to the external customer. The transfer price represents revenue for the selling division and an input cost to the buying division and therefore has an impact on the financial performance of both divisions. The assumptions used to formulate the transfer price based on absorption costing will have a significant impact on divisional financial performance.

Product profitability

The choice of apportionment and absorption basis can have a significant impact on the cost of a product. I recall a recent example when HR costs were charged to the production lines in a factory based on tonnes produced. When discussing this method with the production line manager who was responsible for the line, which produced the majority of the firm's output, I was astonished to find out that the line was apportioned with a large percentage of HR cost. In fact, the line was an automatic one and had only a small number of employees working on it. This line was taking more indirect costs when other lines were not, effectively cross-subsidizing the other products produced on the other lines, which will have an impact on product profitability.

Inventory valuation

The key benefit of absorption costing for the supply chain is that it provides an approach to value inventory at the various stages of the production process, including raw materials, work in progress and finished goods. The inventory valuation includes a proportion of the indirect costs at each stage of the production process. The method conforms to the inventory value rule relating to lower of cost or net realizable value and matching concept.

8.10 Summary

The aim of this chapter was to introduce you to the application of absorption costing and variance analysis in the context of supply chains.

At the end of this chapter you are now able to:

- identify direct and indirect costs that make up a product or service using absorption costing;
- explain the different cost units and cost centres within an organization's supply chain;
- appreciate the differences between allocation, apportionment and absorption, which are used to distribute indirect costs to cost units;
- recognize how indirect costs are charged to products and services;
- explain the difference between mark-up and margin and calculate them;
- explain why absorption costing is important in placing a value on inventory;

- calculate typical price and usage variances for direct costs;
- recognize the benefits and limitations of absorption costing.

8.11 References

CIMA (2005) *CIMA Official Terminology*, CIMA Publishing, Oxford

UK Government (2018) *Being a Goods Vehicle Operator*, available at www.gov.
uk/being-a-goods-vehicle-operator/fees-for-goods-vehicle-licences (Accessed 30
October 2018)

8.12 Solutions to the activities

Activity 8.1 solution

Table 8.36 illustrates the profit for each of the four factories using five
different apportionment bases.

Table 8.36 Factory profit by different apportionment basis used by the organization

Profit (£ million)	Production (%)	People (%)	Sales (%)	Factory costs (%)	Apportioned equally	Range
Factory A	28	58	28	22	40	36
Factory B	54	48	54	54	60	12
Factory C	47	35	53	59	35	24
Factory D	51	39	45	45	45	12
Total profit	180	180	180	180	180	

Activity 8.2 solution

Table 8.37 illustrates the overhead recovery rates for Mega plc.

Table 8.37 Mega plc overhead recovery rates

Overhead recovery rates	Calculation	Rate
Rate per direct labour hour	fixed overheads for the period direct labour hours	£10
Direct labour wage percentage	fixed overheads for the period direct labour wages * 100	100%
Rate per machine hour	fixed overheads for the period machine hours	£50
Direct materials percentage	fixed overheads for the period direct materials * 100	25%
Rate per unit	fixed overheads for the period number of units produced	£200
Prime cost percentage	fixed overheads for the period prime cost * 100	20%

Activity 8.3 solution

Figure 8.3 illustrates the material variances for product AF53.

Figure 8.3 AF53 material variances

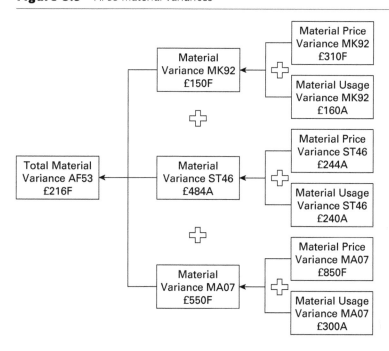

8.13 Study questions

Study question 8.1

You have been asked to calculate a budgeted overhead absorption rate for Department A and Department B within the factory. Both are production cost centres and they share a common purchasing department (service centre). You have been supplied with the budget information in Tables 8.38 to 8.40.

Table 8.38   Budgeted indirect costs

Budgeted indirect costs	£
Heating and lighting	90,000
Supervisors' wages	300,000
Cleaning contract	60,000
Rent and rates	120,000
Plant and machinery maintenance contract	50,000
Plant and machinery insurance	80,000
Plant and machinery depreciation	800,000
Total	**1,500,000**

Table 8.39   Cost centre data

Cost centre data	Dept A	Dept B	Purchasing	Total
Floor area m²	2,700	1,500	300	4,500
Number of stores requisitions	40	160	0	200
Number of supervisors	7	4	1	12
Plant and machinery value £	2,000,000	5,500,000	500,000	8,000,000
Number of breakdowns	4	34	2	40
Machine hours		10,000		
Labour hours	5,000			

Table 8.40   Product data

Product data	Emerald	Diamond	Topaz
Budgeted prime cost per unit (£)	60	120	90
Dept A (hours) per unit	0.50	1.00	0.75
Dept B (hours) per unit	2.00	0.50	1.00

You are required to:

1 Apportion the indirect costs to the production cost centres and the purchasing service centre.

2 Use a suitable basis to apportion the total cost of the stores service centre between the Department A and Department B cost centres.

3 Calculate a suitable overhead recovery rate for Department A and Department B cost centres.

4 Using the information in Table 8.40 for the products Emerald, Diamond and Topaz, calculate the total cost using the overhead absorption rates derived in part 3.

5 Calculate the selling price for each product. The company expects to earn a 25% profit margin.

Study question 8.2

The company's shareholders require a profit margin of 30% on Batch Z62.

Table 8.41   Annual factory production budget and batch Z62 details

Annual factory production budget		Batch Z62
Direct labour hours	200,000	420
Direct labour wages £	2,000,000	5,000
Machine hours	40,000	105
Direct materials consumed £	8,000,000	15,000
Number of units produced	12,500	30
Overheads for the period £	4,000,000	

Using the data in Table 8.41, calculate the following:

1 Calculate the selling price for Batch Z62 (two decimal places) if direct labour hours are used to absorb overheads to production.

   A £42,285.71

   B £43,571.43

   C £40,571.43

   D £39,285.71

2 Calculate the profit for Batch Z62 (two decimal places) if the direct material percentage is used to absorb overheads to production.

A £11,785.71

B £12,685.71

C £12,857.14

D £13,071.43

3 Calculate the profit for Batch Z62 (two decimal places) if the prime cost percentage is used to absorb overheads to production.

A £13,071.43

B £12,171.43

C £12,000.00

D £11,785.71

4 Calculate the total cost for Batch Z62 if units produced are used to absorb overheads to production.

A £30,000

B £29,600

C £28,000

D £27,500

5 Calculate the selling price for Batch Z62 (two decimal places) if direct machine hours are used to absorb overheads to production.

A £42,285.71

B £43,571.43

C £40,571.43

D £39,285.71

6 Calculate the profit for Batch Z62 (two decimal places) if the direct wage percentage is used to absorb overheads to production.

A £11,785.71

B £12,685.71

C £12,857.14

D £13,071.43

Study question 8.3

HR service centre costs are apportioned based on the number of people in each production cost centre. The company's shareholders require a 20% profit margin.

Table 8.42 Service centre apportion data

Cost centre	Cost	People	Capacity hours
Machine shop	£600,000	10	20,000
Finishing shop	£1,600,000	40	80,000
HR service centre	£400,000	10	

Table 8.43 Product data

Product	Prime cost per unit	Machining hours per unit	Finishing hours per unit
Ruby	£100	1.0	3.0
Diamond	£125	1.5	1.0
Emerald	£200	2.0	1.5
Quartz	£225	0.5	0.5

Using the data in Tables 8.42 and 8.43, answer the following:

1 What is the overhead recovery rate per hour for the machine shop?

2 What is the overhead recovery rate per hour for the finishing shop?

3 What is the total cost for making a unit of Ruby?

4 What is the selling price for a unit of Emerald?

5 How much profit does a unit of Quartz produce?

6 How much machine shop overhead costs are charged to a unit of Ruby?

7 How much finishing shop overhead costs are charged to a unit of Diamond?

8 How much profit does a unit of Emerald produce?

9 How much of the HR service centre's costs are apportioned to the finishing shop?

10 What would be the overhead rate for the finishing shop if the HR service centre costs were apportioned equally between the two production cost centres?

Study question 8.4

To make one unit of TZ96, the materials illustrated in Table 8.44, the product's bill of materials, are required.

Table 8.44   TZ96 bill of materials

Raw material component	Price per kg	Quantity of kg
KB6	£30	8
GW5	£15	12
DQ6	£10	5

The actual figures for this month's production of 150 units of TZ96 were as follows:

- KB6 1,320kg at a cost of £35,640;
- GW5 1,950kg at a cost of £31,200;
- DQ6 825kg at a cost of £8,250.

1   What is the total material variance for the monthly production of TZ96?

2   What is the material variance for the raw material component KB6 when 150 units of TZ96 are produced?

3   What is the material price variance for the raw material component KB6 when 150 units of TZ96 are produced?

4   What is the material usage variance for the raw material component KB6 when 150 units of TZ96 are produced?

5   What is the material variance for the raw material component GW5 when 150 units of TZ96 are produced?

6   What is the material price variance for the raw material component GW5 when 150 units of TZ96 are produced?

7   What is the material usage variance for the raw material component GW5 when 150 units of TZ96 are produced?

8   What is the material variance for the raw material component DQ6 when 150 units of TZ96 are produced?

9   What is the material price variance for the raw material component DQ6 when 150 units of TZ96 are produced?

10 What is the material usage variance for the raw material component DQ6 when 150 units of TZ96 are produced?

Table 8.45 Apportion and absorption calculations

Budgeted indirect costs	£	Apportionment basis	Dept A £	Dept B £	Purchasing £	Total £
Heating and lighting	90,000	Floor area m²	54,000	30,000	6,000	90,000
Supervisors' wages	300,000	Number of supervisors	175,000	100,000	25,000	300,000
Cleaning contract	60,000	Floor area m²	36,000	20,000	4,000	60,000
Rent and rates	120,000	Floor area m²	72,000	40,000	8,000	120,000
Plant and machinery maintenance contract	50,000	Number of breakdowns	5,000	42,500	2,500	50,000
Plant and machinery insurance	80,000	Plant and machinery value	20,000	55,000	5,000	80,000
Plant and machinery depreciation	800,000	Plant and machinery value	200,000	550,000	50,000	800,000
Total	**1,500,000**		**562,000**	**837,500**	**100,500**	**1,500,000**
Purchasing		Number of stores requisitions	20,100	80,400		
		Total	**582,100**	**917,900**		**1,500,000**
		Absorption rates	**116.42**	**91.79**		

8.14 Study question solutions

Study question 8.1 solution

Table 8.46 Selling prices

Product	Emerald £	Diamond £	Topaz £
Prime cost	60.00	120.00	90.00
Dept A indirect	58.21	116.42	87.32
Dept B indirect	183.58	45.90	91.79
Total cost	301.79	282.32	269.11
Mark-up	100.60	94.11	89.70
Selling price	402.39	376.42	358.81
Sales margin %	25.00%	25.00%	25.00%

Study question 8.2 solution

1 C

2 A

3 C

4 B

5 B

6 C

Study question 8.3 solution

Table 8.47 Absorption rates for the machine and finishing shop

Cost centre	Machine shop	Finishing shop	HR service centre
Cost £	600,000	1,600,000	400,000
HR apportionment	80,000	320,000	(400,000)
Total cost	680,000	1,920,000	0
Capacity hours	20,000	80,000	
Recovery rate £ per hour	34.00	24.00	

Overhead recovery rate for the machine shop is £680,000/20,000 = £34.00 per hour.

Overhead recovery rate for the finishing shop is £1,920,000/80,000 = £24.00 per hour.

The product's total cost is the prime cost plus the indirect costs. A unit of Ruby requires 1 hour in the machine shop; therefore £34.00 is added to its prime cost of £100.00, to give a work in progress cost of £134.00. The product spends 3 hours in the finishing shop, where the recovery rate is £24.00 per hour, so an additional £72.00 is added, making the total cost £206.00. The company requires a 20% profit margin. Using the following formula we can generate the product's selling price. Table 8.48 illustrates the selling price for all four products.

selling price = product cost/(1 − the profit margin percentage expressed as a decimal)

Ruby's selling price = £206.00/0.8 = £257.50.

Table 8.48 illustrates the total cost, mark-up, selling price and profit margin for all four products.

1　The overhead recovery rate per hour for the machine shop is £34.00.

2　The overhead recovery rate per hour for the finishing shop is £24.00.

3　The total cost for making a unit of Ruby is £206.00.

4　The selling price for a unit of Emerald is £380.00.

5　Quartz produces a profit per unit of £63.50.

Table 8.48　Total cost, mark-up, selling price and profit margin for the four products

Product	Ruby	Diamond	Emerald	Quartz
Prime cost £	100.00	125.00	200.00	225.00
Machine shop costs	34.00	51.00	68.00	17.00
Finishing shop costs	72.00	24.00	36.00	12.00
Total cost	206.00	200.00	304.00	254.00
Mark-up	51.50	50.00	76.00	63.50
Selling price	257.50	250.00	380.00	317.50
Profit margin	20%	20%	20%	20%

6 A unit of Ruby is charged £34 of machine shop overheads.

7 A unit of Diamond is charged £24 of finishing shop overheads.

8 A unit of Emerald makes a profit of £76.00.

9 The finishing shop will be apportioned £320,000 of the HR service centre's costs.

10 Both production centres would be charged £200,000; therefore the total cost of the finishing shop would be £180,000 and the recovery rate would be £22.50 an hour and the machine shop would now be £40.00 per hour. The revised selling prices for the four products are illustrated in Table 8.49.

Table 8.49   Total cost, mark-up, selling price and profit margin for the four products

Product	Ruby	Diamond	Emerald	Quartz
Prime cost £	100.00	125.00	200.00	225.00
Machine shop costs £	40.00	60.00	80.00	20.00
Finishing shop costs £	67.50	22.50	33.75	11.25
Total cost F	207.50	207.50	313.75	256.25
Mark-up £	51.88	51.88	78.44	64.07
Selling price £	259.38	259.38	392.19	320.32
Profit margin	20%	20%	20%	20%
Change in selling price £	1.88	9.38	12.19	2.82

Study question 8.4 solution

Workings

The total material variance for 150 units of product TZ96 is £4,590, which is an overspend of 6.51%. The variances for each material component are as follows:

Table 8.50   TZ96 material variances

TZ96 150 units	Budget	Actual	Variance	Percentage
Material KB6 £	36,000	35,640	360F	1.00 F
Material GW5 £	27,000	31,200	4,200A	15.56A
Material DQ6 £	7,500	8,250	750A	10.00A
Total £	70,500	75,090	4,590A	6.51A

KB6   360F

GW5   4,200A

DQ6   750A

The material price variance is calculated by subtracting the actual price per kg from the standard price per kg and then multiplying by the actual kg used:

KB6   (£30 – £27) * 1,320 = £3,960F

GW5   (£15 – £16) * 1,950 = £1,950F

DQ6   (£10 – £10) * 9,000 = No variance

The material usage variance is calculated by subtracting the actual kg used from the standard kg planned for production and then multiplying by the standard price per kg.

KB6   (1,200Kg – 1,320Kg) * £30 = £3,600A

GW5   (1,800Kg – 1,950Kg) * £15 = £2,250A

DQ6   (750Kg – 825Kg) * £10 = £750A

Figure 8.4 illustrates the material variances for product TZ96.

Figure 8.4   TZ96 material variances

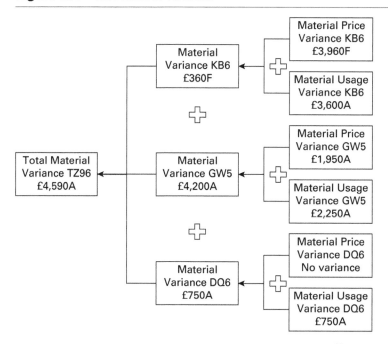

Contemporary 09
costing methods

This chapter introduces you to three contemporary costing methods that emerged towards the end of the twentieth century and have had a significant impact on the decisions taken by SC practitioners, directly affecting the financial performance of an organization: activity-based costing, total cost of ownership and target costing. Each method has led to radical change in the way that functions such as management accounting, sales and marketing, information technology and supply chain management now work together. No longer can these functions exist in their formal silos; today they now overlap, but they need to collaborate, cooperate and become more integrated to achieve the strategic objectives of their organization. Technology, big data and analytics are becoming powerful agents of change and they act as facilitators of integration, breaking down the traditional boundaries of these functions and enabling them to have an ever-increasing role in assisting future value-creation.

In their own way these three costing methods have changed the relationship between management accounting, IT, marketing and supply chain management with regard to costing supply chain activities, understanding the cost to serve different customers, redefining procurement decisions and new product introductions.

From my own perspective, I was fortunate to have witnessed the arrival of these costing methods first-hand, and have been involved with the implementation of some of them into practice, especially activity-based costing, and have experienced the benefits and challenges of implementing them.

9.1 Aim and objectives

The aim of this chapter is to introduce you to three contemporary costing methods used in practice that can have a significant impact on the decisions taken by SC practitioners and contribute to the financial performance of any organization.

At the end of this chapter you will be able to:

- explain the rationale for adopting them;
- identify the benefits of adopting activity-based costing;
- explain the benefits of adopting total cost of ownership (TCO) compared with traditional purchasing based on purchase price;
- recognize the role of target costing when launching new products.

9.2 Activity-based costing (ABC)

Activity-based costing (ABC) is a costing method for distributing indirect costs to products and services as an alternative to full/absorption costing to derive the total cost of the item produced or service delivered. However, Lin *et al* (2001:704) argue that 'ABC does not replace traditional accounting systems and records; ABC merely attempts to define further the data aggregated in traditional accounts into a more advantageous decision-making form for managers.'

The ABC approach, according to Lin *et al* (2001:704), 'traces the consumption of resources back to the consuming activity and then traces those activities to particular cost objects such as specific products, territories, customers, or departments of the corporation'.

CIMA (2005:3) define ABC as an:

> Approach to the costing and monitoring of activities which involves tracing resource consumption and costing final outputs. Resources are assigned to activities, and activities to cost objectives based on consumption estimates. The latter utilize cost drivers to attach activity costs to outputs.

The interest in ABC was fuelled by the disillusionment and dissatisfaction with traditional cost methods that are based on apportionment and absorption, and, depending on the assumptions made, can result in different product costs. As Kaplan and Cooper (1997:89) argue:

> One does not need extensive time-and-motion studies to link resource spending to activities performed. The goal is to be approximately right, rather than precisely wrong, as is the case with virtually all traditional product costing systems.

Cooper (1989:77) argued that 'strategies may be conceptually brilliant, but if they are based on faulty information about the cost of a product, they are likely to fail in the marketplace. Many have.'

The logic supporting ABC is illustrated with this simple example that we can all relate to. You have attended a meal at a restaurant and had a great evening – the meal was fantastic, you enjoyed the very good company and the occasion was extremely enjoyable. And then finally the bill arrives to be paid. Typically, in my experience and probably yours as well, the bill gets divided by the number of people equally. For example, if the cost is £600 and there are 10 people, each person pays £60, because that is the easiest and quickest way to apportion the (you have been doing full costing already) cost; however, is it the fairest way? After you have said goodbye to everybody, you start to analyse the bill in your head as you are walking home. You sum up the cost of the menu items you had and realize that you have paid £60, but have only consumed £35; you have paid £25 more than you should, but it was a great evening. We have all been there!

Table 9.1 illustrates the difference between what each guest paid and what they actually consumed based on the itemized bill.

The first thing to notice about ABC is that it doesn't reduce cost; it just illustrates costs differently. In Table 9.1, four people (A, B, D and G) paid more than they should have for their meal, while five diners (C, E, F, H and J) paid less than they should have, and one person (K) paid the correct amount. If you wanted to, you could now redistribute the costs between the guests based on their actual consumption and suffer the consequences, but it's the fairer approach. It's only a meal, I hear you say.

Table 9.1 Full costing vs. ABC

Guest	A	B	C	D	E	F	G	H	J	K	Total
Full costing £ per person	60	60	60	60	60	60	60	60	60	60	600
ABC £ per person	35	55	80	45	65	70	50	75	65	60	600
Difference £ per person	−25	−5	20	−15	5	10	−10	15	5	0	0

However, say they were not people, but production lines in manufacturing plants, and the cost is not £600, but £6,000,000. There then becomes significant implications regarding the total cost of the products being produced by each line, as some products are being cross-subsidized by others, which can have serious implications for a business. We will revisit this point after the case study example.

ABC case study

The CEO of Mega Manufacturing plc recently attended a breakfast briefing on ABC at a trade show and has asked you to compare next month's budgeted production, which is based on full costing, with an ABC approach. Currently, budgeted production overheads are charged to products based on their budgeted volumes. The company manufactures five products and next month's production volumes for each product as a percentage of total production is illustrated in Table 9.2.

Table 9.2   Mega Manufacturing plc October 20XX production

Product	AD5	KP9	GY7	WQ7	GZ4	Total
Production %	20	25	10	35	10	100

Mega Manufacturing plc's budgeted production overheads for October 20XX are £25,000.

Step 1

The first activity is to calculate the budgeted production overhead to be charged to each product. This is an apportionment, which is based on each product's percentage of the total volume for the period. To calculate the production overhead apportionment, take the product's percentage of the total production and then multiply it by the production overhead for the month. For example, product AD5 has 20% of the budgeted production for October 20XX, therefore it is apportioned 20% of £25,000, which is £5,000. Table 9.3 illustrates the budgeted production overhead that each product would be apportioned for October 20XX.

Table 9.3   October 20XX budgeted production overhead by product for October 20XX

Product	AD5	KP9	GY7	WQ7	GZ4	Total
Production overhead £	5,000	6,250	2,500	8,750	2,500	25,000

Product WQ7 will be charged with £8,750, the highest amount of production overheads; it has 35% of the monthly budgeted production, while GY7 and GZ4 have equal amounts of production overhead, as these products each have 10% of the planned volume for October 20XX.

Step 2

The management accountant and the factory's industrial engineer have managed to translate the production overhead budget into the five cost pools that support the production activity and have also agreed appropriate cost drivers for each cost pool. The budget for each cost pool, their cost driver and the budgeted volumes for each cost driver are illustrated in Table 9.4. The rate per cost driver is calculated by dividing the budget for the cost driver by its budgeted volume; for example, the cost per maintenance callout takes £6,000 and divides by budgeted volume of 50 to give a callout cost of £120.

Table 9.4   Cost pool, cost drives and budgeted volumes cost per drive for October 20XX

Production cost pool	Production cost driver	Budgeted cost pool overhead £	Budget cost driver volumes	Budgeted cost £ per driver
Maintenance	Number of callouts	6,000	50	120
Stores	Number of purchase orders	4,000	40	100
Calibration	Number of set-ups	8,000	160	50
Inspection	Number of checks	2,500	100	25
Cleaning	Number of changeovers	4,500	50	90
		25,000		

Step 3

The industrial engineer, based on experience and past production runs, has budgeted the consumption of each cost driver by product. This information is presented in Table 9.5.

Table 9.5   Cost driver consumption by product

Product	Maintenance	Stores	Calibration	Inspection	Cleaning
AD5	8	5	38	10	7
KP9	12	10	45	15	10
GY7	15	7	30	30	15
WQ7	5	8	15	5	5
GZ4	10	10	32	40	13
Total	**50**	**40**	**160**	**100**	**50**

Step 4

Applying the cost driver rates calculated in Table 9.4 and the volume consumed of each activity by every product in Table 9.5, the total production overhead cost for each product for the month of October 20XX can be calculated. For example, product KP9 is budgeted to consume 12 maintenance callouts in October; the cost per callout is £120; therefore, product KP9 will incur a maintenance cost of £1,440. This calculation is then repeated for all the products to ascertain the maintenance cost for each product and will be reconciled with the total overhead cost for the maintenance cost pool. The process will then be repeated for every cost pool until all the production overhead costs for October have been charged to the five products, as illustrated in Table 9.6.

Table 9.6   Budgeted production overheads by product using ABC for October 20XX

Product	Maintenance	Stores	Calibration	Inspection	Cleaning	Total
AD5	960	500	1,900	250	630	4,240
KP9	1,440	1,000	2,250	375	900	5,965
GY7	1,800	700	1,500	750	1,350	6,100
WQ7	600	800	750	125	450	2,725
GZ4	1,200	1,000	1,600	1,000	1,170	5,970
Total	**6,000**	**4,000**	**8,000**	**2,500**	**4,500**	**25,000**

Step 5

The next stage is to compare the differences between the current method of charging production overheads to products using production volumes with the ABC approach based on consumption of activities by product. Table 9.7 illustrates the cost differences for each product by each costing approach.

In Table 9.7 we can see that ABC does not take cost out, as the production overhead budget remains the same: £25,000. However, an ABC approach presents the costs in a different way, therefore giving the user of the

Table 9.7 Production overhead cost for each product using the two costing approaches

Product	AD5	KP9	GY7	WQ7	GZ4	Total
Apportioned	5,000	6,250	2,500	8,750	2,500	25,000
ABC	4,240	5,965	6,100	2,725	5,970	25,000
Difference	**760**	**285**	**(3,600)**	**6,025**	**(3,470)**	**–**

information a different perspective. The ABC approach to charging production overheads to products based on consumption has redistributed costs between the five products. The impact of the ABC approach is to reduce the production overhead costs of products AD5, KP9 and WQ7 and increase the costs of GY7 and GZ4.

However, changing from the current costing method to ABC will have implications for:

- product profitability;
- sales and product pricing issues;
- internal conflict between functions;
- greater visibility of cost associated with products;
- increased cost ownership and accountability;
- performance management;
- highlight waste in processes;
- opportunities to reduce cost.

The final point above is where ABC can be used to highlight opportunities to reduce costs in processes and activities, which were not possible before. This point is illustrated in Table 9.8, which shows the percentage of cost

Table 9.8 Percentage of cost driver consumption by product

Product	Maintenance	Stores	Calibration	Inspection	Cleaning
AD5	16%	12%	24%	10%	14%
KP9	24%	25%	28%	15%	20%
GY7	30%	18%	19%	30%	30%
WQ7	10%	20%	9%	5%	10%
GZ4	20%	25%	20%	40%	26%
Total	100%	100%	100%	100%	100%

driver volumes consumed by each of the five products. This now provides Mega Manufacturing plc's management accountant and industrial engineer with an opportunity to explore the production process further and in more depth by asking a number of 'why' questions.

The first set of 'why' questions are:

1 Why do production lines GY7 (30%) and KP9 (24%) account for 54% of the maintenance callouts?

2 Why do production lines GZ4 (25%) and KP9 (25%) account for 50% of the total purchase orders?

3 Why does KP9 production line account for 28% of the total set-ups?

4 Why does GZ4 have 40% of the number of checks, but only produces 10% of the factory's production volumes?

5 Why do GY7 and GZ4 account for 20% of the factory's production, but are responsible for 56% of the cleaning costs?

The implementation journey for ABC provides the opportunity to study the organization's processes and activities in more depth. When used in conjunction with time-based process mapping, the synergies are significant in identifying non-value-adding activities, waste and opportunities to reduce cost.

Calculating descriptive statistics generated by the ABC implementation illustrated in Table 9.9 include:

Table 9.9   Minimum, maximum, range and multiple

Product	Maintenance	Stores	Calibration	Inspection	Cleaning
AD5	8	5	38	10	7
KP9	12	10	45	15	10
GY7	15	7	30	30	15
WQ7	5	8	15	5	5
GZ4	10	10	32	40	13
Minimum	5	5	15	5	5
Maximum	15	10	45	40	15
Range	10	5	30	35	10
Multiple	3	2	3	8	3

- identifying minimum and maximum values to related activity consumption;
- calculating the range;
- calculating the multiple (dividing maximum value by the minimum value).

The analysis can generate additional questions worth investigating, including:

1 Why is the inspection range 35 and the multiple between the maximum and minimum value 8?

2 Why are the multiples for maintenance, calibration and cleaning three times the minimum values?

Now have a go at the next activity.

Activity 9.1

Ultra Ltd currently apportions its monthly overheads of £40,000 to product lines using the percentage of monthly production. The company wants to move to activity-based costing to distribute overheads to products. The management accountant has been taken ill. Complete the shaded areas in Tables 9.10, 9.11 and 9.12, and then solve questions 1 to 5.

Table 9.10   Monthly production by product line

Production line	Alpha	Beta	Gamma	Delta
Monthly production %	15		25	20

Table 9.11   Cost driver volumes by product line

Production line	Plant maintenance	Quality control	Engineering
Cost driver	Number of breakdowns	Number of inspections	Number of set-ups
Alpha	40	80	
Beta		20	18
Gamma	20	60	24
Delta	30	40	48
Total	100		120

Table 9.12 Activity-based costs by product line

Production line	Plant maintenance £	Quality control £	Engineering £
Alpha	10,000		1,500
Beta	2,500	900	900
Gamma		2,700	1,200
Delta	7,500	1,800	2,400
Total	25,000	9,000	

1 How much overhead cost will be apportioned to the Beta production line based on the monthly production percentage?

   A £10,000

   B £8,900

   C £11,700

   D £16,000

2 What is the activity-based cost per breakdown?

   A £50

   B £75

   C £100

   D £250

3 How much of the monthly overhead is charged to Gamma production line if activity-based costing is used?

   A £11,700

   B £8,900

   C £4,300

   D £10,000

4 Which production lines' overhead costs will increase using activity-based costing?

   A Alpha and Beta

   B Beta and Gamma

   C Gamma and Alpha

   D Delta and Alpha

5 Which product line will benefit the most if activity-based costing is introduced?

A Alpha

B Beta

C Gamma

D Delta

9.3 Total cost of ownership

Here is a simple everyday example that reinforces the rationale for taking a total cost of ownership (TCO) approach. My daughter decided to purchase an ink jet printer instead of a laser printer while at university, as the initial purchase cost for the laser was more expensive than the ink jet. However, the running costs of the ink jet printer turned out to be more expensive than the laser. A cost per page calculation undertaken by her father revealed this to be the case!

Ellram and Siferd (1993:164) define a total cost of ownership approach as: 'All costs associated with the acquisition, use and maintenance of an item must be considered in evaluating that item and not just the purchase price.' Therefore, a TCO approach will need to take into consideration all the relevant costs associated with procuring an item, including any pre-transaction costs, transaction costs and post-transaction costs. Have a go at the following activity:

Activity 9.2

Your organization is considering adding to its road haulage fleet by purchasing a new articulated truck and trailer to launch its new trucking service, which will specialize in operating full truck deliveries for B2B. This will be a substantial purchase and they have asked you to help them with a total cost of ownership approach to identify the relevant costs they should include in their cost analysis. Complete Table 9.13 by identifying as many relevant costs as you can think of that they should incorporate in their cost model.

Table 9.13   Total cost of ownership approach for a truck and trailer purchase

Pre-transaction costs	Transaction costs	Post-transaction costs

Total cost of ownership case study

The inspiration for this fictitious total cost of ownership (TCO) case study came from this fascinating example from Ryals and McDonald (2008:226):

> An interesting example was given to one of the authors by a director of a specialist construction company which built and fitted out operating theatres. The customer's procurement guidelines initially resulted in the cheapest suitable light bulbs being specified in the operating theatres.

Increasing and extending cost visibility with a TCO approach (Ryals and McDonald, 2008:226):

> However, a TCO analysis after the theatres had been in use for a while revealed that these light bulbs blew more frequently than the more expensive ones. This meant the expense and disruption of shutting down the operating theatre, calling in a maintenance contractor, and then re-sterilizing the operating theatre – all to change a light bulb!

The Hippocratic Hospital Trust's procurement manager has approached you to supply specialist light bulbs for their operating theatres in the hospitals they manage. They have supplied you with the following information regarding one of their hospitals, The Socrates Royal Infirmary. The hospital has eight operating theatres in use and the theatres are used on average 10 hours per day, 300 days per annum. The hospital has contracted out the maintenance and cleaning of their theatres to a specialized cleaning firm. When a light bulb fails, the operating theatre cannot be used and will have to be deep-cleaned after the bulb has been replaced. The cost to the trust is £1,000 for the changeover and sterilization of the theatre. The trust is charged £50 per bulb for disposal of a bulb.

You have two bulbs that meet the specialist requirements of the Hippocratic Hospital Trust. Their details are shown in the Table 9.14.

Table 9.14   Light bulbs' cost, life and running costs

Light bulb	Price	Life span	Running cost
Sunburst 2000	£400	3,000 hours	£0.30 per hour
Starlight 660	£100	1,200 hours	£0.35 per hour

The trust's charter states that they have adopted a 'value for money' ethos regarding their procurement decisions. This would be a good contract to win. Recommend to the trust which light bulb they should buy.

In a TCO costing approach to purchase a light bulb, the first step is to calculate the amount of light required. The hospital has eight operating theatres in use throughout the year and the theatres are used on average 10 hours per day for 300 days per annum. Therefore the hospital requires light for 24,000 hours (8 theatres * 10 hours * 300 days).

If they buy the Sunburst 2000, they require 8 bulbs (24,000 hours/3,000 hours).

If they buy the Starlight 660, they require 20 bulbs (24,000 hours/1,200 hours).

The costings for each bulb are illustrated in Table 9.15.

Table 9.15   Total cost of ownership for Sunburst 2000 and Starlight 660

Light bulb	Sunburst 2000	Starlight 660
Purchase cost	8 bulbs @ £400 = £3,200	20 bulbs @ £100 = £2,000
Running cost	£0.30 @ 24,000 hours = £7,200	£0.35 @ 24,000 hours = £8,400
Changeover	8 bulbs @ £1,000 = £8,000	20 bulbs @ £1,000 = £20,000
Disposal cost	8 bulbs @ £50 = £400	20 bulbs @ £50 = £1,000
Total cost	**£18,800**	**£31,400**

If the hospital procurement department is just concerned with purchasing the cheapest light bulb, they will purchase the Starlight 660 at a cost of £2,000, which is a saving of £1,200.

If the purchase and running costs are taken into consideration, the cost of the Starlight 660 is £10,400; the cost of the Sunburst 2000 is also £10,400.

Finally, if the total cost of ownership is calculated for both bulbs, factoring in the changeover and disposal costs, the hospital's procurement department will purchase the Sunburst 2000, as its total cost is £18,800, which is £12,600 cheaper than the Starlight 660.

The key factor is that the procurement decision needs to take into consideration not just the purchase costs but total cost of ownership of the item, which means they need to be aware of all the costs associated with the purchase of the item, including the pre-transaction costs, the transaction cost and the post-transaction costs

Ryals and McDonald (2008:266) argue: 'There are many examples of transactions where the cheapest product or service turns out to be of poorer value than buying a more expensive product which lasts longer and requires less maintenance.'

The next time you buy a printer, try adopting a TCO approach.

9.4 Target costing

Target cost is defined by CIMA (2005:15) as: 'Product cost estimate derived by subtracting a desired profit margin from a competitive market price.' Cooper and Slagmulder (1997:52) offer an enhanced definition:

> A structured approach to determine the life-cycle cost at which a proposed product with specified functionality and quality must be produced to generate the desired level of profitability over its life cycle when sold at its anticipated selling price.

The following example illustrates the logic relating to target costing. TC plc wanted to sell their new product XXG4 for £250; however, a recent marketing study has revealed that they will only be able to charge £220. Their shareholders require a 25% profit margin (M). How much will they have to reduce the current cost of making XXG4 to achieve their target profit margin if the product now sells for £220?

The current cost of making a unit of XXG4 can be calculated by using the following formula: $SP*(1 - M)$, where M is the target profit margin expressed as a decimal. Therefore the cost of making XXG4 is £250.00 * 0.75 = £187.50. The calculation is now repeated for the new target price of £220.00, which is £165.00. Therefore, the target cost reduction is the difference between £187.50 and £165.00, which equates to £22.50. This is the amount that TC plc will need to engineer out of the product's supply chain. The following case study explores this aspect of reducing a product's cost across its supply chain.

The example also illustrates the argument put forward by Cooper and Chew (1996:88) with regard to introducing new products into the marketplace, but also reinforcing the need for greater functional integration with regard to pricing and costing a new product or service:

> Before a company launches a product (or family of products), senior managers determine its selling price, establish the feasibility of meeting that price, and then control costs to ensure that the price is met. They are using a management process known as target costing.

Target costing is market-led and is a totally different mindset and approach to pricing a product compared with the traditional cost-plus pricing that is underpinned by full costing. Full costing takes the product's prime cost (sum of all the direct costs), then adds on the indirect costs (overheads) to achieve a total cost; a mark-up is added to achieve the desired margin, deriving the product's selling price. This approach is typically referred to as 'bottom–up', while a target approach follows the logic described by Cooper and Chew (1996) and takes a 'top–down' approach.

Cooper and Slagmulder (1997:55) advocate using seven questions in relation to target costing:

> What are the firm's long-term sales and profit objectives?
> Where will the new product's survival zone be when it's launched?
> What is the target profit margin?
> What level of cost reduction is realistic?
> How can we achieve this cost reduction objective?
> Are there extraneous circumstances that allow the target?
> How can we distribute the cost reduction among the components?

The target cost approach is explored further in the following fictitious case study example.

Target costing case study

Ultra plc is prepared to launch its new product ZXT 23B. It will sell for £1,250 and the organization's shareholders expect to earn a profit margin of 20%. The product's supply chain is illustrated in Figure 9.1. There are four organizations that make up the supply chain.

Figure 9.1 ZXT 23B supply chain

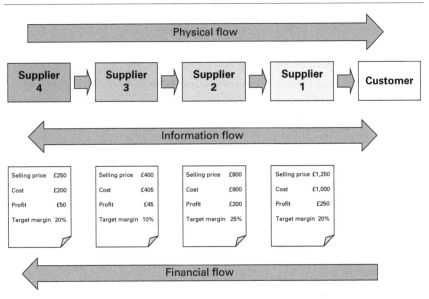

Supplier 4 sells the components that are incorporated into supplier 3's sub-frame, which is sold to supplier 2, who attaches their control system to the sub-frame, which is incorporated by Ultra plc into the finished product ZXT 23B, which is then sold to the customer. All of the organizations have agreed as part of their collaboration agreement to adopt open-book accounting and are prepared to share their costs with each other.

Ultra plc's marketing team have just returned from an international trade show where ZXT 23B was extremely well received by its potential customers; however, feedback from customers indicated that the proposed price was too high and that £1,150 was a fair price.

If ZXT 23B sells for £1,150, Ultra plc will only achieve a profit of £150, which equates to a profit margin of 13% (£150/£1,150 * 100), not the expected profit margin of 20% that their shareholders desire. Achieving a target margin of 20% when the selling price is £1,150 requires a target cost of £920; currently the cost of making the product is £1,000. The current selling prices, cost breakdown and profit margins for each organization as per the open-book accounting agreement are illustrated in Table 9.16.

Ultra plc is unable to absorb all of the cost reduction and has asked all the members of ZXT 23B supply chain to attend a meeting to identify opportunities to reduce the cost of the product but still maintain their individual target profit margins.

Table 9.16 Product ZXT 23B open-book accounting data by organization

Original	Ultra plc	Supplier 2	Supplier 3	Supplier 4
Selling price £	1,250.00	800.00	450.00	250.00
In-house cost £	200.00	150.00	155.00	200.00
Bought-in cost £	800.00	450.00	250.00	0.00
Total cost £	1,000.00	600.00	405.00	200.00
Profit £	250.00	200.00	45.00	50.00
Margin	20%	25%	10%	20%

Each of the organizations was asked to identify opportunities to reduce the costs associated with making the product ZXT 23B. Table 9.17 illustrates the revised costing for making the product at a target cost of £920 per unit.

Table 9.17 Product ZXT 23B target cost reductions from £1,000 to £920 per unit

Target cost reduction	Ultra plc	Supplier 2	Supplier 3	Supplier 4
Selling price £	1,150.00	750.00	427.50	239.75
In-house cost £	170.00	135.00	145.00	191.80
Bought-in cost £	750.00	427.50	239.75	0.00
Total cost £	920.00	562.50	384.75	191.80
Profit £	230.00	187.50	42.75	47.95
Margin	20%	25%	10%	20%

Target costing can also be applied within an organization to reduce costs of internal transactions between internal buyers and sellers. The price charged for the internal transaction is referred to as the transfer price. Mehafdi (2004:639) defines the transfer price as 'the prices charged for products exchanged in internal transactions between sellers (or transferors) and buyers (or transferees) who belong to the same organization, usually a decentralised company'.

If an existing supplier node in either an internal or external supply chain is unable to achieve its target cost reduction, the buyer node will have to seek an alternative source of supply. In the case of an internal supply chain this will result in a make or buy decision being made, resulting in the selection of an external supplier to the detriment of the existing internal supplier. The make or buy decision is illustrated in Figure 9.2.

Figure 9.2 Make or buy decision

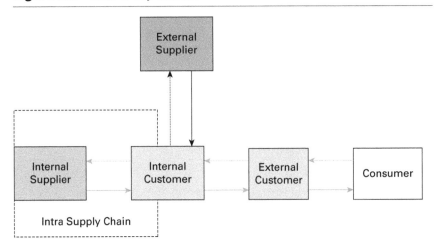

Now have a go at the following target costing activity.

Activity 9.3

a Ultra plc has designed and produced a new product WHY363H, which has a total cost of £90. They would like to make a profit margin of 40%. What will be the product's selling price?

b Mega plc wanted to sell their new product for £200; however, a recent marketing study has revealed that they will only be able to charge £180. The shareholders require a 25% profit margin. How much will they have to reduce the current cost to achieve their target profit margin if the product sells for £180?

c TC plc had planned to sell their new product X40 for £200, which would generate a profit margin of 35%; however, at a recent trade show potential customers liked the product but were only prepared to place orders if the product's price was reduced by 20%. TC plc shareholders still require a margin of 35%. Currently X40's total cost is made up of 70% in-house components and 30% from a third-party supplier. If the cost reduction is apportioned based on the current cost split, what will be the third party's target price?

d SCT plc's new product costs £120. What is the mark-up percentage required to achieve a profit margin of 25%?

9.5 Other contemporary costing methods

Templar *et al* (2004:510) identified a number of contemporary costing methods, including the three introduced in this chapter, in their supply chain costing road map. These are illustrated in Table 9.18 on page 312. Their road map highlights the main area of application in the supply chain for each costing method using the SCOR activities (plan, source, make, deliver and return). The road map briefly introduces the benefits and typical impacts of each costing approach.

Templar *et al* (2004:514) argue that:

> Traditional costing systems, based on arbitrary rules of overhead recovery, are not effective in providing cost information in an accurate way to support supply chain managers in their decision-making. A range of contemporary costing systems has emerged to address the needs of specific supply chain costing applications.

9.6 Summary

The aim of this chapter is to introduce you to three contemporary costing methods used in practice that can have a significant impact on the decisions taken by SC practitioners and contribute to the financial performance of any organization.

Of the three costing methods you were introduced to in this chapter, activity-based costing is the most versatile as it can be used across all the activities highlighted in Porter's value chain as well as the SCOR activities. You are now able to explain the rationale for the adoption of these costing methods in the SC and can identify their benefits and their impact on the different areas of an organization's SC operation.

9.7 References

CIMA (2005) *CIMA Official Terminology*, CIMA Publishing, Oxford

Cooper, R (1989) You need a new cost system when, *Harvard Business Review* (January – February), pp 77–82

Cooper, R and Chew, W (1996) Control tomorrow's costs through today's design, *Harvard Business Review*, 74 (1), pp 88–97

Cooper, R and Slagmulder, R (1997) *Target Costing and Value Engineer*, Productivity Press, Portland

Table 9.18 Supply chain costing road map

Costing method	Primary focus	P	S	M	D	R	Major benefit	Typical impacts
Activity-based costing	Deriving more accurately the costs associated with an organization's processes	X	X	X	X	X	Greater visibility of indirect costs associated with activities	Highlights the cost associated with business processes. Reduces the impact of cross-subsidization. Increased accountability and ownership of supply chain costs
Cost to serve	Identify costs associated with different customers, products and channels to market				X		Translates functional expenditure to customers, products and channels highlighting profitability issues	Improved visibility of customer segment profitability Highlighting product profitability issues Comparing channel-to-market costs
Direct product profitability	Understanding retail profitability by product				X		Maps retail handling and storage costs to individual products based on each product's specific characteristics	Compare product profitability for a range of products Will identify loss-making products Maximize profit per retail floor space
Target costing	Achieving a target cost through business process re-engineering	X	X	X	X	X	Enables customer-focused cost reductions without destroying customer value	Targeted cost reduction Evaluating sourcing decisions Improved communication across supply chain processes
Throughput accounting	Maximizing throughput based on known constraints			X	X		Maximizing profitability based on constraints	Increased profitability
Total cost of ownership	Optimizing procurement decisions	X					All cost associated with the acquisition and maintenance of an item should be included in the total cost	Establishes selection criteria Enables make or buy decisions to be evaluated

Ellram, L and Siferd, SP (1993) Purchasing: the cornerstone of the total cost of ownership concept, *Journal of Business Logistics*, **14** (1), pp 163–184

Kaplan, RS and Cooper, R (1997) *Cost and Effect: Using integrated cost systems to drive profitability and performance*, Harvard Business Review Press, Boston

Lin, B, Collins, J and Su, RK (2001) Supply chain costing: an activity based approach, *International Journal of Physical Distribution and Logistics Management*, **31** (10), pp 702–713

Mehafdi, M (2004) Transfer pricing, in *Handbook of Management Accounting*, 3rd edn, ed J Innes, pp 639–658, CIMA Publishing, Oxford

Ryals, L and McDonald, M (2008) *Key Account Plans: The practitioners' guide to profitable planning*, Butterworth-Heinemann, Oxford

Templar, S, Bernon, M and Fan, M (2004) Supply chain costing – a road map, in *Logistics Research Network Conference 2004*, Dublin, September

9.8 Solutions to the activities

Activity 9.1 solution

Ultra Ltd currently apportions its monthly overheads of £40,000 to product lines using the percentage of monthly production. Table 9.19 illustrates the current costing method of apportioning overhead costs to production lines based on volume.

Table 9.19   Monthly production by product line

Production line	Alpha	Beta	Gamma	Delta	Total
Monthly production %	15	40	25	20	**100**
Overhead apportionment £	6,000	16,000	10,000	8,000	**40,000**

Table 9.20 illustrates the completed table for the consumption of activities by product line.

Table 9.21 illustrates the overhead costs that have now been charged to the individual production lines based on their consumption of the activities.

The cost driver rate is calculated by dividing the cost for each cost pool by the cost driver volume, illustrated in Table 9.22.

The redistribution of costs between the production lines based on the application of activity-based costing is illustrated in Table 9.23.

The solutions to the questions are as follows:

Table 9.20   Cost driver volumes by product line

Production line	Plant-maintenance	Quality control	Engineering
Cost driver	Number of breakdowns	Number of inspections	Number of set-ups
Alpha	40	80	210
Beta	10	20	18
Gamma	20	60	24
Delta	30	40	48
Total	**100**	**200**	**120**

Table 9.21   Activity-based costs by product line

Production line	Plant maintenance £	Quality control £	Engineering £
Alpha	10,000	3,600	1,500
Beta	2,500	900	900
Gamma	5,000	2,700	1,200
Delta	7,500	1,800	2,400
Total	**25,000**	**9,000**	**6,000**

Table 9.22   Cost driver rates

Production line	Plant maintenance £	Quality control £	Engineering £
Cost pool £	25,000	9,000	6,000
Cost driver volumes	100	200	120
Cost driver rate £	250	45	50

Table 9.23   Monthly production by product line

Production line	Alpha	Beta	Gamma	Delta	Total
Overhead apportionment £	6,000	16,000	10,000	8,000	**40,000**
Activity-based costs £	15,100	4,300	8,900	11,700	**40,000**
Difference £	–9,100	11,700	1,100	–3,700	**0**

1 £16,000 will be apportioned to the Beta production line based on the line's monthly production, which is 40% of the total production of the factory.
Answer = D

2 The activity-based cost per breakdown is £250.
Answer = D

3 If overheads are charged to production lines using activity-based costing, the monthly overhead charged to Gamma production will be £8,900.
Answer = B

4 The production lines that will have an increase in their monthly overhead costs when using activity-based costing are Alpha and Delta.
Answer = D

5 The product line which will benefit the most if activity-based costing is introduced is Beta, as £11,700 costs will be redistributed to the product lines that produce Alpha and Delta.
Answer = B

Activity 9.2 solution

When considering the purchase of a new articulated truck and trailer, a total cost of ownership approach can be used to identify the relevant costs to be included in a cost analysis. Table 9.24 identifies a list of relevant costs that should be incorporated into a TCO costing model.

Table 9.24 Total cost of ownership approach for a truck and trailer purchase

Pre-transaction costs	Transaction costs	Post-transaction costs
Supplier visits	Vehicle price	Fuel
Test driving the vehicle	Additional specifications costs	Tyres
Evaluating alternatives		Maintenance
Preparing the business case		Depreciation
Negotiating with supplier		Taxes
Evaluating different finance options		Insurance
		Spares
		Interest

Activity 9.3 solution

a To calculate the selling price for the new product WHY363H, which will generate a profit margin of 40%, you need to apply the following formula:

$$SP = C/(1-M)$$

Where:

$$SP = \text{selling price} ;$$
$$C = \text{product's cost};$$
$$M = \text{the target margin expressed as a decimal};$$
$$SP = £90/ (1-0.4) = £90/0.6 = £150.$$

The selling price for WHY363H that will generate a profit margin of 40% will be £150; the product's profit will be £60 (£150 – £90). To calculate the profit margin, we divide the profit of £60 by the selling price of £150 and multiply by 100 to give a margin of 40%.

b First of all we need to derive the current cost of making the product. This is done by multiplying the selling price by 1 minus the profit margin expressed as a decimal, which is 0.75. Multiplying the selling price of £200 by 0.75 derives the cost of the product, which is £150. The process is repeated for the new price: £180 multiplied by 0.75 equals £135, which is the target cost; therefore the target cost reduction is £15.

c X40 revised selling price will be £200 * 0.8, which is £160. TC expects to make a profit margin of 35%; therefore the target cost will be £104. The third party's target price will be £31.20, which is a reduction of £7.80.

d Use the formula $SP = C/(1-M)$ to derive the selling price for the product, which will be £160, so the profit will be £40. The mark-up percentage is calculated by dividing the product's profit by its cost, which is a mark-up percentage of 33.334% (£40/£120).

9.9 Study question

Study question 9.1

JIT Manufacturing Ltd currently absorbs its monthly overheads of £60,000 to product lines using the percentage of monthly production. The company wants to move to activity-based costing to distribute overheads to products. Complete Tables 9.25, 9.26 and 9.27, and then solve questions 1 to 10.

Table 9.25 Monthly production by product line

Production line	Red	Green	Yellow	Blue
Monthly production %	10		30	20

Table 9.26 Cost driver volumes by product line

Production line	Plant maintenance	Quality control	Engineering
Cost driver	Number of breakdowns	Number of inspections	Number of set-ups
Red	15		20
Green	24	20	10
Yellow	26	65	15
Blue	35	40	
Total		200	50

Table 9.27 Activity based costs by product line

Production line	Plant maintenance £	Quality control £	Engineering £
Red	4,200	8,250	4,000
Green		2,200	2,000
Yellow	7,280	7,150	3,000
Blue	9,800		1,000
Total	28,000	22,000	

1 How much overhead cost will be absorbed to the Green production line based on the monthly production percentage?

2 What is the activity-based cost per breakdown?

3 How much of the monthly overhead is charged to Red's production line if activity-based costing is used?

4 Which product's production line overhead costs will increase using activity-based costing?

5 Which product line will benefit the most if activity-based costing is introduced?

6 What is the activity-based cost per set-up?

7 What is the cost per inspection?

8 Which product has the highest percentage of breakdowns?

9 How much overhead cost will be absorbed to Yellow's production line based on the monthly production percentage?

10 Which product line has the highest number of quality control inspections?

9.10 Study question solution

Study question 9.1 solution

JIT Manufacturing Ltd is considering changing from apportioning its monthly overheads of £60,000 to product lines based on the monthly production percentage. Table 9.28 illustrates the overhead costs to production lines based on volume.

Table 9.28   Monthly production by product line

Production line	Red	Green	Yellow	Blue	Total
Monthly production %	10	40	30	20	100
Overhead apportionment £	6,000	24,000	18,000	12,000	60,000

The consumption of activities volumes by product line is presented in Table 9.29.

Table 9.29   Cost driver volumes by product line

Production line	Plant maintenance	Quality control	Engineering
Cost driver	Number of breakdowns	Number of inspections	Number of set-ups
Red	15	75	20
Green	24	20	10
Yellow	26	65	15
Blue	35	40	5
Total	100	200	50

The overhead costs charged to the individual production lines based on their consumption of the activities are depicted in Table 9.30.

Table 9.30 Activity-based costs by product line

Production line	Plant maintenance £	Quality control £	Engineering £
Red	4,200	8,250	4,000
Green	6,720	2,200	2,000
Yellow	7,280	7,150	3,000
Blue	9,800	4,400	1,000
Total	28,000	22,000	10,000

The cost driver rate is derived by dividing the cost pool's cost by its driver volume cost, as illustrated in Table 9.31.

Table 9.31 Cost driver rates

Production line	Plant maintenance £	Quality control £	Engineering £
Cost pool £	28,000	22,000	10,000
Cost driver volumes	100	200	50
Cost driver rate £	280	110	200

Table 9.32 illustrates the redistribution of costs between the production lines based on the JIT Manufacturing Ltd decision to switch to activity-based costing.

Table 9.32 Monthly production by product line

Production line	Red	Green	Yellow	Blue	Total
Overhead apportionment £	6,000	24,000	18,000	12,000	**60,000**
Activity-based costs £	16,450	10,920	17,430	15,200	**60,000**
Difference £	−10,450	13,080	570	−3,200	**0**

The solutions to the questions are as follows:

1 Under the current cost method, Green's production line will be charged with 40% of the company's overheads, which is £24,000.

2 The activity-based cost per breakdown will be £280.

3 Red's production line monthly overhead charge will be £16,450 if the organization adopts activity-based costing.

4 Using activity-based costing, Red and Blue production lines' overhead costs will increase.

5 The product line which will benefit the most if the organization adopts activity-based costing is Green.

6 The cost per set-up will be £200.

7 The cost per inspection is £110.

8 The product line that has the highest percentage of breakdowns is Blue.

9 Yellow's production line based on the monthly production percentage will be charged £18,000.

10 The production line that has the highest number of quality control inspections is Red.

Investment appraisal   10

In previous chapters you were introduced to two types of asset: non-current and current (Chapter 3); you were also introduced to different categories of expenditure, revenue and capital (Chapter 2) and depreciation (Chapter 5). In this chapter we will revisit these topics from the perspective of capital investment appraisal decisions taken by supply chain management practitioners.

Before we jump into the topic of investment appraisal, I would like to share with you a description of my typical rail journey to London, but it could be any commuter's rail journey, in any geographical location, and perhaps even yours.

I press the flashing button on the car park barrier and a ticket is issued. I finally find a space on the top floor and park my car, then take the lift down to the railway station concourse. I walk over to the booking office and purchase my train ticket from the ticket vending machine using my credit card. I take my ticket and then pass through the automatic barrier onto the station platform. I check the computer display: my train is on time and I also have time to grab a coffee. I walk into a café and order a double espresso. The machine hisses and my coffee is served. While it's cooling, I text my first meeting to inform them that the train is on time. I drink my coffee and as I leave I purchase a newspaper for the journey. An intermodal freight train travels through the station carrying an assortment of different types of containers. My train pulls into the station; I get on, find a seat and sit down for the 42-minute journey to work. As the train departs an automated announcement informs the passengers of the calling points along the way.

We will explore this journey a little later in the context of investment appraisal.

10.1 Aim and objectives

The aim of this chapter is to explore the rationale for organizations to apply investment appraisal (IA), with an emphasis on supply chain management decisions. The chapter will use examples taken from practice, and a range of activities and study questions will be used to introduce you to the tools and techniques relating to investment appraisal.

At the end of this chapter you will be able to:

• state the reasons for undertaking investment appraisal;

• identify the accounting techniques used in the appraisal process;

• apply six techniques that are typically used in an investment appraisal.

10.2 Revenue and capital expenditure

There are two types of expenditure that exist in business: revenue and capital. CIMA (2005:77) defines revenue expenditure as:

> Expenditure on the manufacture of goods, the provision of services or on the general conduct of the entity which is charged to the income statement in the period the expenditure is incurred. This will include charges for depreciation and impairment of non-current assets as distinct from the cost of the assets.

Capital expenditure (CIMA, 2005:61) is defined as 'costs incurred in acquiring, producing or enhancing non-current assets (both tangible and intangible)'.

Capital investment projects typically involve spending money on non-current assets such as property, plant and equipment (see earlier chapters relating to the balance sheet and depreciation). A non-current asset is defined by CIMA (2005:74) as a 'tangible or intangible asset, acquired for retention by an entity for the purpose of providing a service to the entity and not held for resale in the normal course of trading'.

Here is an example of both revenue and capital expenditures in a quotation by Rail Delivery Group Chief Executive Paul Plummer (2018), who said on the BBC News website in regard to rail fares:

> For every pound paid in fares, 98p goes back in to running and improving the railway. We are ready to work with all parts of the rail industry to improve value for money for our customers.

Running costs are revenue expenditure and improving the railway would be capital expenditure; another term mentioned in the quote is 'value for money'. We will look into this term later in this chapter when exploring the reasons why organizations adopt IA.

Now let's revisit my train journey to London and identify the non-current assets that I came into contact with, from arriving at the car park until I sat down on my seat in the train.

- multi-storey car park, including all its equipment such as the barrier and lift;
- station complex, including the building and all its fixtures and fittings;
- café fixtures and fittings, including the coffee machine;
- the water company's distribution network that supplies the water to make the coffee;
- mobile telephone network and its supporting infrastructure;
- newspaper stand;
- the freight locomotive, its intermodal wagons and the containers it is carrying;
- the passenger train's rail cars and coaches;
- the railway infrastructure, including the track, platform, signalling and overhead cables to power the train;
- the electricity company's transmission and generating infrastructure to supply the electricity to power the train.

Activity 10.1

Now list all the non-current assets that you interact with in a single day, or alternatively list the non-current assets you may find in a typical supermarket's regional distribution centre (RDC).

10.3 Shareholder value

Investors make financial decisions to invest (buying shares) their cash into businesses, which will fulfil customer demand for their products or services and therefore make a profit. Investors will expect a return on their investment in terms of dividends paid to them from the profits but will also have expectation of capital growth (a rising share price) as the business is successful, therefore increasing their shareholder value.

CIMA's official terminology (2005:96) defines shareholder value as:

> Total return to the shareholders in terms of both dividends and share price growth, calculated as the present value of future free cash flows of the business discounted at the weighted average cost of capital less the market value of debt.

Don't be alarmed. We will explore this definition later in this chapter.

I passionately believe that the decisions that supply chain practitioners take will have a positive impact on the financial performance of the organizations that employ them. There is anecdotal evidence to suggest that over 70% of an organization's total assets is supply chain related. Therefore, it is extremely important to an organization that investment opportunities are evaluated to ensure that they generate returns that enhance value for the owners of the business.

10.4 Capital investment appraisal

Organizations as well as individuals have to make choices when it comes to making future investments, as they do not have infinite resources in terms of surplus cash to fund all the investment opportunities they would like to pursue. Cash is a limited resource and organizations are looking to get the best return that they can, whether they operate in the private (return on investment) or public (value for money) sector. Investment opportunities therefore have to be compared, analysed, evaluated, prioritized and then a final decision made. When organizations and individuals are considering investing a large amount of money into an investment, there are a number of important questions that need to be answered, including:

- How much will the investment cost?
- What are the risks associated with the investment?

- When will I get my money back?
- What return will I make on the investment?
- What are the alternative investments?

Typically, within an organization the management accounting function will provide the answers to these questions, using a set of techniques grouped together under the heading of capital investment appraisal. CIMA (2005:86) defines capital investment appraisal as:

> Application of a set of methodologies (generally based on the discounting of projected cash flows) whose purpose is to give guidance to managers with respect to decisions as to how best to commit long-term investment funds.

There are many reasons why organizations use investment appraisal techniques to evaluate investment opportunities. They fall into two areas: maximizing financial performance and reducing risk. Financial performance is maximized by increasing profitability, ensuring value for money and enhancing liquidity. The risk of failure is minimized by comparing alternative investments as part of the management's stewardship duty.

All of these reasons are applicable to the types of decision that supply chain managers take when designing their supply chain operation. Examples of supply chain decisions that commit long-term investment funds include:

- investing in non-current assets such as a fleet of road freight vehicles – just think of all the alternative vehicle types that could be evaluated;
- different make or buy decisions, including outsourcing, offshoring, toll manufacturing, insourcing, and so on;
- an acquisition of a supply chain function, such as a rival road freight distribution operator;
- a change in a process, converting a manual to an automated process, such as capturing a customer's order;
- changing the method of employee remuneration may involve buying out an existing agreement over a period of time;
- calculating the lifetime value of a major customer;
- developing a new product or service.

Investment appraisal techniques can be used to assist supply chain managers with these decisions. An important economic concept that underpins investment appraisal is opportunity cost.

10.5 Opportunity cost

Let's now explore the concept of opportunity cost with a simple example. You have saved £1,000. You could spend the money on a second-hand car, which would cost you the whole amount, or alternatively you can buy a two-week holiday for the same amount. Your opportunity cost of purchasing the car is the benefit that you could have had from your holiday in the sun, which you have now sacrificed for your second-hand car. Alternatively, the opportunity cost of the holiday is the car. CIMA (2005:14-15) defines opportunity cost as:

> The value of the benefit sacrificed when one course of action is chosen in preference to an alternative. The opportunity cost is represented by the forgone potential benefit from the best rejected course of action.

Organizations also have to make sacrifices when considering investing in alternative capital projects, which is compared with the interest they could expect to earn from investing the cash in a bank. The underlying rationale is that an investment opportunity must not destroy shareholder value.

10.6 Case study: warehouse management system upgrade

A fictional case study will be used throughout this section to introduce you to the typical investment appraisal tools that are used in practice.

A FMCG company is proposing an upgrade to its warehouse management system (WMS) in its RDC. It will cost £100,000 and it is anticipated that the new hardware will produce the following cash savings over its six-year life by improving the replenishment process and reducing stock-outs at the picking locations, as illustrated in Table 10.1.

Table 10.1 WMS upgrade cash flows

Year	0	1	2	3	4	5	6
Cash flows £	−100,000	45,000	35,000	20,000	20,000	10,000	6,000

This activity will introduce you to six investment appraisal tools that are typically used in practice to compare alternative capital investment projects:

- cost–benefit analysis;
- accounting rate of return;
- payback;
- net present value;
- discounted payback;
- internal rate of return.

Cost–benefit analysis

The cost–benefit analysis compares the relevant costs associated with a project with its relevant benefits. If the benefits are greater than the costs, the project achieves its first investment appraisal hurdle. The upgrade to the WMS will cost £100,000 and over six years the WMS generates savings of £136,000, by improving the replenishment process and reducing stockouts at the picking locations, resulting in a surplus of £36,000. The cash flows for the WMS upgrade are illustrated in Table 10.2.

Table 10.2 WMS upgrade cash flows

Year	0	1	2	3	4	5	6	Total
Cash flow £k	−100	45	35	20	20	10	6	36

In Table 10.2 you are introduced to year 0. You may not have come across year 0 until now; however, in investment appraisal it is incredibly important. It represents the day that the cash flows out of the business to purchase the investment. On a time line, year 0 is 1 January 20XX and year 1 is the last day of 31 December 20XX. The analysis assumes that cash flow adopts a straight-line basis during a single year; for example, in year 6, £6,000 savings will be divided by 12 to give a monthly flow of £500.

Accounting rate of return

For those of you who had thought we had left financial ratios behind in ratio analysis, here's a surprise for you! The accounting rate of return is a proxy profitability ratio similar to return on investment (ROI) and is based on average profit and average investment. It is calculated using the following formula:

*(average annual profit an investment * 100)/average investment*

Let's calculate the accounting rate of return for the WMS upgrade by producing a proxy income statement for the five years (Table 10.3). Where savings are revenue and capital expenditure are costs, revenue minus costs equals a profit.

Table 10.3   WMS upgrade income statement

Revenue	£136,000
Less costs	£100,000
Equals profit	£36,000

The average profit is now calculated by dividing the profit produced from the project over its life by the number of years.

$$£36,000/6 = £6,000 \text{ per annum}$$

We have derived the numerator, which is £6,000, and now we have to calculate the denominator. For those of a nervous disposition, you may want to shield your eyes or retreat behind your comfortable sofa, as this formula is not for the faint-hearted: it is bizarre in nature. You have been warned.

Taking the investment in the project and dividing by 2 derives the average investment in the project. Therefore £100,000/2 = £50,000.

The accounting rate of return for the WMS is:

$$(£6,000/£50,000) * 100 = 12\%.$$

Why 2, you ask. There is a start date and an end date to the project period. If the project's life was 10 or 20 years, the investment would still be divided by 2. I leave the final sentence concerning the accounting rate of return with CIMA (2005:21):

> Sometimes used in investment appraisal, derived in the same way as return on investment. Unlike net present value and internal rate of return, the ratio is based on profits not cash flows. Exclusive use of this ratio is not recommended.

Payback period

The payback period is the time it takes to recover the investment in the project. It is a measure of liquidity, not profitability, as investments that are more profitable will be rejected in favour of an investment that pays back faster but returns less. Payback aligns with a risk-averse mindset: rather recoup your investment quickly than wait for higher returns over a long time period, which may never materialize if the market conditions change. CIMA (2005:93) terminology defines payback as 'time required for the cash inflows from a capital investment project to equal the cash outflows'.

The payback calculation for the WMS upgrade is illustrated in Table 10.4. The original cash flows are taken, and the cumulative cash flow is calculated in a new column.

Table 10.4   WMS upgrade payback period

Year	Cash flows £	Cumulative cash flow £
0	−100,000	−100,000
1	45,000	−55,000
2	35,000	−20,000
3	20,000	0
4	20,000	20,000
5	10,000	30,000
6	6,000	36,000

The upgrade to the WMS recovers the initial outlay of £100,000 at the end of year 3, when the cumulative cash flow is 0. However, what would be the payback period if the initial outlay were £90,000 instead of £100,000? Table 10.5 illustrates the new cumulative cash flow based on the WMS upgrade costing £90,000.

Table 10.5   WMS upgrade payback period version 2

Year	Cash flows £	Cumulative cash flow £
0	−90,000	−90,000
1	45,000	−45,000
2	35,000	−10,000
3	20,000	10,000
4	20,000	30,000
5	10,000	40,000
6	6,000	46,000

Now the payback period is between years 2 and 3; therefore, to ascertain the payback period, an apportionment needs to be undertaken. In this instance, at the end of year 2 we still require £10,000 to recover the initial outlay of £90,000; at the end of year 3 we have a surplus of £10,000. The apportionment calculation takes the outstanding amount required and divides it by the total cash inflow for the year when the project goes from deficit to surplus. At the end of year 2 the WMS has £10,000 outstanding, and in year 3 the project will produce savings of £20,000. Hence £10,000/20,000 = 1/2 of year, or 6 months, or 182.5 days. The payback period for the upgrade is 2 years and 6 months.

The major weakness of the payback method is that if the major objective is to recoup the initial investment, projects that generate higher profits but have longer payback periods will be rejected. Project B in Table 10.6 will be selected as it pays back in 1.5 years, even though it is the least profitable of the three projects, returning a surplus of £6,000 over the four years, compared with Project A, which generates £10,000, and Project C, whose profit is 2.5 times that of Project B.

Table 10.6 Payback vs. profitability

	Project A £		Project B £		Project C £	
Year	Cash flow	Cumulative	Cash flow	Cumulative	Cash flow	Cumulative
0	−10,000	−10,000	−10,000	−10,000	−10,000	−10,000
1	5,000	−5,000	7,500	−2,500	2,500	−7,500
2	5,000	0	5,000	2,500	5,000	−2,500
3	5,000	5,000	2,500	5,000	7,500	5,000
4	5,000	10,000	1,000	6,000	10,000	15,000
Total	10,000		6,000		15,000	
	Payback = 2 years		Payback = 1.5 years		Payback = 2.34 years	

Net present value

The WMS upgrade will produce savings for the business of £36,000 over the six years. The big question that needs to be answered now is: would the business have made a greater return if they had invested their money in an alternative investment or project? Discounted cash flow techniques can be used to compare a return from a potential investment with the organization's hurdle rate (CIMA 2005:91):

> Rate of return which a capital investment proposal must achieve if it is to be accepted. Set by reference to the cost of capital, the hurdle rate may be increased above the base cost of capital to allow for different levels of risk.

For example, if a company could expect to receive a 5% return on their money on deposit in the bank, an alternative investment must earn more than 5%, which is the company's hurdle rate.

Comparing like with like

We now need to know the answer to this question: will the savings generated by the WMS upgrade be in excess of what we could have earned if the money had been deposited in a bank? We need to 'compare like with like' the returns from both investments at one point in time, which is year 0. Discounted cash flow is a technique that enables us to do this, as every future value is discounted back to year 0, by discounting by the hurdle rate – in this example the interest the company would have received if they had chosen to leave their money in the bank. The hurdle rate, which is also referred to as the test discount rate (CIMA, 2005:87), is defined as the 'percentage rate used to discount future cash flows generated by a capital project'.

The adjusted future value is referred to as the present value, which the value of a future sum is discounted back to year 0 by the organization's cost of capital. CIMA (2005:91) defines present value as the 'cash equivalent now of a sum receivable or payable at a future date'.

We are able to calculate the discount factor that will be used to determine the present value for any future sum using the following formula:

$$\text{discount factor} = 1/(1+r)^n$$

where

    r = test discount rate expressed as a decimal;
    n = number of years.

In section 10.11 a discount factor table (Table 10.23) illustrates a range of factors from 1% to 30% by year 0 to year 15.

The discount rate factor for five years at a test discount rate of 10% = $1/(1+0.1)^5 = 0.621$.

In year 5 the WMS upgrade delivers savings of £10,000. This figure is multiplied by the discount factor of 0.621 to give a present value of £6,210. In other words, if we were to invest £6,215 for five years at a compound interest rate of 10%, it would increase to £10,000 (£6,210 multiplied by $[1.1]^5$); therefore, discounting is the inverse of compounding. Discounting tables can be used to derive the discount factor and a sample of factors is illustrated in section 10.11. It is important to understand that the higher the discount rate percentage and the greater the time from year 0, the bigger impact the discount factor will have on the future value. Table 10.7 illustrates the impact of the discount rate on the present value of £10,000 received in five years' time. For instance, £10,000 received in five years' time if the discount rate was 5% would generate a present value at year 0 of £7,840; if the rate changes to 50%, the present value would fall to £1,320.

Table 10.7 How much is a £10,000 investment worth in five years' time?

Discount rate %	Discount factor	Present value
5	0.784	£7,840
10	0.621	£6,210
15	0.497	£4,970
20	0.402	£4,020
25	0.328	£3,280
30	0.269	£2,690
35	0.223	£2,230
40	0.186	£1,860
45	0.156	£1,560
50	0.132	£1,320

Figure 10.1 illustrates present value of £10,000 received in five years' time for a range of discount rates. For instance, £10,000 received in five years' time if the discount rate was 10% would generate a present value at year 0 of £6,210; if the rate changes to 30%, the present value would fall to £2,690.

Figure 10.1 How much is a £10,000 investment worth in five years' time?

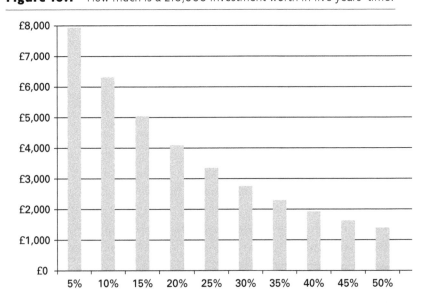

The sum of all the present values over an investment's life is referred to as the net present value (NPV). CIMA (2005:93) defines NPV as the 'difference between the sum of the projected discounted cash inflows and outflows attributed to a capital project or other long-term project'.

If the NPV is positive, the investment has generated greater returns than would have been produced if the money was invested at the organization's hurdle rate and should be accepted. If the outcome is a negative NPV, the investment should be rejected, as leaving the money in the bank can generate greater returns. If the NPV is zero, the investment breaks even and will also be accepted, as there may be additional benefits associated with the investment that are non-financial.

The NPV calculations for the WMS upgrade are illustrated in Table 10.8; the company's hurdle rate is 10%.

Table 10.8   WMS upgrade net present value at 10% discount rate

Year	Cash flows £	10% discount factor	Present value £
0	−100,000	1.000	−100,000
1	45,000	0.909	40,905
2	35,000	0.826	28,910
3	20,000	0.751	15,020
4	20,000	0.683	13,660
5	10,000	0.621	6,210
6	6,000	0.564	3,384
	36,000		8,089

The present value for each financial year is calculated by multiplying the cash flow by the discount factor. Notice in year 0 that the cash outflow of £100,000 is not impacted by the discount factor, giving a negative £100,000. The NPV is the sum of all the years including year 0, which results in £8,089; as it is a positive figure the project is accepted because it has generated higher returns than the discount rate of 10%. The project originally generated savings of £36,000; after deducting the cost of capital, the investment returns £8,089. The cost of capital (CIMA, 2005:87) is defined as:

Minimum acceptable return on an investment generally computed as a discount rate for use in investment appraisal exercise. The computation of the optimal cost of capital can be complex, and many ways of determining this opportunity cost have been suggested.

Often the hurdle rate is the organization's weighted average cost of capital.

Weighted average cost of capital

The weighted average cost of capital (WACC) is defined by CIMA (2005:98) as 'the average cost of the company's finance (including equity, debentures and bank loans) weighted to the proportion each element bears to the total pool of capital'. Table 10.9 illustrates the weighted average cost of capital calculation for an organization that is valued at £100 million, which is funded 75% by equity (shareholders) and 25% by long-term debt (bank). The shareholders are expecting a return of 12% on their investment, while the bank will receive 4%. Currently the shareholders are looking for a return that is three times that of the bank, as they are exposed to a higher level of risk if the venture fails.

Table 10.9   Weighted average cost of capital calculation

Capital	Value	Return	Proportion	WACC
Equity	£75 million	12%	0.75	9%
Debt	£25 million	4%	0.25	1%
Total	**£100 million**			**10%**

The WACC is 10%. This will be the hurdle rate that is used to evaluate investment opportunities, as this rate will be sufficient to meet the expectations of the shareholders at 12% and the loan providers who want 4%. If the proportion changes in favour of debt, the WACC will decrease; if the opposite occurs, the WACC will increase. This chapter adopts a simplified WACC calculation which does not include a tax shield.

Discounted payback period

The discounted payback period applies the same logic as the traditional payback calculation; however, it uses the discounted cash flows rather than the original flows, factoring the cost of capital into the analysis. When calculating the discounted payback period, the time to recoup the original investment should always be longer than the traditional payback figure; if not, check your calculations. CIMA (2005:88) defines the discounted payback period as a 'capital investment method with the aim of determining the period of time required to recover initial cash outflow when net cash inflows are discounted at the opportunity cost of capital'.

The cumulative discounted cash flows have been calculated in Table 10.10 for the WMS upgrade and the payback period is between years 4 and 5.

To calculate the payback period, an apportionment is required. The outstanding amount required at the end of year 4 is £1,505. This figure is

Table 10.10   WMS upgrade discounted payback period

Year	Cash flows £	Cumulative cash flow £
0	−100,000	−100,000
1	40,905	−59,095
2	28,910	−30,185
3	15,020	−15,165
4	13,660	−1,505
5	6,210	4,705
6	3,384	8,089

divided by the total cash inflow for the year when the project goes from deficit to surplus, which is £6,210. Therefore, £1,505/£6,210 = 0.242 of a year, or 88 days; thus, the discounted payback period for the upgrade is 4 years and 88 days, or 4.242 years.

Internal rate of return

The sixth and final technique is the internal rate of return (IRR) and is defined as (CIMA, 2005:91) the 'annual percentage return achieved by a project, at which the sum of the discounted cash inflows over the life of the project is equal to the sum of the discounted cash outflows'. In other words, the IRR is the test discount rate, which results in zero NPV. When comparing projects, the project with the highest IRR percentage will be chosen as it has the highest yield and the lowest risk.

When calculating the IRR, you require two things: a test discount rate that generates a positive NPV and a rate that produces a negative test rate. Typically, the rate that provides a positive NPV is the organization's hurdle rate; however, the rate for a negative rate is based on an iterative process that involves choosing a rate and then calculating the NPV to see if it produces a negative value.

Table 10.11 illustrates a positive NPV of £8,089 using a 10% discount rate, and Table 10.12 depicts a negative NPV of £10,975 when using a 20% rate.

Now that we have a positive and negative rate, we can derive the IRR. This can be done in two ways: graphically or by formula.

Let's first derive the IRR graphically. From Tables 10.11 and 10.12 we have two pairs of coordinates, which are shown in Table 10.13. The coordinates are now plotted onto a chart and a straight line is drawn between the two points; where the line intersects the x-axis derives the IRR. Assumption

Table 10.11   WMS upgrade positive net present value at 10% discount rate

Year	Cash flows £	10% discount factor	Present value £
0	−100,000	1.000	−100,000
1	45,000	0.909	40,905
2	35,000	0.826	28,910
3	20,000	0.751	15,020
4	20,000	0.683	13,660
5	10,000	0.621	6,210
6	6,000	0.564	3,384
			8,089

Table 10.12   WMS upgrade negative net present value at 20% discount rate

Year	Cash Flows £	20% Discount Factor	Present Value £
0	−100,000	1.000	−100,000
1	45,000	0.833	37,485
2	35,000	0.694	24,290
3	20,000	0.579	11,580
4	20,000	0.482	9,640
5	10,000	0.402	4,020
6	6,000	0.335	2,010
			−10,975

Table 10.13   IRR coordinates

	X	Y
Positive	10%	£8,089
Negative	20%	£−10,975

warning is now required: a straight line is used to give an approximation; in reality the curve is not a straight one. Figure 10.2 illustrates the graphical solution for the WMS upgrade; the chart indicates that the IRR is around 12%.

Figure 10.2 WMS upgrade internal rate of return graphical solution

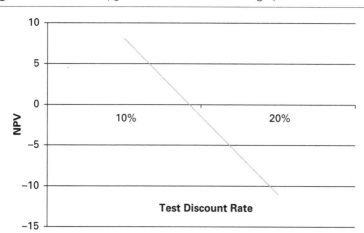

The alternative is to derive the IRR by using the following formula:

$$i1 + \left\{ (i2 - i1) * \left[\frac{npv1}{npv1 - npv2} \right] \right\}$$

i1=Discount rate which produces a positive npv1
i2=Discount rate which produces a negative npv2

The formula is basically an apportionment (remember full costing); we take the positive NPV as a proportion of the absolute difference between the positive NPV and negative NPV, and use this fraction to apportion the difference between the two discount rates and then add the difference to the hurdle rate to derive the IRR. Let's break it down into a series of activities:

1 positive NPV = £8,089;

2 absolute difference = £8,089 – –£10,975 = £19,064 (note two minuses make a plus);

3 £8,089/£19,064 = 0.4243;

4 the difference between the two rates used is 20 – 10 = 10;

5 10 * 0.0.4243 = 4.243;

6 add the difference to the hurdle rate to give the IRR = 10% + 4.243% = 14.243%.

Please see below the solution using the IRR formula:

$$10+\left\{(20-10)*\left[\frac{8,089}{8,089-10,975}\right]\right\}$$

$$10+\left(10*\left[\frac{8,089}{19,064}\right]\right)$$

$$10+(10*0.4243)$$

$$= 14.243$$

WMS upgrade summary of results

It is important that you present the findings of your capital investment appraisal analysis in such a way that informs the decision-maker; a summary table is an excellent format to use, as illustrated in Table 10.14 for the WMS upgrade.

Table 10.14   Capital investment appraisal: summary of results

Capital investment appraisal techniques	WMS upgrade
Cost–benefit analysis (CBA)	£36,000
Accounting rate of return percentage (ARR)	12%
Payback period (PB)	3 years
Discounted payback period (DPB)	4.11 years
Net present value 10% (NPV1)	£8,089
Net present value 20% (NPV2)	–£10,975
Internal rate of return percentage (IRR)	14.243%

Overall the findings of the analysis are:

1 The WMS upgrade has a CBA of £36,000 over its lifetime.

2 The project has an ARR of 12% based on the average investment over the period.

3 The project pays back the original investment of £100,000 in three years and discounted payback period of 4.11 years.

4 The WMS upgrade has net present value of £8,089 using the organization's hurdle rate of 10%.

5 The project has a negative NPV of £10,975 at 20% discount rate.

6 The internal rate of return for the project is 14.243%.

There may be alternative solutions to the WMS upgrade that will need to be evaluated before finally making a recommendation. Now have a go at Activity 10.2.

Activity 10.2

You now have two additional options supplied to you by two competing vendors, illustrated in Table 10.15. You now need to evaluate these with the original WMS (option 1).

Table 10.15   WMS options 1 to 3

	Option 1 (original)	Option 2	Option 3
Year	Cash flows £	Cash flows £	Cash flows £
0	−100,000	−100,000	−100,000
1	45,000	60,000	70,000
2	35,000	32,000	30,000
3	20,000	16,000	15,000
4	20,000	12,000	9,000
5	10,000	8,000	5,000
6	6,000	5,000	1,000

Complete Table 10.16 and recommend to the company, based on your analysis, which option they should invest in.

Table 10.16   WMS options 1 to 3 summary of results

Investment appraisal tool	Option 1	Option 2	Option 3
Cost–benefit analysis £	36,000		
Accounting rate of return %	12		
Payback period years	3.0		
Net present value 10% £	8,089		
Discount payback period 10% years	4.2		
Net present value 20% £	−10,975		
Internal rate of return %	14.243		

A more complex investment appraisal question is provided in section 10.13.

10.7 Equivalent annualized cost

Occasionally you may have the need to evaluate projects which have different life spans and also do not generate income or provide cost savings; therefore, the key decision criteria will be based on lowest cost, when all other factors are equal. The project that will be chosen is the one with the lowest annualized cost. Your organization is evaluating two packing machines for the outbound logistics operation in its RDC. Both packaging machines meet the operational specification required for the cost centre; however, they have different purchase prices, operational cost life spans and disposal costs, as illustrated in Table 10.17.

Table 10.17   Packaging machines option 1 and option 2

	Packaging machine option 1			Packaging machine option 2	
Year	Cash flow out £	Cash flow in £	Year	Cash flow out £	Cash flow in £
0	−12,000	0	0	−18,000	0
1	−800	0	1	−500	0
2	−800	0	2	−500	0
3	−800	0	3	−500	0
4	−800	0	4	−500	0
5	−800	0	5	−500	0
6	−800	2,400	6	−500	0
			7	−500	0
			8	−500	0
			9	−500	3,300

Annualized cost is defined by Investopedia (2018) as:

> Equivalent annual cost (EAC) is the annual cost of owning, operating and maintaining an asset over its entire life. EAC is often used by firms for capital budgeting decisions, as it allows a company to compare the cost effectiveness of various assets that have unequal lifespans.

Therefore, we need to calculate the EAC for both machines, and the one with the lowest cost will be chosen. The company uses a test discount rate of 10% to evaluate capital projects. Table 10.18 illustrates the EAC calculations for option 1.

Table 10.18 Packaging machines option 1 EAC calculation

Year	Cash flow Out £	Cash flow in £	Net cash flow £	10% Discount factor	Present value 10% £
0	−12,000	0	−12,000	1.0000	−12,000.00
1	−800	0	−800	0.9091	−727.28
2	−800	0	−800	0.8264	−661.12
3	−800	0	−800	0.7513	−601.04
4	−800	0	−800	0.6830	−546.40
5	−800	0	−800	0.6209	−496.72
6	−800	2,400	1,600	0.5645	−903.20
	−16,800	2,400	−14,400	4.3552	−14,129.36
					−3,244.25

Typically, the calculation takes a very similar approach to calculating the NPV for a project. The stages for calculating the EAC are illustrated in 10.19.

Table 10.19 Stages in calculating the EAC for a project

Stage 1	The first thing to do is to identify the annual cash outflows. In the case of option 1, the purchase price is £12,000, and over the machine's life, £800 per annum is expensed, making the total cost of the packing machine £16,800.
Stage 2	In this stage we need to account for any cash inflows that are relevant to the capital project; in this example in year 6, when the packaging machine is sold, there is a disposal value of £2,400.
Stage 3	Involves calculating the net cash flow for each; for example in year 6 the net cash flow is a positive figure, as −£800 + £2,400 = £1,600.
Stage 4	The present value for the year is calculated by taking the net cash flow for each year and multiplying by the relevant discount factor for that particular year. In year 5, −£800 is multiplied by 0.6209 to give a present value of −£496.72.
Stage 5	The net present value is calculated by adding up all the project's present values from year 0 to year 6, which equates to −£14,129.36, as shown in Table 10.18.
Stage 6	To calculate EAC we now add up the discount factors for all the years, from 0 to 6, and then subtract 1.0. The reason we subtract 1.0 is that year 0 is not required in the calculation to determine the EAC. 1.0000 + 0.9091 + 0.8264 + 0.7513 + 0.6830 + 0.6209 + 0.5645 = 5.3552. 5.3552 − 1.0 = 4.3552.

(continued)

Table 10.19   (*Continued*)

Stage 7	To calculate the EAC, the net present value in stage 5 is divided by the sum of the discount factors calculated in stage 6. Therefore the EAC for option 1 is −£14,129.36/4.3552, which equates to an EAC of −£3,244.25, as shown in Table 10.20.
Stage 8	The final stage is to check if the annualized cost reconciles back to the project's NPV; therefore for each year of the project's life, the annualized cost is multiplied by the relevant discount factor to derive the present value for the year and then aggregated to calculate the NPV.

Table 10.20   Packaging machines option 1 NPV reconciliation

Year	Annualized cost £	10% discount factor	Present value 10% £
1	−3,244.25	0.9091	−2,949.35
2	−3,244.25	0.8264	−2,681.05
3	−3,244.25	0.7513	−2,437.41
4	−3,244.25	0.6830	−2,215.82
5	−3,244.25	0.6209	−2,014.36
6	−3,244.25	0.5645	−1,831.38
			−14,129.36

Table 10.21   Packaging machines option 2 EAC calculation

Year	Cash flow out £	Cash flow in £	Net cash flow £	10% Discount factor	Present value 10% £
0	−18,000		−18,000	1.0000	−18,000.00
1	−500		−500	0.9091	−454.55
2	−500		−500	0.8264	−413.20
3	−500		−500	0.7513	−375.65
4	−500		−500	0.6830	−341.50
5	−500		−500	0.6209	−310.45
6	−500		−500	0.5645	−282.25
7	−500		−500	0.5132	−256.60
8	−500		−500	0.4665	−233.25
9	−500	3,300	2,800	0.4241	1,187.48
	−22,500	3,300	−19,200	5.7590	−19,479.97
					−3,382.53

The process is now repeated to calculate the EAC for the second packaging machine, as illustrated in Tables 10.21 and 10.22.

Table 10.22 Packaging machines option 2 NPV reconciliation

Year	Annualized cost £	10% discount factor	Present value 10% £
1	-3,382.53	0.9091	-3,075.05
2	-3,382.53	0.8264	-2,795.32
3	-3,382.53	0.7513	-2,541.29
4	-3,382.53	0.6830	-2,310.27
5	-3,382.53	0.6209	-2,100.21
6	-3,382.53	0.5645	-1,909.44
7	-3,382.53	0.5132	-1,735.91
8	-3,382.53	0.4665	-1,577.95
9	-3,382.53	0.4241	-1,434.53
			-19,479.97

The company can now compare the EAC for each packaging machine and will choose the machine which has the lowest EAC. Option 1 has EAC of £3,244.25 compared with £3,382.53 for option 2; therefore option 1 will be chosen.

Activity 10.3

You have been supplied with the net cash flows for three machines your company is evaluating in Table 10.23. Calculate the EAC for each machine and recommend to the business which machine they should buy.

Table 10.23 Packaging machines option 2 npv reconciliation

Year	Machine A £	Machine B £	Machine C £
0	-20,000	-15,000	-10,000
1	-2,500	-3,500	-5,000
2	-2,500	-3,500	-4,000
3	-2,500	-2,000	
4	-2,500		
5	-2,500		
6	-500		

10.8 Practical applications of investment appraisal in supply chains

Investment appraisal is used in a variety of supply chain decisions, including:

- evaluating the future costs and benefits of introducing new products and services;
- procurement decisions, including make or buy, outsourcing, insourcing and offshoring decisions;
- lifecycle costing;
- total cost of ownership;
- financing decisions regarding the alternative financing of non-current assets;
- customer lifetime value;
- procurement of non-current assets;
- acquisitions and other investments.

Activity 10.4

Your task is to understand further the application of investment appraisal in the context of supply chain decisions. Therefore, your task is to:

- get a copy of your organization's investment appraisal policy;
- find out your organization's discount rate or hurdle rate for evaluating capital investment decisions;
- identify which investment appraisal tools your organization uses to evaluate capital expenditure;
- from your organization's balance sheet, calculate the value of non-current assets as a percentage of total assets.

10.9 Summary

The chapter highlighted the reasons why organizations use investment appraisal techniques to evaluate an investment opportunity. Organizations need to maximize returns to stakeholders, obtain value for money and improve liquidity. They also want to reduce risk by comparing different investment opportunities as part of the management duty of stewardship.

You were introduced to six accounting techniques used in the appraisal process, three of which don't incorporate the impact of time on the value of money:

- cost–benefit analysis;
- accounting rate of return;
- payback period.

And three that do factor in the impact of time on the value of money:

- net present value;
- discounted payback period;
- internal rate of return.

Finally, the importance of taking a holistic perspective to investment appraisal by incorporating all of the accounting techniques into your decision-making process, not just relying on a single technique, was emphasized.

10.10 References

BBC (2018) *Rail Fares: Commuters 'pay fifth of salary' on season tickets*, available at www.bbc.co.uk/news/uk-england-45174496 (accessed 15 August 2018)

CIMA (2005) *CIMA Official Terminology*, CIMA Publishing, Oxford

Investopedia (2018) *Equivalent Annual Cost*, available at www.investopedia.com/terms/e/eac.asp#ixzz5ONkYsivE (accessed 19 August 2018)

10.11 Discount factor tables

The discount factors for 1% to 30% are illustrated in Table 10.24.

Table 10.24 Discount factors for 1% to 30% for 15 years

Year	1	2	3	4	5	6	7	8	9	10
0	1.0000	1.0000	1.0000	1.0000	1.0000	1.0000	1.0000	1.0000	1.0000	1.0000
1	0.9901	0.9804	0.9709	0.9615	0.9524	0.9434	0.9346	0.9259	0.9174	0.9091
2	0.9803	0.9612	0.9426	0.9246	0.9070	0.8900	0.8734	0.8573	0.8417	0.8264
3	0.9706	0.9423	0.9151	0.8890	0.8638	0.8396	0.8163	0.7938	0.7722	0.7513
4	0.9610	0.9238	0.8885	0.8548	0.8227	0.7921	0.7629	0.7350	0.7084	0.6830
5	0.9515	0.9057	0.8626	0.8219	0.7835	0.7473	0.7130	0.6806	0.6499	0.6209
6	0.9420	0.8880	0.8375	0.7903	0.7462	0.7050	0.6663	0.6302	0.5963	0.5645
7	0.9327	0.8706	0.8131	0.7599	0.7107	0.6651	0.6227	0.5835	0.5470	0.5132
8	0.9235	0.8535	0.7894	0.7307	0.6768	0.6274	0.5820	0.5403	0.5019	0.4665
9	0.9143	0.8368	0.7664	0.7026	0.6446	0.5919	0.5439	0.5002	0.4604	0.4241
10	0.9053	0.8203	0.7441	0.6756	0.6139	0.5584	0.5083	0.4632	0.4224	0.3855
11	0.8963	0.8043	0.7224	0.6496	0.5847	0.5268	0.4751	0.4289	0.3875	0.3505
12	0.8874	0.7885	0.7014	0.6246	0.5568	0.4970	0.4440	0.3971	0.3555	0.3186
13	0.8787	0.7730	0.6810	0.6006	0.5303	0.4688	0.4150	0.3677	0.3262	0.2897
14	0.8700	0.7579	0.6611	0.5775	0.5051	0.4423	0.3878	0.3405	0.2992	0.2633
15	0.8613	0.7430	0.6419	0.5553	0.4810	0.4173	0.3624	0.3152	0.2745	0.2394

Year	11	12	13	14	15	16	17	18	19	20
0	1.0000	1.0000	1.0000	1.0000	1.0000	1.0000	1.0000	1.0000	1.0000	1.0000
1	0.9009	0.8929	0.8850	0.8772	0.8696	0.8621	0.8547	0.8475	0.8403	0.8333
2	0.8116	0.7972	0.7831	0.7695	0.7561	0.7432	0.7305	0.7182	0.7062	0.6944
3	0.7312	0.7118	0.6931	0.6750	0.6575	0.6407	0.6244	0.6086	0.5934	0.5787
4	0.6587	0.6355	0.6133	0.5921	0.5718	0.5523	0.5337	0.5158	0.4987	0.4823
5	0.5935	0.5674	0.5428	0.5194	0.4972	0.4761	0.4561	0.4371	0.4190	0.4019
6	0.5346	0.5066	0.4803	0.4556	0.4323	0.4104	0.3898	0.3704	0.3521	0.3349
7	0.4817	0.4523	0.4251	0.3996	0.3759	0.3538	0.3332	0.3139	0.2959	0.2791
8	0.4339	0.4039	0.3762	0.3506	0.3269	0.3050	0.2848	0.2660	0.2487	0.2326
9	0.3909	0.3606	0.3329	0.3075	0.2843	0.2630	0.2434	0.2255	0.2090	0.1938
10	0.3522	0.3220	0.2946	0.2697	0.2472	0.2267	0.2080	0.1911	0.1756	0.1615
11	0.3173	0.2875	0.2607	0.2366	0.2149	0.1954	0.1778	0.1619	0.1476	0.1346
12	0.2858	0.2567	0.2307	0.2076	0.1869	0.1685	0.1520	0.1372	0.1240	0.1122
13	0.2575	0.2292	0.2042	0.1821	0.1625	0.1452	0.1299	0.1163	0.1042	0.0935
14	0.2320	0.2046	0.1807	0.1597	0.1413	0.1252	0.1110	0.0985	0.0876	0.0779
15	0.2090	0.1827	0.1599	0.1401	0.1229	0.1079	0.0949	0.0835	0.0736	0.0649

(continued)

Table 10.24 *(Continued)*

Year	21	22	23	24	25	26	27	28	29	30
0	1.0000	1.0000	1.0000	1.0000	1.0000	1.0000	1.0000	1.0000	1.0000	1.0000
1	0.8264	0.8197	0.8130	0.8065	0.8000	0.7937	0.7874	0.7813	0.7752	0.7692
2	0.6830	0.6719	0.6610	0.6504	0.6400	0.6299	0.6200	0.6104	0.6009	0.5917
3	0.5645	0.5507	0.5374	0.5245	0.5120	0.4999	0.4882	0.4768	0.4658	0.4552
4	0.4665	0.4514	0.4369	0.4230	0.4096	0.3968	0.3844	0.3725	0.3611	0.3501
5	0.3855	0.3700	0.3552	0.3411	0.3277	0.3149	0.3027	0.2910	0.2799	0.2693
6	0.3186	0.3033	0.2888	0.2751	0.2621	0.2499	0.2383	0.2274	0.2170	0.2072
7	0.2633	0.2486	0.2348	0.2218	0.2097	0.1983	0.1877	0.1776	0.1682	0.1594
8	0.2176	0.2038	0.1909	0.1789	0.1678	0.1574	0.1478	0.1388	0.1304	0.1226
9	0.1799	0.1670	0.1552	0.1443	0.1342	0.1249	0.1164	0.1084	0.1011	0.0943
10	0.1486	0.1369	0.1262	0.1164	0.1074	0.0992	0.0916	0.0847	0.0784	0.0725
11	0.1228	0.1122	0.1026	0.0938	0.0859	0.0787	0.0721	0.0662	0.0607	0.0558
12	0.1015	0.0920	0.0834	0.0757	0.0687	0.0625	0.0568	0.0517	0.0471	0.0429
13	0.0839	0.0754	0.0678	0.0610	0.0550	0.0496	0.0447	0.0404	0.0365	0.0330
14	0.0693	0.0618	0.0551	0.0492	0.0440	0.0393	0.0352	0.0316	0.0283	0.0254
15	0.0573	0.0507	0.0448	0.0397	0.0352	0.0312	0.0277	0.0247	0.0219	0.0195

10.12 Solutions to the activities

Activity 10.1 solution

The list of non-current assets you may find in a typical supermarket's regional distribution centre (RDC) are illustrated in Table 10.25.

Table 10.25   Non-currents assets you may find in a supermarket's regional distribution centre

Electric pallet trucks for picking	Hand pallet trucks
Roll-cage pallets	Pallet stacker
Different types of racking	Conveyors
Counterbalance forklift trucks	Reach forklift trucks
Warehouse management system	Tractor units
Shrink wrapper	Trailers, various sizes
Sortation equipment	Ridge trucks
Pallets	Tote bins
Automated guided vehicles	Stacker crane
Building	Office equipment

Activity 10.2 solution

Tables 10.26 to 10.28 illustrate the net present value calculations for the three options.

Table 10.29 summarizes the results of the investment appraisal analysis for the three alternative options.

An alternative summary of the output of the investment appraisal analysis is illustrated in Table 10.30, where a ranking of 1 is the best and 3 is the worst.

Table 10.26   Option 1

Year	Cash flows £	Cumulative cash flow £	10% discount factor	Present value 10% £	Cumulative cash flow £	20% discount factor	Present value 20% £
0	−100,000	−100,000	1.000	−100,000	−100,000	1.000	−100,000
1	45,000	−55,000	0.909	40,905	−59,095	0.833	37,485
2	35,000	−20,000	0.826	28,910	−30,185	0.694	24,290
3	20,000	0	0.751	15,020	−15,165	0.579	11,580
4	20,000	20,000	0.683	13,660	−1,505	0.482	9,640
5	10,000	30,000	0.621	6,210	4,705	0.402	4,020
6	6,000	36,000	0.564	3,384	8,089	0.335	2,010
	36,000			8,089			−10,975

Table 10.27   Option 2

Year	Cash flows £	Cumulative cash flow £	10% discount factor	Present value 10% £	Cumulative cash flow £	20% discount factor	Present value 20% £
0	−100,000	−100,000	1.000	−100,000	−100,000	1.000	−100,000
1	60,000	−40,000	0.909	54,540	−45,460	0.833	49,980
2	32,000	−8,000	0.826	26,432	−19,028	0.694	22,208
3	16,000	8,000	0.751	12,016	−7,012	0.579	9,264
4	12,000	20,000	0.683	8,196	1,184	0.482	5,784
5	8,000	28,000	0.621	4,968	6,152	0.402	3,216
6	5,000	33,000	0.564	2,820	8,972	0.335	1,675
	33,000			8,972			−7,873

Table 10.28   Option 3

Year	Cash flows £	Cumulative cash flow £	10% discount factor	Present value 10% £	Cumulative cash flow £	20% discount factor	Present value 20% £
0	−100,000	−100,000	1.000	−100,000	−100,000	1.000	−100,000
1	70,000	−30,000	0.909	63,630	−36,370	0.833	58,310
2	30,000	0	0.826	24,780	−11,590	0.694	20,820
3	15,000	15,000	0.751	11,265	−325	0.579	8,685

(continued)

Table 10.28   *(Continued)*

Year	Cash flows £	Cumulative cash flow £	10% discount factor	Present value 10% £	Cumulative cash flow £	20% discount factor	Present value 20% £
4	9,000	24,000	0.683	6,147	5,822	0.482	4,338
5	5,000	29,000	0.621	3,105	8,927	0.402	2,010
6	1,000	30,000	0.564	564	9,491	0.335	335
	30,000			**9,491**			**−5,502**

Table 10.29   Summary of results

Investment appraisal tool	Option 1	Option 2	Option 3
Cost–benefit analysis £	36,000	33,000	30,000
Accounting rate of return %	12	11	10
Payback period years	3.0	2.5	2.0
Net present value 10% £	8,089	8,972	9,491
Discount payback period 10% years	4.24	3.86	3.05
Net present value 20% £	−10,975	−7,873	−5,502
Internal rate of return %	14.243	15.326	16.330

Table 10.30   Summary table by rankings

Investment appraisal tool	Option 1	Option 2	Option 3
Cost–benefit analysis £	1	2	3
Accounting rate of return %	1	2	3
Payback period years	3	2	1
Net present value 10% £	3	2	1
Discount payback period 10% years	3	2	1
Net present value 20% £	3	2	1
Internal rate of return %	3	2	1

Activity 10.3 solution

The EAC calculations for the three machines are illustrated in Tables 10.31 to 10.33.

The company should choose Machine A as it has the lowest EAC.

Table 10.31 Machine A EAC calculations

Year	Machine A	20% discount factor	Present value 20%
0	−20,000	1.000	− 20,000.00
1	−2,500	0.833	−2,082.50
2	−2,500	0.694	− 1,735.00
3	−2,500	0.579	−1,447.50
4	−2,500	0.482	−1,205.00
5	−2,500	0.402	− 1,005.00
6	−500	0.335	−167.50
	−33,000	3.325	−27,642.50
		EAC=	**−8,313.53**

Table 10.32 Machine B EAC calculations

Year	Machine B	20% discount factor	Present value 20%
0	−15,000	1.000	−15,000.00
1	−3,500	0.833	−2,915.50
2	−3,500	0.694	−2,429.00
3	−2,000	0.579	−1,158.00
	−24,000	2.106	−21,502.50
		EAC=	**−10,210.11**

Table 10.33 Machine C EAC calculations

Year	Machine C	20% discount factor	Present value 20%
0	−10,000	1.000	−10,000.00
1	−5,000	0.833	−4,165.00
2	−4,000	0.694	−2,776.00
	−19,000	1.527	−16,941.00
		EAC=	**−11,094.30**

10.13 Study questions

Study question 10.1

Your company is considering investing in a new opportunity. They have provided you with details of the four opportunities they are currently evaluating in Table 10.34. The company uses a test discount rate of 5% to evaluate capital projects in Table 10.35.

Table 10.34 Four projects

Year	Red £m	Yellow £m	Green £m	Blue £m
0	−8	−8	−8	−8
1	4	3	4	5
2	2	3	2	2
3	2	3	2	2
4	1	1	2	2

Table 10.35 5% discount factors

Year	0	1	2	3	4
5%	1.000	0.952	0.907	0.864	0.823

1 Which investment has the shortest payback period?

  A Red

  B Yellow

  C Green

  D Blue

2 Which investment has the largest accounting rate of return?

  A Red

  B Yellow

  C Green

  D Blue

3 Which product has the smallest cost–benefit analysis?

  A Red

  B Yellow

  C Green

  D Blue

4 What is Red's net present value when the test discount rate is 5%?

    A £0.173 million

    B £0.189 million

    C £0.203 million

    D £0.217 million

5 What is Red's internal rate of return (two decimal places) if it has a negative net present value of £–0.527 million when the test discount rate is 10%?

    A 5.24%

    B 6.24%

    C 7.24%

    D 8.24%

Study question 10.2

Using the data contained in Table 10.36, for the three projects calculate the following for each project:

Table 10.36   Three investment opportunities

	Brass	Chrome	Steel
Year	Cash flow £	Cash flow £	Cash flow £
0	–£290,000	–£290,000	–£290,000
1	£55,000	£145,000	£100,000
2	£85,000	£115,000	£100,000
3	£115,000	£85,000	£100,000
4	£145,000	£55,000	£100,000

1 cost–benefit analysis;

2 accounting rate of return;

3 payback;

4 net present value using a 6% and 12% test discount rate;

5 discounted payback;

6 internal rate of return.

Summarize your analysis and recommend to the organization which project they should invest in, supporting your recommendation with your findings.

Study question 10.3

You have been supplied with the net cash flows for two machines your company is evaluating in Table 10.37.

Table 10.37   Net cash flows for machines A and B

Year	Option A £	Option B £
0	−50,000	−35,000
1	−3,500	−5,000
2	−3,500	−5,000
3	−3,500	2,000
4	−3,500	
5	−3,500	
6	6,500	

Calculate the EAC for each machine and recommend to the business which machine they should buy. The company uses a test discount rate of 20% to evaluate capital investment decisions.

Your organization is funded by £150m of share capital, whose investors expect a return of 12% on their funds, and £50m from loan capital, whose investors expect a return of 8% on their investment. What is your organization's weighted average cost of capital?

Study question 10.4

Your company is evaluating a new inventory management system that will cost them £4m and will produce efficiency savings over four years, which are illustrated in Table 10.38. The company's cost of capital is 10%.

Table 10.38   Inventory management system cash flow data

Year	Cash flows £m	10% discount factors
0	−4.0	1.000
1	1.8	0.909
2	1.5	0.826
3	1.2	0.751
4	1.0	0.683

1 Calculate the project's cost–benefit.

A £3.0 million

B £2.5 million

C £2.0 million

D £1.5 million

2 What is the project's accounting rate of return (to two decimal places)?

A 75.00%

B 9.38%

C 18.75%

D 37.50%

3 How long does the project take to recover its initial investment?

A 213 days

B 578 days

C 943 days

D 1,308 days

4 What is the project's net present value using the company's test discount rate of 10%?

A £1.239 million

B £0.901 million

C £0.683 million

D £0.459 million

5 What is the project's internal rate of return, if a test discount rate of 20% produces a negative net present value of £–0.2828m?

A 6.19%

B 16.19%

C 26.19%

D 36.19%

Study question 10.5

Primary Colours Ltd is evaluating four future investment opportunities, as illustrated in Table 10.39.

Table 10.39 Four future investment opportunities

Project	Purple	Pink	Green	Orange
Year	Cash flows £m	Cash flows £m	Cash flows £m	Cash flows £m
0	−7.0	−7.0	−7.0	−7.0
1	3.5	3.0	3.0	3.0
2	2.5	2.5	2.5	3.0
3	2.0	2.0	1.5	2.0
4	1.0	1.0	1.0	1.5

The company's cost of capital is 10% and the discount factors are illustrated in Table 10.40.

Table 10.40 10% discount factors

Year	0	1	2	3	4
10% discount factors	1.000	0.9091	0.8264	0.7513	0.6830

Using the information supplied in the two tables, answer the following questions:

1 Which project has the lowest cost–benefit figure?

A Purple

B Pink

C Green

D Orange

2 Which project has the highest accounting rate of return (to two decimal places)?

A Purple

B Pink

C Green

D Orange

3 Which project has a payback period of 2.75 years?

A Purple

B Pink

C Green

D Orange

4 What is Purple's net present value using the company's test discount rate of 10%?

A £0.2335 million

B £0.3335 million

C £0.4335 million

D £0.5335 million

5 What is Purple's internal rate of return, if a test discount rate of 15% produces a negative net present value of £–0.177m.

A 14.55%

B 13.55%

C 12.55%

D 11.55%

10.14 Study question solutions

Study question 10.1 solution

1 D = Blue pays back in 2.5 years.

2 D = Blue has the highest accounting rate of return of 19%.

3 A = Red has the smallest cost–benefit of £1 million.

4 A = Red has a net present value of £0.173m at a 5% discount rate.

5 B = Red has an internal rate of return of 6.24%.

Study question 10.2 solution

Cost–benefit analysis

In this example all three projects have the same capital investment of £290,000, but they also generate the same amount of cash inflows, £400,000; therefore they have the same cost–benefit analysis of £110,000; however, their cash flow profiles are different, as illustrated in Table 10.41.

Table 10.41   Cost–benefit analysis results

	Brass	Chrome	Steel
Year	Cash flow £	Cash flow £	Cash flow £
0	−£290,000	−£290,000	−£290,000
1	£55,000	£145,000	£100,000
2	£85,000	£115,000	£100,000
3	£115,000	£85,000	£100,000
4	£145,000	£55,000	£100,000
	£110,000	**£110,000**	**£110,000**

Accounting rate of return

All three projects have the same accounting rate of return. The average profit is calculated by dividing the profit produced from the project over its life by the number of years of the project.

$$£110,000/4 = £27,500 \text{ per annum}$$

The investment is the same for all the projects, £290,000, and dividing by 2 derives the average investment in the project. Therefore, £290,000/2 = £145,000.

The accounting rate of return for all three projects is:

$$(£27,500/£145,000) * 100 = 19\%.$$

Payback period

To derive the payback period, it is essential to calculate the cumulative cash flow for each project, as outlined in Table 10.42.

Table 10.42   Payback periods

Project	Brass cash flow		Chrome cash flow		Steel cash flow	
Year	Annual	Cumulative	Annual	Cumulative	Annual	Cumulative
0	−£290,000	−£290,000	−£290,000	−£290,000	−£290,000	−£290,000
1	£55,000	−£235,000	£145,000	−£145,000	£100,000	−£190,000
2	£85,000	−£150,000	£115,000	−£30,000	£100,000	−£90,000
3	£115,000	−£35,000	£85,000	£55,000	£100,000	£10,000
4	£145,000	£110,000	£55,000	£110,000	£100,000	£110,000
	£110,000		**£110,000**		**£110,000**	

Of the three projects, Project Chrome has the shortest payback period of 2.35 years, compared with Project Brass, which has a payback period of 3.24 years, as depicted in the summary in Table 10.43.

Table 10.43 Payback periods

Project	Brass	Chrome	Steel
PB years	3.24	2.35	2.90

Net present value

Tables 10.44 to 10.46 illustrate the NPV calculations for the three projects.

Table 10.44 Project Brass: net present value at 12% discount rate

Year	Cash flow £	Discount rate 12%	Present value 12%	Cumulative cash flow £
0	−£290,000	1.0000	−£290,000	−£290,000
1	£55,000	0.8929	£49,110	−£240,891
2	£85,000	0.7972	£67,762	−£173,129
3	£115,000	0.7118	£81,857	−£91,272
4	£145,000	0.6355	£92,148	£876
	£110,000		**£876**	

Table 10.45 Project Chrome: net present value at 12% discount rate

Year	Cash flow £	Discount rate 12%	Present value 12%	Cumulative cash flow £
0	−£290,000	1.0000	−£290,000	−£290,000
1	£145,000	0.8929	£129,471	−£160,530
2	£115,000	0.7972	£91,678	−£68,852
3	£85,000	0.7118	£60,503	−£8,349
4	£55,000	0.6355	£34,953	£26,604
	£110,000		**£26,604**	

Table 10.46 Project Steel: net present value at 12% discount rate

Year	Cash flow £	Discount rate 12%	Present value 12%	Cumulative cash flow £
0	−£290,000	1.0000	−£290,000	−£290,000
1	£100,000	0.8929	£89,290	−£200,710
2	£100,000	0.7972	£79,720	−£120,990
3	£100,000	0.7118	£71,180	−£49,810
4	£100,000	0.6355	£63,550	£13,740
	£110,000		**£13,740**	

Project Chrome has the highest net present value of the three projects, which is £26,604.

Internal rate of return

Tables 10.47 to 10.49 illustrate the IRR calculations for the three projects.

Table 10.47 Project Brass: internal rate of return calculation 18% discount rate

Year	Cash flow £	Discount rate 12%	Present value 12%	Discount rate 18%	Present value 18%
0	−£290,000	1.0000	£−290,000	1.0000	−£290,000
1	£55,000	0.8929	£49,110	0.8475	£46,613
2	£85,000	0.7972	£67,762	0.7182	£61,047
3	£115,000	0.7118	£81,857	0.6086	£69,989
4	£145,000	0.6355	£92,148	0.5158	£74,791
	£110,000		**£876**		**−£37,561**

Table 10.48 Project Chrome: internal rate of return calculation 18% discount rate

Year	Cash flow £	Discount rate 12%	Present value 12%	Discount rate 18%	Present value 18%
0	−£290,000	1.0000	−£290,000	1.0000	−£290,000
1	£145,000	0.8929	£129,471	0.8475	£122,888
2	£115,000	0.7972	£91,678	0.7182	£82,593
3	£85,000	0.7118	£60,503	0.6086	£51,731
4	£55,000	0.6355	£34,953	0.5158	£28,369
	£110,000		**£26,604**		**−£4,420**

Table 10.49   Project Steel: internal rate of return calculation 18% discount rate

Year	Cash flow £	Discount rate 12%	Present value 12%	Discount rate 18%	Present value 18%
0	−£290,000	1.0000	−£290,000	1.0000	−£290,000
1	£100,000	0.8929	£89,290	0.8475	£84,750
2	£100,000	0.7972	£79,720	0.7182	£71,820
3	£100,000	0.7118	£71,180	0.6086	£60,860
4	£100,000	0.6355	£63,550	0.5158	£51,580
	£110,000		£13,740		−£20,990

Of the three projects, Project Chrome has the highest IRR of 17.15%, compared with Project Brass, which has the lowest IRR of 12.14%, as depicted in the summary in Table 10.50.

Table 10.50   Summary of IRR results

Project	Brass	Chrome	Steel
IRR %	12.14	17.15	14.37

Project Chrome has the highest internal rate of return of 17.15%; if the test discount rate was to increase to 17%, Chrome would still generate a positive net present value.

Internal rate of return (graphical solution)

Figure 10.3 presents the graphical internal rate of return solution for the three projects. The chart confirms that Project Chrome has the highest internal rate of return.

Capital investment appraisal: summary of results

A summary of the results for each project is presented in Table 10.51.

Figure 10.3 Internal rate of return (graphical solution)

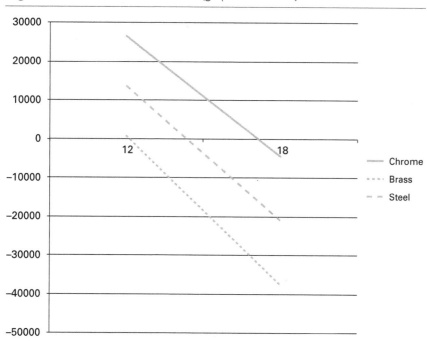

Table 10.51 Capital investment appraisal: summary of results

Project	Brass	Chrome	Steel
CBA	£110,000	£110,000	£110,000
ARR %	19	19	19
PB years	3.24	2.35	2.90
DPB years	3.99	3.24	3.78
NPV 12%	£876	£26,604	£13,740
NPV 18%	−£37,561	−£4,420	−£20,990
IRR %	12.14	17.15	14.37

Overall the analysis recommends that the organization should invest in Project Chrome for the following reasons:

1 The project has the best payback period of the three projects. It pays back the original investment of £110,000 in 2.35 years; similarly, the discounted payback period is also the shortest. Therefore, Project Chrome has the best liquidity of the three projects.

2 Project Chrome has the highest net present value, £26,604, of the three projects, making it the most profitable.

3 The project with the largest internal rate of return is also Chrome, with 17.15%, which means it produces the highest yield and also has the lowest risk.

4 The cost–benefit analysis and the accounting rate of return are equal for all of the projects and therefore, from a comparison perspective, we can ignore them.

Study question 10.3 solution

1 Table 10.52 illustrates the equivalent annualized cost for options A and B.

Table 10.52   Equivalent annualized cost for options A and B

Year	Option A	20% discount factor	Present value 20%
0	–50,000	1.000	–50,000.00
1	–3,500	0.833	–2,915.50
2	–3,500	0.694	–2,429.00
3	–3,500	0.579	–2,026.50
4	–3,500	0.482	–1,687.00
5	–3,500	0.402	–1,407.00
6	6,500	0.335	2,177.50
	–61,000	3.325	–58,287.50
		EAC=	–17,530.08

Year	Option B	20% discount factor	Present value 20%
0	–35,000	1.000	–35,000.00
1	–5,000	0.833	–4,165.00
2	–5,000	0.694	–3,470.00
3	2,000	0.579	1,158.00
	–43,000	2.106	–41,477.00
		EAC=	–19,694.68

The company should invest in option A as it has the lowest EAC of £17,530 per annum.

2 Your organization's weighted average cost of capital is 11%.

Workings

Total capital employed is £200m.

Equity £150m/£200m = 0.75 * 12% = 9%.

Debt £50m/£200m = 0.25 * 8% = 2%.

Add them together = 11%.

Study question 10.4 solution

1 The project's cost–benefit analysis is calculated by adding up the project's positive and negative cash flows; therefore the project has a cost–benefit analysis of £1.5m.

Answer = D

2 The project's accounting rate of return is calculated by using the following equation:

$$\frac{Average\ profit}{Average\ investment} * 100$$

The average profit is calculated by dividing the project's profit by the life span of the project. The average profit for the project is £1.5m divided by 4 = £0.375m.

The average investment is calculated by dividing the project's investment by 2. The average investment for the project is £4.0m divided by 2 = £2.0m.

$$\frac{£375,000}{£2,000,000} * 100 = 18.75\%$$

Answer = D

3 The time taken for the project to recover its initial investment is referred to as the payback period. The project's investment was £4m, and by calculating the cumulative cash flow it can be seen in Table 10.53 that the project will recover its original investment between year 2 and year 3.

Table 10.53 Payback calculations

Year	Cash flows £m	Cumulative cash flow £m
0	−4.0	−4.0
1	1.8	−2.2
2	1.5	−0.7
3	1.2	0.5
4	1.0	1.5
	1.5	

The table reveals that at the end of year 2 the project has a cash shortfall of £0.7m, and by the end of year 3 the project has a cash surplus of £0.5m, but when does the sign change from negative to positive? To find this point we do an apportionment. The amount outstanding at the end of year 2 is divided by the cash received in year 3; this proportion is then multiplied by 365 to calculate the number of days in year 3 when the sign changes.

$$\frac{£0.7\,million}{£1.2\,million} * 365 = 213\,days$$

The project will recover its investment in 2 years 213 days, or 943 days. Answer = **C**

4   The project's net present value using the company's test discount rate of 10% is £0.459m, as illustrated in Table 10.54.

Table 10.54   NPV calculations

Year	Cash flows £m	10% discount factors	Present value £m
0	−4.0	1.000	−4.000
1	1.8	0.909	1.636
2	1.5	0.826	1.239
3	1.2	0.751	0.901
4	1.0	0.683	0.683
	1.5		0.459

To calculate the project's net present value, each annual cash flow is multiplied by its respective discount factor for that year to generate the present value; for example in year 3 the cash flow of £1.2m is multiplied by 0.751 to arrive at £0.901m. All the individual present values are aggregated to calculate the net present value for the project, which is £0.459m.

Answer = **D**

5   The project's internal rate of return is the discount rate that will result in a net present value of zero. When the test discount rate is 20%, the project will have a negative net present value of −£0.2828m. To derive the internal rate of return, an apportionment is used, as we know that the discount rate will be between 10% and 20%. To find this point the respective net present values are used in the following calculation. The proportion calculated is then multiplied by the difference between the two discount rates used to derive the net present values, which is 10%

(20% – 10%), and added to the discount rate that generated the positive net present value to calculate an internal rate of return of 16.19%.

$$10\% + \left[10\% * \left(\frac{£0.459m}{£0.459m - -£0.2828} \right) \right] = 16.19\%$$

Answer = **B**

Study question 10.5 solution

1 To find the project which has the lowest cost–benefit figure, we just add together the positive and negative cash flows for each project, as illustrated in Table 10.55.

Table 10.55 Cost–benefit analysis calculations

Project	Purple	Pink	Green	Orange
Year	Cash flows £m	Cash flows £m	Cash flows £m	Cash flows £m
0	–7.0	–7.0	–7.0	–7.0
1	3.5	3.0	3.0	3.0
2	2.5	2.5	2.5	3.0
3	2.0	2.0	1.5	2.0
4	1.0	1.0	1.0	1.5
Total	2.0	1.5	1.0	2.5

Project Green has the lowest cost–benefit of £1.0m, compared with Project Orange's £2.5m, which is the highest.

Answer = **C**

2 The accounting rate of return (ARR) is calculated by using the following equation:

$$\frac{Average\ profit}{Average\ investment} * 100$$

The average profit is calculated by dividing the project's profit by the life span of the project.

The average investment is calculated by dividing the project's investment by 2.

The project with the highest ARR of 18% is Orange, while Green has the lowest percentage of 7%, as illustrated in Table 10.56.

Table 10.56   ARR calculations

Project	Purple	Pink	Green	Orange
Profit £m	2.00	1.50	1.00	2.50
Average profit £m	0.50	0.38	0.25	0.63
Average investment £m	3.50	3.50	3.50	3.50
ARR %	14%	11%	7%	18%

Answer = **D**

3 The payback period (PP) is the time taken for the project to recover its initial investment. Therefore, we need to calculate for each project its cumulative cash flow. When the cumulative cash flow changes from negative to positive it indicates the point in time when the project recovers its initial investment. The cumulative cash flows for each project are illustrated in Table 10.57. Let's focus first on project Green. Look at its cumulative cash flow. The cash flow changes from negative to positive exactly at the end of year 3; therefore its payback is three years. The other three projects change from negative to positive between years 2 and 3, but we need to find the project that has a payback period of 2.75 years. To find the exact PP, we do an apportionment by taking the amount outstanding at the end of year 2 and dividing it by the cash received in year 3. In the case of project Pink, at the end of year 2 £1.5m is needed to recover the initial investment, and in year 3 the forecast cash flow received is £2.0m. To calculate the point when the sign changes, we now divide £1.5m by £2.0m, which equals 0.75. Therefore, project Pink will have a PP of 2.75 years, or 2 years 274 days approximately.

It is important to point out that in the PP calculation, we assume that the cash flows are a straight line over time; we assume that the forecast cash flow is the same for every day in a specific year, which in practice is not the case.

Therefore, the project that has a payback period of 2.75 years is Pink.

Answer = **C**

Table 10.57 Payback period calculations

Project	Purple	Purple	Pink	Pink	Green	Green	Orange	Orange
Year	Cash flows £m	Cumulative £m	Cash flows £m	Cumulative £m	Cash flows £m	Cumulative £m	Cash flows £m	Cumulative £m
0	-7.0	-7.0	-7.0	-7.0	-7.0	-7.0	-7.0	-7.0
1	3.5	-3.5	3.0	-4.0	3.0	-4.0	3.0	-4.0
2	2.5	-1.0	2.5	-1.5	2.5	-1.5	3.0	-1.0
3	2.0	1.0	2.0	0.5	1.5	0.0	2.0	1.0
4	1.0	2.0	1.0	1.5	1.0	1.0	1.5	2.5
Total	2.0		1.5		1.0		2.5	
	PP = 2.50 years		PP = 2.75 years		PP = 3.00 years		PP = 2.50 years	

4 To calculate the project's net present value (NPV), we need to calculate the present value for each year. We do this by multiplying the cash flow for each year by it relevant discount factor for that year. Let's take year 1 for project Purple. Its cash flow is £3.5m, the discount factor at 10% for that year is 0.9091; we multiply them to derive the present value of £3.1819. We do the same present value calculation for every year, even year 0, and then add them all together to arrive at the NPV for the project, as illustrated in Table 10.58 for project Purple. Purple's NPV using the company's test discount rate of 10% will be £0.4335m. Purple's NPV is positive when a 10% discount rate is adopted; therefore, the project's returns are greater than the cost of capital (opportunity cost) and should be accepted.

Answer = C

Table 10.58   Project Purple NPV calculation

Project	Purple	Discount factor	Present value
Year	Cash flows £m	10%	£m
0	−7.0	1.0000	−7.0000
1	3.5	0.9091	3.1819
2	2.5	0.8264	2.0660
3	2.0	0.7513	1.5026
4	1.0	0.6830	0.6830
Total	2.0		0.4335

5 The internal rate of return (IRR) is the discount rate that will result in an NPV of zero. When the test discount rate is 15%, Purple has a negative NPV of −£0.177m; however, when the test discount rate is 10%, the project has a positive NPV of £0.4335m. The IRR will be located somewhere between 10% and 15%. The following formula, which is an apportionment, will be used to approximate the IRR:

$$10\% + \left[5\% * \left(\frac{£0.4335m}{£0.4335m - - £0.177} \right) \right] = 13.55\%$$

Answer = B

INDEX

CPSIA information can be obtained
at www.ICGtesting.com
Printed in the USA
BVHW021038150320
575060BV00015B/825